COLLABORATION RESEARCH IN MANAGEMENT

COLLABORATION RESEARCH IN MANAGEMENT

Ankush Arya

RANDOM PUBLICATIONS

NEW DELHI - 110 002 (INDIA)

Collaboration Research in Management

ISBN 978-93-51117-18-6

Published in 2015 in India by

RANDOM PUBLICATIONS

Reprint 2017

4376-A/4B, Gali Murari Lal, Ansari Road
New Delhi-110 002
Phone: +9111-43580356, 23289044
E-mail: randomexports@gmail.com; sales@randompublications.com;
info@randompublications.com

Type Setting by: Friends Media, Delhi-110089
Digitally Printed at: Replika Press Pvt. Ltd.

Preface

Collaboration is working with others to do a task and to achieve shared goals. It is a recursive process where two or more or organizations work together to realize shared goals, (this is more than the intersection of common goals seen in co-operative ventures, but a deep, collective determination to reach an identical objective) — for example, an endeavour that is creative in nature—by sharing knowledge, learning and building consensus. Most collaboration requires leadership, although the form of leadership can be social within a decentralized and egalitarian group. In particular, teams that work collaboratively can obtain greater resources, recognition and reward when facing competition for finite resources. Collaboration is also present in opposing goals exhibiting the notion of adversarial collaboration, though this is not a common case for using the word.

Collaboration in business can be found both inter- and intra-organization and ranges from the simplicity of a partnership and crowd funding to the complexity of a multinational corporation. Collaboration between public, private and voluntary sectors can be effective in tackling complex policy problems, but may be handled more effectively by committed boundary-spanning teams and networks than by formal organizational structures. Collaboration between team members allows for better communication within the organization and throughout the supply chains. It is a way of coordinating different ideas from numerous people to generate a wide variety of knowledge. Collaboration with a selected few firms as opposed to collaboration with a large number of different firms has been shown to positively impact firm performance and innovation outcomes. The recent improvement in technology has provided the world with high speed internet, wireless connection, and web-based collaboration tools like blogs, facebook, twitter has created a "mass collaboration." People from all over the world are efficiently able to communicate and share ideas through the internet, or even conferences, without any geographical barriers. The power of social networks it beginning to permeate into business culture where many collaborative uses are being found including file sharing and knowledge transfer. A plethora of studies have shown that collaboration can be a powerful tool towards higher achievement and increased productivity since collective efficacy can significantly boost groups' aspirations, motivational investment, morale, and resilience to challenges. However, a four-year study of interorganizational collaboration by Fischer and colleagues at the University of Oxford, found that successful collaboration can be rapidly derailed through external policy steering, particularly where it undermines relations built on trust. On a more specific level, coworking spaces are businesses dedicated to providing an space for freelancers to work with others in a collaborative environment. Collaboration is one of the five coworking core values: Collaboration, openness, community, accessibility and sustainability. Collaboration relies on openness and knowledge sharing but also some level of focus and accountability on the part of the business organizations. Governance should be established addressing the creation and closing of team workspaces with assignment of responsibility for capturing the emergent results of the collaborative effort.

The true partnership ideal and emergent enquiry process make collaborative research complex and difficult to organize, lead, and manage. The present book addresses these needs by revisiting traditional research ideals.

I thank all members of my team who have helped in the preparation of the book. My special thanks go to "Random Publications" who have published the book.

— Ankush Arya

Contents

Chapter 1

Collaborative Research

Collaborative research is any research project that is carried out by at least two people. Collaborative research happens in many ways, and is more common in some fields than others. It is very common in the sciences, and less so in the humanities. Working with others on a research project can have several benefits, but there can be drawbacks as well. Often, researchers will choose to collaborate when a project is large or involved, or to pool their areas of expertise. For example, let's imagine that two researchers are interested in a similar scientific topic. One researcher is an expert in statistical methods, and the other has collected a lot of data from a field experiment. If they collaborate, the researchers can combine their strengths and do sophisticated statistical analyses of the data from the field experiments. Usually the goal of collaborative research is to publish the results, and the researchers will divide up the work of writing up the results and navigating the publication process.

Another example of collaborative research is a large survey, such as the U.S. Census. The Census involves thousands of people at different levels of involvement. Several things must be accomplished in order for the census to be successful. There is a hierarchical structure for the census and large teams of interviewers and analysts that carry out the work of collecting information.

When done in the right spirit, collaborative research can result in more reliable and powerful results that come to publication faster than they would if the research were done independently. Researchers can pool their knowledge and critique each other's work before starting the publication process.

There can be some drawbacks to collaborative research, however. Sometimes it is hard to know whether collaboration will be fruitful. A collaborator may be difficult to work with, or researchers may not reach a consensus about their results. Another common pitfall is struggles over authorship or ownership of the research. In many academic publications, being the "first author," or having one's name listed first as the author on an article, carries the most professional prestige, and may be important for career advancement. Therefore, deciding who will be the "first" author is potentially contentious.

Research

Research comprises "creative work undertaken on a systematic basis in order to increase the stock of knowledge, including kstems for the advancement of human knowledge. Approaches to research depend on epistemologies, which vary considerably both within and between humanities and sciences. There are several forms of research: scientific, humanities, artistic, economic, social, business, marketing, practitioner research, etc.

Forms of Research

Scientific research is a systematic way of gathering data, a harnessing of curiosity. This research provides scientific information and theories for the explanation of the nature and the properties of the world. It makes practical applications possible. Scientific research is funded by public authorities, by charitable organisations and by private groups, including many companies. Scientific research can be subdivided into different classifications according to their academic and application disciplines. Scientific research is a widely used criterion for judging the standing of an academic institution, such as business schools, but some argue that such is an inaccurate assessment of the institution, because the quality of research does not tell about the quality of teaching (these do not necessarily correlate totally).

Research in the humanities involves different methods such as for example hermeneutics and semiotics, and a different, more relativist epistemology. Humanities scholars usually do not search for the ultimate correct answer to a question, but instead explore the issues and details that surround it. Context is always important, and context can be social, historical, political, cultural or ethnic. An example of research in the humanities is historical research, which is embodied in historical method. Historians use primary sources and other evidence to systematically investigate a topic, and then to write histories in the form of accounts of the past.

Artistic research, also seen as 'practice-based research', can take form when creative works are considered both the research and the object of research itself. It is the debatable body of thought which offers an alternative to purely scientific methods in research in its search for knowledge and truth.

Definitions

Research has been defined in a number of different ways. A broad definition of research is given by Martyn Shuttleworth - "In the broadest sense of the word, the definition of research includes any gathering of data, information and facts for the advancement of knowledge."

Another definition of research is given by Creswell who states that - "Research is a process of steps used to collect and analyze information to increase our understanding of a topic or issue". It consists of three steps: Pose a question, collect data to answer the question, and present an answer to the question.

The Merriam-Webster Online Dictionary defines research in more detail as "a studious inquiry or examination; especially : investigation or experimentation aimed at the discovery and interpretation of facts, revision of accepted theories or laws in the light of new facts, or practical application of such new or revised theories or laws".

Steps in Conducting Research

Research is often conducted using the hourglass model structure of research. The hourglass model starts with a broad spectrum for research, focusing in on the required information through the method of the project (like the neck of the hourglass), then expands the research in the form of discussion and results. The major steps in conducting research are:

- Identification of research problem
- Literature review
- Specifying the purpose of research
- Determine specific research questions
- Specification of a Conceptual framework - Usually a set of hypotheses
- Choice of a methodology (for data collection)
- Data collection
- Analyzing and interpreting the data
- Reporting and evaluating research

- Communicating the research findings and, possibly, recommendations

The steps generally represent the overall process, however they should be viewed as an ever-changing iterative process rather than a fixed set of steps. Most researches begin with a general statement of the problem, or rather, the purpose for engaging in the study. The literature review identifies flaws or holes in previous research which provides justification for the study. Often, a literature review is conducted in a given subject area before a research question is identified. A gap in the current literature, as identified by a researcher, then engenders a research question. The research question may be parallel to the hypothesis. The hypothesis is the supposition to be tested. The researcher(s) collects data to test the hypothesis. The researcher(s) then analyzes and interprets the data via a variety of statistical methods, engaging in what is known as Empirical research. The results of the data analysis in confirming or failing to reject the Null hypothesis are then reported and evaluated. At the end the researcher may discuss avenues for further research.

Rudolph Rummel says, "... no researcher should accept any one or two tests as definitive. It is only when a range of tests are consistent over many kinds of data, researchers, and methods can one have confidence in the results."

Scientific Research

Generally, research is understood to follow a certain structural process. Though step order may vary depending on the subject matter and researcher, the following steps are usually part of most formal research, both basic and applied:

1. Observations and Formation of the topic: Consists of the subject area of ones interest and following that subject area to conduct subject related research. The subject area should not be randomly chosen since it requires reading a vast amount of literature on the topic to determine the gap in the literature the researcher intends to narrow. A keen interest in the chosen subject area is advisable. The research will have to be justified by linking its importance to already existing knowledge about the topic.
2. Hypothesis: A testable prediction which designates the relationship between two or more variables.
3. Conceptual definition: Description of a concept by relating it to other concepts.

4. Operational definition: Details in regards to defining the variables and how they will be measured/assessed in the study.
5. Gathering of data: Consists of identifying a population and selecting samples, gathering information from and/or about these samples by using specific research instruments. The instruments used for data collection must be valid and reliable.
6. Analysis of data: Involves breaking down the individual pieces of data in order to draw conclusions about it.
7. Data Interpretation: This can be represented through tables, figures and pictures, and then described in words.
8. Test, revising of hypothesis
9. Conclusion, reiteration if necessary

A common misconception is that a hypothesis will be proven (see, rather, Null hypothesis). Generally a hypothesis is used to make predictions that can be tested by observing the outcome of an experiment. If the outcome is inconsistent with the hypothesis, then the hypothesis is rejected. However, if the outcome is consistent with the hypothesis, the experiment is said to support the hypothesis. This careful language is used because researchers recognise that alternative hypotheses may also be consistent with the observations. In this sense, a hypothesis can never be proven, but rather only supported by surviving rounds of scientific testing and, eventually, becoming widely thought of as true.

A useful hypothesis allows prediction and within the accuracy of observation of the time, the prediction will be verified. As the accuracy of observation improves with time, the hypothesis may no longer provide an accurate prediction. In this case a new hypothesis will arise to challenge the old, and to the extent that the new hypothesis makes more accurate predictions than the old, the new will supplant it. Researchers can also use a null hypothesis, which state no relationship or difference between the independent or dependent variables. A null hypothesis uses a sample of all possible people to make a conclusion about the population.

Historical Method

The historical method comprises the techniques and guidelines by which historians use historical sources and other evidence to research and then to write history. There are various history guidelines that are commonly used by historians in their work, under the headings of external criticism, internal criticism, and synthesis. This includes lower criticism and sensual criticism. Though items may vary depending on the subject matter and researcher, the following concepts are part of most formal historical research:

- Identification of origin date
- Evidence of localization
- Recognition of authorship
- Analysis of data
- Identification of integrity
- Attribution of credibility

Research Methods

The goal of the research process is to produce new knowledge or deepen understanding of a topic or issue. This process takes three main forms (although, as previously discussed, the boundaries between them may be obscure):

- Exploratory research, which helps to identify and define a problem or question.
- Constructive research, which tests theories and proposes solutions to a problem or question.
- Empirical research, which tests the feasibility of a solution using empirical evidence.

There are two major types of research design: qualitative research and quantitative research. Researchers choose qualitative or quantitative methods according to the nature of the research topic they want to investigate and the research questions they aim to answer:

Qualitative Research

Understanding of human behaviour and the reasons that govern such behaviour. Asking a broad question and collecting data in the form of words, images, video etc that is analyzed and searching for themes. This type of research aims to investigate a question without attempting to quantifiably measure variables or look to potential relationships between variables. It is viewed as more restrictive in testing hypotheses because it can be expensive and time consuming, and typically limited to a single set of research subjects. Qualitative research is often used as a method of exploratory research as a basis for later quantitative research hypotheses. Qualitative research is linked with the philosophical and theoretical stance of social constructionism.

Quantitative Research

Systematic empirical investigation of quantitative properties and phenomena and their relationships. Asking a narrow question and collecting numerical data to analyze utilising statistical methods. The quantitative research designs are experimental, correlational, and survey (or descriptive). Statistics derived from quantitative research can be used to establish the existence of associative or causal relationships between variables. Quantitative research is linked with the philosophical and theoretical stance of positivism.

The Quantitative data collection methods rely on random sampling and structured data collection instruments that fit diverse experiences into predetermined response categories. These methods produce results that are easy to summarize, compare, and generalize. Quantitative research is concerned with testing hypotheses derived from theory and/ or being able to estimate the size of a phenomenon of interest. Depending on the research question, participants may be randomly assigned to different treatments (this is the only way that a quantitative study can be considered a true experiment). If this is not feasible, the researcher may collect data on participant and situational characteristics in order to statistically control for their influence on the dependent, or outcome, variable. If the intent is to generalize from the research participants to a larger population, the researcher will employ probability sampling to select participants.

In either qualitative or quantitative research, the researcher(s) may collect primary or secondary data. Primary data is data collected specifically for the research, such as through interviews or questionnaires. Secondary data is data that already exists, such as census data, which can be re-used for the research. It is good ethical research practice to use secondary data wherever possible.

Mixed-method research, i.e. research that includes qualitative and quantitative elements, using both primary and secondary data, is becoming more common.

Research Funding

Most funding for scientific research comes from three major sources: corporate research and development departments; private foundations, for example, the Bill and Melinda Gates Foundation; and government research councils such as the National Institutes of Health in the USA and the Medical Research Council in the UK. These are managed primarily through universities and in some cases through military contractors. Many senior researchers (such as group leaders) spend a significant amount of their time applying for grants for research funds. These grants are necessary not only for researchers to carry out their research, but also as a source of merit. The Social Psychology Network provides a comprehensive list of U.S. Government and private foundation funding sources.

Original Research

This material is of a primary source character. The purpose of the original research is to produce new knowledge, rather than to present the existing knowledge in a new form (*e.g.*, summarized or classified).

Different Forms

Original research can take a number of forms, depending on the discipline it pertains to. In experimental work, it typically involves direct or indirect observation of the researched subject(s), e.g., in the laboratory or in the field, documents the methodology, results, and conclusions of an experiment or set of experiments, or offers a novel interpretation of previous results. In analytical work, there are typically some new (for example) mathematical results produced, or a new way of approaching an existing problem. In some subjects which do not typically carry out experimentation or analysis of this kind, the originality is in the particular way existing understanding is changed or re-interpreted based on the outcome of the work of the researcher.

The degree of originality of the research is among major criteria for articles to be published in academic journals and usually established by means of peer review. Graduate students are commonly required to perform original research as part of a dissertation.

Business and Management Research

Business and management research is a systematic inquiry that helps to solve business problems and contributes to management knowledge. It Is an applied research.

Four factors (Easterby-Smith, 2008) combine to make business and management a distinctive focus for research :

- Transdiscipline approach
- Information access is difficult since managers see information as comptetivive advantage on the market
- Managers are educated and want some information produced by the classical research method
- Finding must resolve practical management problems

Managers often need information of high quality to help them to make the right decision.

Research Process

- Define and clarifying a research topic
- Literature review on this subject
- Research Philosophies
- Formulate research design
- Ethics and access to information
- Defining a sample
- Using Secondary data
- Collecting primary data through observations, questionnaires and interview
- Analysing data
- Draw conclusions from data analysis

Co-opetition

Co-opetition describes a strategic framework that enables organisations to classify relevant actors in their industry and beyond. The model uses insights from game theory to understand and influence the behaviour of these players.

Adam Brandenburger and Barry Nalebuff, professors in economics at Harvard and Yale University and specialists in the field of game theory, developed their co-opetition model in the mid-1990's. Based on case studies across different industries, they argued that cooperation and competition are both necessary and desirable when doing business. Cooperation is required to increase benefits to all players (focus on market growth), and competition is needed to divide the existing benefits among these players (focus on market share). Game theory provided the economic foundation to determine circumstances when cooperation is the preferential strategy. Their research added to previous industry analysis literature such as Porter's five forces, which focused almost exclusively on competition.

Game theory studies how interactions between players and the choices each player makes lead to different outcomes or end states of the game. The objective to develop advantageous strategies provides insights for strategic management. The theory, developed in 1944 by Von Neumann and Morgenstern, has found application in other fields such as politics, economics, ethics and the military.

Brandenburg and Nalebuff use "Value Net" as their core concept. They identified four types of players that every company faces:

Customers

Parties to which the company directs its products and services. In return, money goes from the customers to the company.

Suppliers

Parties who flow resources to the company. In return, money goes from the company to the suppliers.

Competitors

The definition depends on perspective:

- *Customer perspective*: "A player is your competitor if customers value your product less when they have the other player's product than when they have your product by itself." Your product behaves as a substitute for a competitor's product – your increase in market share will directly decrease your competitor's share. Substitutes can be both direct, e.g. two bakeries competing as well as indirect, e.g. bread versus rice.
- *Supplier perspective*: "A player is your competitor if it is less attractive for a supplier to provide resources to you when it is also supplying the other player than when it is supplying you alone." Any firm competes for resources in quantity, quality and price with other organisations.

Complementors

The definition also depends on perspective.

- Customer perspective: "A player is your complementor if customers value your product more when they have the other player's product than when they have your product by itself." Complementors are the inverse of a competitor because more demand for their products will lead to more demand for your product.
- Supplier perspective: "A player is your complementor if it is more attractive for a supplier to provide resources to you when it is also supplying the other player than when it is supplying you alone." When a market is small, it is difficult to get resources delivered exactly on spec. When the market increases, suppliers begin to tailor their offering and make the purchasing efforts easier on all acquiring firms.

Importantly, a single player can have more than one role simultaneously. A player can even be both competitor and complementor at the same time. Competitors Sony and Philips acted as complementors in the joint development of a standard for the Compact Disc.

Brandenburger and Nalebuff continued by describing the PARTS of a business strategy — five dimensions a company can use to identify strategies that change the game, the companies business, to its own advantage.

Players

The Value Net can be used to identify and categorize the current players in the game. Bringing more players (customers, suppliers, complementors and competitors) into the game can have positive effects on a company - eg: increasing suppliers can decrease costs; extra complementors give more value to a company's product; and a competitor can be brought in to give customers the feeling that they have choice.

Added Value

At this point, a company can identify its added value from the other players' point of view and take action to increase this added value in order to increase profitability - eg: a monopolist company can limit supply; in a competitive market, a company can introduce affinity programs to create loyal customers or suppliers.

Rules

In every business, many written and unwritten rules apply. Although many rules cannot be changed due to governmental enforcement, contracts provide opportunities to change the rules on a smaller scale. Brandenburger and Nalebuff elaborate on "most favoured customer clauses" (MFCs) and "meet the competition clauses" (MCCs) as ways to change the game. As a purchaser, an MFC gives the right to buy supplies against the lowest price offered to anyone else and as a supplier, an MCC gives the right to meet a competitor's lowest bid.

Tactics

Tactics are defined as: "actions that players take to shape the perceptions of other players". Brandenburger and Nalebuff argue that actions of a player are always rational in light of that player's perception of reality. A company can influence other players' perceptions and actions by deliberately sending out certain signals. It is necessary, however, to be aware of these perceptions in order to be able to influence them.

Scope

Often, a game is not isolated, but linked to other games via its players. A firm can extend its business to other games when it adds value to the other game and increases its profitability. On the other hand, a firm can deliberately keep two games separate when linking the games would cannibalize its traditional business. Linking and de-linking games can occur by recognising complementary markets, by special clauses in contracts or by influencing the perception of other players.

The co-opetition model provides a framework to identify and explain the underlying mechanisms in a firm's environment and how these mechanisms can be changed to the firm's advantage. Its main academic contribution is the identification and justification of the role that complementors play. Business is more than competing for market share in the current market.

Pros

The framework is based on the well established foundations of game theory. The co-opetition model provides a framework to organise available information on a company's market and to discover gaps. It is, therefore, a valuable framework to use in strategic planning exercises.

The model builds on the mindset that cooperation is as important in business as competition, and that a company can simultaneously have a competitive and a cooperative relationship with another player.

The PARTS of business strategy show that an organisation can influence the market on dimensions other than price and quality.

In contrast to Porter, Brandenburg and Nalebuff departed from the concept of industry, because this concept limits available opportunities. The most interesting business opportunities arise from intersections between traditional industries.

The model is highly abstract. The definition of competitors, complementors and co-opetition is broad. Although the model can stimulate creative thinking, it does not provide clear-cut answers to everyday problems. For example, the model does not provide practical propositions on how to create successful co-opetitive relations with other organisations. Bengtsson and Kock (2000) have tried to fill this gap.

Cooperation among competitors often occurs when an industry standard needs to be set, — a process that Brandenburger and Barry Nalebuff did not discuss. Hax (2001) built on the Value Net framework by describing how the 'standard' or platform owner could best behave. Hax further broke down the concept of complementors.

The model is based on the principles of game theory and has inevitably inherited some of its limitations; i.e. the application of the theory becomes exponentially more complex as more players or options are added.

The term "Tactics" in the PARTS acronym might be misleading because this element only focuses on influencing perceptions. The other components can also be regarded as tactics.

Research and Development Management?

Research and Development (R&D) management involves overseeing and controlling the research and development department of a given company. Research and development is the process of developing new ideas in order to patent, market or sell those ideas. Research and development exists in many industries but is most common in the technology industry and the drug industry where there is a consistent need for newer, better and more innovative projects and where more extensive research and work must be done to make those products a functional reality.

There are a number of different things that go into research and development management, depending on the industry and the type of project being done. One of the main components of research and development management involves overseeing, managing and allocating the budget assigned to given research projects. Research and development, or R&D, when conducted by for-profit companies, is designed to produce a product that will be profitable for the company when patented or sold.

R&D managers must ensure that funds are allocated only to products likely to produce a good return-on-investment (ROI) and that any funds invested are reasonable in light of what the ROI will ultimately be if the product is developed properly. For example, it would not be logical to allocate millions in funds to create a drug used to treat a minor illness that only a small portion of the population has, since there would be both a small market and little willingness to pay high prices for the given drug. On the other hand, allocating millions to research cures for cancer is a more appropriate investment since there are many people with cancer who would pay large sums of money to be made healthy.

Research and development management also involves overseeing the process of R&D and ensuring that all requirements are complied with. This is especially important in the drug industry, where there are generally stringent controls put in place by the government before a drug can be approved for use and sale. For example, in the United States, the Food and Drug Administration (FDA) imposes standards for how drugs must be tested and requires a set amount of clinical trials before a drug is approved. Research and development management entails overseeing the programs to ensure that no R&D process breaks the laws associated with human testing. They also ensure sufficient records are kept so that the records may be submitted to the FDA when applying for approval of the drug.

What are The Core Principles of Collaboration?

The notion of how we collaborate has been one that whilst often discussed has never really been nailed down. Game theory offers up the basic tit-for-tat principle whereby we collaborate until the other party proves themselves untrustworthy, at which point collaboration breaks down.

A new Harvard paper delves into this issue in more detail. Author Nicholas Christakis has form in this area as he's the author of *Connected: The Surprising Power of our Social Networks*. His latest research required participants to play a collaboration-testing game over the Internet. The obvious benefit of this approach is that it attracted a much larger sample than is traditionally the case for laboratory research. Courtesy of Amazon's Mechanical Turk over 750 volunteers were signed up for the experiment.

Participants in the game were allocated points. During each round of the game they can donate points to their neighbours if they wish, with each donation matched by the 'game'. Obviously if everyone donates equally then each player gets significantly richer as a result. As game theory suggests however, should a participant defect and not donate, they stand to gain significantly from the donations of others without giving up any of their own points, at least in the short term before people cotton on and stop playing their game.

The mechanics of the game saw it split into three distinct rule sets. The first saw players interacting with the same people all the time, therefore their historical behaviour was known to the others. The second variation meanwhile players were randomly reshuffled at the end of each round, whilst the final variation 1/3 of the players were shuffled.

In each of the variations one player from each pair was reminded how the other had acted in the previous round, but only in the third variation could they act on this information and decide whether to play with their partner or ask for a new one. To add spice to the game, at the end all of the points people have attained were converted into actual money. This was done to ensure that participants played the game as realistically as possible.

In all versions of the game approximately 60% of players co-operated to begin with. In the first two variants however this dropped significantly once the impact of free loaders began to hit home. Tit-for-tat was being played out and after a few rounds collaboration was massively hit, down to around 15% on average.

Obviously the first two variants however gave players no choice over their partner, but in the third they could act upon previous behaviour. In this version of the game collaboration remained stable throughout the game as players simply chose not to participate with the free loaders. This simple feedback mechanism enabled the community to become smarter and for collaboration to survive.

The research found that not only were collaborators wealthier at the end of the game, they had also gained significantly more connections than the free loaders. Perhaps not surprising in itself, but one ray of light emerged when the free loaders, as a result of being shunned, began to change their behaviour to a more collaborative approach.

Furthermore, as they were shunned, the defectors began to change their behaviour. A defector's likelihood of switching to co-operation increased with the number of players who had broken links with him in the previous round. Unlike straightforward tit-for-tat, social retaliation was having a marked effect.

So What Lessons can We Take from This for Real World Collaboration?

The research clearly shows that it pays to be generous. It wasn't merely the selfish that were punished in future rounds but also the stingy. So here are a few principles that you should try to encourage in your organisation if you wish to encourage a collaborative approach amongst employees and other stakeholders.

Principles of Collaboration

1. Participation – You want to encourage participation from across your organisation. As we've seen from the experiment, this could involve you removing, or at least educating, people that don't act collaboratively.
2. Collective – As collaboration will involve taken relatively narrow perspectives and making them broad, you will need to help the

group reach a consensus and then take action collectively on the decisions they make.

3. Transparency – Feedback and trust are essential elements of collaboration. Being transparent with information is crucial if that is to be achieved. Make sure that all debates are had in the open and that the entire group has access to the latest information.
4. Independence – James Surowiecki emphasized the importance of independent thought in his book *Wisdom of Crowds*, so you'll need to ensure that group-think does not emerge and that people are thinking for themselves.
5. Persistence – You will need to be persistent in your application of these principles, to ensure that all content is kept within the community and easily accessible to all members.
6. Emergence – Remember that the point of mass collaboration is to achieve great results, so ensure you focus on the end goal rather than worrying about how that is achieved. You will need your collaborative community to set their own goals and objectives.

Conflict Reduction between Researchers

Effective collaboration is essential for creating value. Indeed, it's one of the reasons we create corporations, because organisations are more effective than individuals at allocating resources. But knowing and doing are two different things. As organisations grow, collaboration can suffer—particularly across silos, as people learn to work for the benefit of their own group rather than the whole. This lost potential in collaboration is a huge, untapped source of competitive advantage, one that executives appear to be aware of. In a 2005 McKinsey survey only 25 percent of senior executives would describe their organisations as effective at sharing knowledge across boundaries, even though nearly 80 percent acknowledged such coordination was crucial to growth.

One of the most difficult and interesting aspects of collaboration is conflict. True collaboration can't exist without personal commitment, and commitment brings with it the possibility of engaging in healthy conflict and debate. If I go to a meeting but don't have the chance to test my views against contrary opinions, I may leave the room saying "yes" to initiatives without feeling any personal commitment to them. Before you can have healthy debate, you need to establish a baseline of trust that makes it safe to voice dissenting views. You may also need to develop people's skills in areas such as how to de-personalize ideas, how to ensure that everyone's views get heard, and how to make it clear that once the debate is done, the decision is binding on everyone taking part, even if their view wasn't adopted.

Since employees watch their managers' behaviour for cues on the organisation's values, managers can signal the acceptability of conflict by engaging in debate with their seniors. If employees see managers acquiesce to their senior managers without open debate, they're likely to follow suit. If on the other hand, there is an open commitment to debate and an explicit understanding that debate moves the organisation to better decisions, then employees are more likely to bring their ideas into the arena.

Role modelling is only one of several ways that management can signal to employees that conflict is a natural part of collaboration, one that can be managed successfully in the organisation. Companies can overtly state that conflict is okay; at McKinsey, for example, the obligation to dissent is a core value because we believe it gets us to better answers when solving complex issues for clients. This obligation is reinforced at every level of training and in company discussions of firm values. Skills in encouraging and managing healthy conflict successfully can be part of ongoing training programs. And of course, managers can reinforce these principles by ensuring that employees don't suffer negative consequences solely for disagreeing or introducing constructive conflict into a conversation.

We've seen many interesting examples of ways to manage conflict effectively and openly in organisations.

- Some groups use a visual symbol – a yellow card, for example – in meetings as a way for individuals to signal that they have an objection or that they feel their view (or someone else's) is being overlooked. Bob Sutton and other management researchers have noted the tendency for senior people to dominate conversation within meetings. Raising the yellow card signals that the objector is acting within the group-defined agreement of behaviour and serves as a cue to remind the others that the group has agreed on the necessity and value of conflicting opinions and debate.
- In a real-time production environment, quick and informal meetings can resolve issues and fix small problems before they become big ones. Following a series of late deliveries (complete with subsequent recriminations) at one aerospace company, the global head of operations began a policy where if a conflict arose or a mistake was discovered along the production line, all work

> in that section stopped immediately. The managers of that section, along with those of the sections immediately upstream and downstream, gathered quickly in a team room for a fast meeting to resolve the issue. These meetings rarely took more than 20 minutes, sometimes less than 10, and occurred only a few times a week. But they were effective in quickly resolving problems that might otherwise simmer or create larger issues. Stopping the production line may look expensive, but it was less costly than the mistakes that would otherwise have occurred.

Both of these examples show how managers implemented simple but effective ways for employees to air their conflicts, to openly debate their opinions in a safe environment.

Of course, managing conflict is only one aspect of creating healthy collaboration. In this series , we'll also explore the roles of people in the collaboration network (brokers and bottlenecks), focusing on collaboration as a means to the organisation's goals, and the need for accountability. We'll also detail the steps that companies must take to make their collaboration deliver effective impact, in terms of business success and employee morale. Finally, we'll also look at other opinions on the role and importance of collaboration, including the views of INSEAD's Morten Hansen who argues in a recent book that a focus on collaboration for its own sake can distract managers from the goals that effective collaboration is intended to achieve and that collaboration should be targeted to the places it adds value.

The Challenges Facing Research

R&D Cost

Research and development (R&D) represents a large and rapidly growing effort in both industrialized and semi-industrialized nations. In 1997 the United States spent $151 billion on industrial R&D and $32 billion on military R&D, for a total of $183 billion, equal to 2.5 percent of the gross national product (GNP). Similar ratios exist for economically advanced countries, such as Germany, France, the United Kingdom, and Japan. In order to compete in the international marketplace, rapidly industrializing countries such as South Korea, Indonesia, and Brazil have national policies in place for developing indigenous R&D. The goal is substitution of strategic imports and development of exports. Major countries not politically aligned with the Western powers—notably Russia, China, and India, and to a certain extent, France and Israel—perform significant levels of R&D for defence purposes, in order (1) to be technologically and logistically independent from Western sources, and (2) to export arms to third world countries. South Africa, Iraq, and North Korea spent inordinate amounts of their limited GNPs for military purposes in the 1990s.

The reason for this increased emphasis on R&D is that it creates new or improved technology that in turn can be converted through technology management into a competitive advantage at the business, corporate, and national level. While the process of technological innovation (of which R&D is the first phase) is complex and risky, the rewards can be very high, as witnessed, for example, by GE Engineering Plastics. Started in 1957 and based on R&D, the business grew to $7 billion in sales by 1997.

The relationship between R&D and economic growth is complex, but several economic studies have come to the conclusion that it is very significant. The "social" rate of return of industrial and agricultural R&D is on the order of 50 to 70 percent, while the "private" rate of return is on the order of 25 to 50 percent. The reason that the private rate is approximately half the social rate is that the originator of R&D cannot appropriate all the benefits of innovations and must share them with customers, the public, and even competitors. The Strategic Management Institute determined that, at the business level, the return of R&D for 42 major U.S. corporations was 33 percent in 1978. Therefore, R&D is a good investment for business, but a risky one—the majority of R&D projects fail to provide the expected financial results, and the successful projects (25 to 50 percent) must also pay for the projects that are unsuccessful or terminated early by management.

Objectives and Types of R&D

The objective of academic and institutional R&D is to obtain new knowledge, which may or may not be applied to practical uses. In contrast, the objective of industrial R&D is to obtain new knowledge *applicable to the company's business needs,* that eventually will result in new or improved products, processes, systems, or services that can increase the company's sales and profits.

The National Science Foundation defines three types of R&D: basic research, applied research, and development. Basic research has as its objective a fuller knowledge or understanding of the subject under study, rather than a practical application thereof. As applied to the industrial sector, basic research is defined as research that advances scientific knowledge but does not have specific commercial objectives, although such investigation may be in the fields of present or potential interest to the company.

Applied research is directed towards gaining knowledge or understanding necessary for determining the means by which a recognised and specific need may be met. In industry, applied research includes investigations directed to the discovery of new specific knowledge having specific commercial objectives with respect to products, processes, or services.

Development is the systematic utilisation of the knowledge or understanding gained from research toward the production of useful materials, devices, systems, or methods, including design and development of prototypes and processes.

At this point, it is important to differentiate development from engineering, which can be defined as utilisation of state-of-the-art knowledge for the design and production of marketable goods and services. In other words, research creates knowledge, and development develops and builds prototypes and proves their feasibility. Engineering then converts these prototypes into products or services that can be offered to the marketplace or into processes that can be used to produce commercial products and services.

In modem industrial practice, the distinction between R (research) and D (development) is not always clear. At General Electric's (GE) R&D Centre, a relatively small percentage (5 to 10 percent) of the total effort is devoted to "exploratory research," with results expected within a span of 10 to 15 years and no specific commercial applications. All the remaining efforts are lumped together and accounted for as R&D. Also, the relative importance of R&D varies according to a company's strategy and culture. Some companies, such as E.I. du Pont de Nemours & Co. and Sony, still rely heavily on research to eventually develop new products such as Kevlar or the VCR. Other companies prefer to conduct little or no research and instead develop new products from the results of research generated by others that may be generally available in the public domain or acquired legally. In the United States, Apple Computer Inc. and Microsoft Corp. conduct relatively little research but are exceptionally creative at development. The Japanese consumer electronics industry initially utilised the results of American and European research creatively and effectively to enter the international marketplace through new low-cost, high-quality products, which were developed, designed, and manufactured in a relatively short time. As technology became harder to acquire, many Japanese companies switched from development to research. For instance, in the 1950s, Toshiba was heavily dependent on GE's technology, but it now has a major independent R&D laboratory. Thanks to this change in R&D strategy, several Japanese firms have become world leaders in specific technological areas, for instance Canon in ink-jet printers, Toray in carbon fibres, Honda in small internal combustion engines, Fanuc in factory automation , and Toshiba in portable computers .

R&D and Technology Acquisition

In many cases, technology required for industrial purposes is available in the marketplace, usually for a price. Before embarking on the lengthy and risky process of performing its own R&D, a company should perform a "make or buy" analysis and decide whether or not the new R&D project is strategically and economically justified.

The following influencing factors should be considered: proprietariness, timing, risk , and cost.

Proprietariness

If a technology can be safeguarded as proprietary, and protected by patents , trade secrets, nondisclosure agreements, etc., the technology becomes the exclusive property of the company and the value is much higher. In fact, a valid patent grants a company a temporary monopoly for 20 years to use the technology as it sees fit, usually to maximize sales and profits. In this case, a high level of R&D effort is justified for a relatively long period (up to ten years) with an acceptable risk of failure. Typical examples are the pharmaceutical companies and some high-tech materials producers. For instance, more than ten years and expenditures in excess of $1 billion dollars were required by Pfizer to develop Viagra, a treatment for male impotence, but the potential market is very large and will continue for a long time. Similarly, GE developed man-made industrial diamonds in its research laboratory in the early 1950s. Although the original patents have expired, GE is still the world's leading supplier. Its major competitor, De Beers, acquired a GE license in the late 1950s and still produces diamonds with the GE process.

On the contrary, if the technology cannot be protected, as is the case with certain software programs, expensive in-house R&D is not justified since the software may be copied by a competitor or "stolen" by a disloyal employee. In this case, the secret of commercial success is staying ahead of the competition by developing continuously improved software packages, supported by a strong marketing effort. MapInfo, a new venture founded in 1986, developed the first software program for displaying maps and related databases on a personal computer. They are still the world leader, thanks to the improved and expanded versions of the original mapping system and to a broad spectrum of application packages issued regularly since first commercialization.

Timing

If the market growth rate is slow or moderate, in-house or contracted R&D may be the best means to obtain the technology. On the other hand, if the market is growing very fast and competitors are rushing in, the "window of opportunity" may close before the technology has been developed by the new entrant. In this case, it is better to acquire the technology and related know-how, in order to enter the market before it is too late. For instance, in December 1998 America Online acquired Netscape, the company with the most expertise in Internet browser software, in order to be able to compete effectively with Microsoft, Yahoo!, and many other Internet providers. Because of the Internet explosion, America Online had neither the people nor the time to develop its own proprietary software, and was consequently willing to pay $4.21 billion for Netscape.

Risk

Inherently, technology development is always riskier than technology acquisition because the technical success of R&D cannot be guaranteed. There is always the risk that the planned performance specifications will not be met, that the time to project completion will be stretched out, and that the R&D and manufacturing costs will be higher than forecasted. On the other hand, acquiring technology entails a much lower risk, since the product, process, or service, can be seen and tested before the contract is signed. This is the reason why rapidly industrializing countries represent a major fast-growing market for technology available from the more advanced nations. In the past such countries acquired older, obsolescent versions of technology, but now they demand the latest, in order to be competitive in the global marketplace.

Regardless of whether the technology is acquired or developed, there is always the risk that it will soon become obsolete and be displaced by a superior technology. This risk cannot be entirely removed, but it can be considerably reduced by careful technology forecasting and planning. If market growth is slow, and no winner has emerged among the various competing technologies, it may be wiser to monitor these technologies through "technology gatekeepers" and be ready to jump in as the winner emerges. For instance, in the development of nonimpact magnetic printers, several technologies were researched and developed: lasers, laser xerography, electrostatic, magnetic, and ink jet. In the 1970s, GE jumped on the magnetic technology bandwagon without considering alternative technologies; after spending nearly $10 million and ten years to develop its product, the company found no takers for its poor performing printer. In the meantime IBM, Xerox, Honeywell, and several Japanese companies had developed successful printers using the other technologies listed above. In retrospect, GE could have reduced its risk by monitoring the various competing technologies through gatekeepers in its R&D centre and by starting a crash program (as it did with computerized axial tomography, a medical diagnostic imaging system) as soon as the market was ready and the winning technology had emerged.

Cost

For a successful product line with a relatively long life, acquisition of technology is more costly, but less risky, than technology development. Normally, royalties are paid in the form of a relatively low initial payment as "earnest money," and as periodic payments tied to sales. These payments continue throughout the period of validity of the licensing agreement . Since these royalties may amount to 2 to 5 percent of sales, this creates an undue burden of continuing higher cost to the licensee, everything else being equal. On the other hand, R&D requires a high front-end investment and therefore a longer period of negative cash flow. There are also intangible costs involved in acquiring technology: the licensing agreements may have restrictive geographic or application clauses, other businesses may have access to the same technology and compete with lower prices or stronger marketing. Finally, the licensee is dependent upon the licensor for technological advances, or even for keeping up to date, and this may be dangerous. As a typical example, GE gave a general design and manufacturing license for heavy electrical equipment (hydraulic turbines, transformers, circuit breakers) to its subsidiaries in Italy, CGE (Compagnia Generale di Elettricita), and in Spain, GEE (General Electrica Espafiola), for only 1.5 percent of sales. The problem arose when GE Power Systems decided to abandon the three businesses and drastically cut back R&D on steam turbines. The GE subsidiaries were stuck with obsolescent technologies and had to scramble to find other sources, since they lacked the resources and the time to perform in-house R&D.

Moving ahead with R&D

Once the decision has been made to perform R&D, the company should decide where and how such R&D should be carried out. There are various possibilities: in-house R&D in the company laboratories, externally contracted R&D, and joint R&D. In-house R&D commands a strategic advantage, since the company is the sole owner of the technology and can protect it from unauthorized uses. In addition, since

R&D is basically a learning process, the company can develop a group of experienced scientists and engineers that can be employed in developing more advanced products and processes and in transferring the results of their R&D to operations and to customers. Since R&D personnel do not like to work alone and are stimulated by peers, however, the laboratory should have a critical mass in the core technologies and support services. In some cases, critical mass may exceed the company resources, and external R&D will have to be contracted.

External R&D is usually contracted out to specialised nonprofit research institutions, such as Battelle Memorial Institute or SRI International in the United States, or to universities. The advantages are that these institutions may already have experienced personnel in the disciplines to be researched, as well as the necessary laboratory and test equipment. This will save money and especially time in comparison with in-house R&D. The disadvantages are that the company will not benefit from the learning experience, and may become overly dependent on the contractor. Also, the technology transfer may be difficult and there is always the possibility of leaks to competitors. In the case of universities, costs are usually lower and there is the additional benefit of identifying graduate students who may be hired later and researchers who may be employed as consultants when needed.

Joint R&D has been carried out systematically in Europe and Japan and has now become popular in the United States after antitrust laws were relaxed and tax incentives offered to research and development consortia. In a consortium, several companies with congruent interests join together to perform R&D, either in a separate organisation (such as SEMATECH, the Semiconductor Manufacturing Technology Consortium), or in a university. The advantages are lower costs, since each company does not have to invest in similar equipment; a critical mass of researchers; and the interchange of information among the sponsors. The disadvantages are that all the sponsors have access to the same R&D results. Because of antitrust considerations, however, the R&D performed must be precompetitive, and each participant in the joint R&D must separately apply to its products, processes, and services the information obtained. In some countries (for example, Japan), this joint research is sponsored, if not imposed, by the government and the companies have no choice but to comply with the "directives" of MITI, the Ministry of Technology and Industry.

R&D Laboratory Organisation and Funding

For reasons of efficiency and control and to facilitate communications and synergy among researchers, R&D is usually performed within R&D laboratories, also called R&D centres. The organisational positioning and the funding of these laboratories is often a controversial matter and is still evolving. There have been three phases in the evolution of R&D in large and medium companies since the 1950s.

Phase I

After World War II, it was believed that R&D was the key to the success of a technology-based company. All that was needed was to have the "best" (in terms of creativity and training) scientists available, give them well-equipped research laboratories, plenty of money, maximum freedom to do their own research, and wait for the inevitable scientific discoveries. According to the director of research of Eastman Kodak Co. "the best person to decide what research shall be done is the man who is doing the research." The laboratory, in order to ensure full independence, was part of the corporate staff and was entirely funded by the corporation, which "assessed" its cost to operations. Little attention was given to how to transfer the research results to operations, or how to couple R&D activities with the company business strategies. In effect, technology management was not practiced.

Unfortunately, this laissez-faire management approach produced few useful results. In some cases, the scientists met insurmountable technical barriers (for instance, high-efficiency low-cost solar cells) or made important discoveries unrelated to the firm's strategic and business thrust (for instance, Nobel prizes in astrophysics and cosmology awarded to a telephone company). Some laboratories were unable to transfer their new technologies to the company operations and, in frustration, turned to more receptive audiences, including competitors. A well-publicized example is the development of the STAR PC by the Xerox Palo Alto Research Centre (PARC). The computer business unit of Xerox was interested only in mainframe computers and disdained the STAR as a toy. Steve Jobs, the founder of Apple Computer, visited PARC, realised the potential of the new technology, hired the PARC researchers, developed the Lisa and Macintosh personal computers, and made a fortune.

Phase II

As a reaction to these problems, operations were encouraged to set up their own laboratories, mostly to do development for a specific business. GE, for instance, had two central laboratories: the Research Laboratory and the General Engineering and Consulting Laboratory (later renamed the Advanced Technology Laboratory), both located in Schenectady, New York. These were later joined to form the present

GE R&D Centre. In addition, GE set up an Electronics Lab in Syracuse, New York, a Space Sciences Lab in Valley Forge, Pennsylvania, an Appliance Lab in Louisville, Kentucky, and a Plastics Application Lab in Pittsfield, Massachusetts. The R&D Centre's mission was to perform research and longer term development of benefit to several operating units. The mission of the other laboratories was to perform shorter term research and mostly development for the businesses to which they were organisationally responsible and from which they received funding. To ensure closer coupling between the R&D Centre and operations, only about two-thirds of the required funds came from the corporation through assessments. The remaining one-third was obtained through contracts that had to be negotiated with the interested operations. Naturally, operations would fund contracts only for short- or medium-term results, usually less than three years, and would not renew the contract annually unless they were satisfied. A separate "liaison office" was set up in the R&D Centre to ensure close coupling with operations, to listen to their requirements (market pull) and to persuade them to adopt the new technologies (technology push), and to help sell the R&D contracts.

Phase III

This system worked relatively well until the economic crises of the 1980s and the intensification of international competition. Many large and medium-sized corporations, faced with staggering losses and major reductions in employment, questioned the need for, and the role of, the corporate laboratory, especially its funding. Some central labs were simply eliminated, or drastically reduced in size, with their mission restricted to R&D for developing new businesses at the corporate level. Most researchers were transferred to operations, where the climate was less benign, others resigned, moving to universities or starting their own businesses. In the case of GE, there was a major cutback in the support functions of the R&D Centre, and the liaison function was eliminated. The laboratory and section managers are now responsible for coupling with operations. At the same time, the funding sources of the laboratory were reversed. Before 1982, the corporation was contributing 67 percent of the budget in assessed funds, and contracts with operations amounted to the remaining 33 percent. Under the new president, Jack Welch, contract funds now amount to 75 percent and assessed funds to 25 percent. In theory, assessed funds are for exploratory research and for new business development. In practice, some may be shared with operations, for projects of longer range impact or higher risk, which operations are unwilling to fund alone. This new funding approach does ensure close coupling with operations, but targets the R&D Centre activities towards the larger, and richer, GE businesses, such as plastics, medical systems and aircraft engines, while neglecting the poorer, less glamorous core businesses, such as power systems.

An R&D laboratory can be organised internally according to three patterns: by functions, by projects, and matrix. In the functional organisation, all researchers working in a specific discipline, for instance laser optics or polymers, are grouped in a unit and report to a manager, who is a recognised expert in the field. This organisation is similar to the various academic departments of a university. The advantages are close interaction with peers and competent evaluations of the scientific value of the researchers' work. The main disadvantage is that most industrial R&D projects require the contributions of different disciplines, and there is often nobody responsible for managing the project and integrating the work of the researchers.

In the project organisation, all researchers working on a given project report to a project manager, who is usually not an expert in the researchers' specific disciplines. The project manager evaluates the researchers on the basis of practical results, time, and money, rather than on the value of their scientific and technical contributions. The advantages are that the project can be professionally managed and corrective actions taken if the results expected are not forthcoming or budgets are not met. The main disadvantage is that projects have, by definition, a limited life. A project team, as an organisation, is disbanded as soon as the work has been completed. The researchers now have no "home" and must look for work on new projects, which may or may not be forthcoming.

The matrix organisation attempts to combine the best features of the functional and project organisations, by assigning every researcher to two supervisors: a functional manager and a project manager. The functional manager is responsible for evaluating the scientific value of the researcher's work, planning his or her career development, and providing a "home" between projects. The project manager is responsible for evaluating the researcher's contributions to the project and giving him or her the resources needed to get the job done. Obviously, the two managers must work closely together in assigning the duties of the researchers, integrating their evaluations, and reporting them to higher management.

In practice, small and shorter term projects are run according to a functional organisation, with one researcher taking on the project administration *(not* management) duties. Larger, longer range projects, such as the GE CAT (computerized axial tomography) and MRI (magnetic resonance imaging) medical diagnostic imaging systems projects, are organised as independent projects with strong professional project management. When project responsibility is transferred to operations, some of the researchers move too, thereby ensuring an effective transfer of technology. In other cases, engineers from operations are invited to join the R&D team, and they transfer back home with the project.

R&D Project Selection, Management, and Termination

Industrial R&D is generally performed according to projects (i.e., separate work activities) with specific technical and business goals, assigned personnel, and time and money budgets. These projects can either originate "top down"—for instance, from a management decision to develop a new product, such as the first IBM PC—or" bottom up" from an idea originated by an individual researcher, such as the Toshiba Japanese language word processor. The size of a project may vary from a part-time effort of one researcher for a few months with a budget of tens of thousands of dollars, to major five- or ten-year projects with large multidisciplinary teams of tens of researchers and budgets exceeding millions of dollars. Therefore, project selection and evaluation is one of the more critical and difficult subjects of R&D management. Of equal importance, although less emphasized in practice, is the subject of project termination, particularly in the case of unsuccessful or marginal projects.

Normally, a company or a laboratory will have requests for a greater number of projects than can be effectively implemented. Therefore, R&D managers are faced with the problem of allocating scarce resources of personnel, equipment, laboratory space, and funds to a broad spectrum of competing projects. Since the decision to start on an R&D project is both a technical and a business decision, R&D managers should select projects on the basis of the following objectives, in order of importance:

- maximizing the long-term return on investment
- making optimum use of the available human and physical resources
- maintaining a balanced R&D portfolio and controlling risk
- fostering a favourable climate for creativity and innovation

Project selection is usually done once a year, by listing all ongoing projects and the proposals for new projects, evaluating and comparing all these projects according to quantitative and qualitative criteria, and prioritizing the projects in "totem pole" order. The funds requested by all the projects are compared with the laboratory budget for the following year and the project list is cut off at the budgeted amount. Projects above the line are funded, those below the line delayed to the following year or tabled indefinitely. Some experienced R&D managers do not allocate all the budgeted funds, but keep a small percentage on reserve to take care of new projects that may be proposed during the year, after the laboratory's official budget has been approved. These unallocated amounts are often purposely disguised as "proposal" or "exploratory" funds, or made available by over-budgeting some "safe" projects, or even hidden by working on "underground projects" without the knowledge of headquarters. For instance, the highly successful Toshiba laptop computer was vetoed twice by Tokyo headquarters, and was developed in the Ome factory by ten engineers who, protected by the general manager, pretended to be working on budgeted military computer projects.

Since R&D projects are subject to the risk of failure, the expected value (EV) of a project can be evaluated *ex ante* according to the following statistical formula:

where *P* is the payoff if the project is successful, that is, the stream of net income accruing to the company over the life of the new product (or process or service) resulting from the project. The payoff *P* is then multiplied by the probability of success, which is the product of three separate probabilities:

- p_t is the probability of technical success, i.e., that the new product or process will meet the technical and functional specifications
- p_c is the probability of commercial success, i.e., that the new product will be accepted by the marketplace and will achieve the forecasted market share
- p_f is the probability of financial success, i.e., that the new product will achieve the forecasted financial goals, in terms of profits, return on investment, and cash flow.

Consequently, project evaluation must be performed along two separate orthogonal real dimensions: technical evaluation, to establish the probability of technical success, and business evaluation, to establish the payoff and the probabilities of commercial and financial success. Once the expected value (EV) of a project has been determined, it should be divided by the forecasted cost C of the project, in order to obtain a benefit/cost ratio *R* of the form R = EV/C. Obviously the higher this ratio, the more desirable the project.

For more advanced and longer term projects, leading to major (rather than incremental) innovation, it may be difficult to establish reliable values of P, C, Pt, Pc, and pf. In this case, a "relative" comparison of projects is made based on their respective "technical quality" and "potential business value."

Technical quality is evaluated by analyzing and rating the clarity of the project goals; the extent of the technical, institutional, and market penetration obstacles that must be overcome; the adequacy of the skills and facilities available in the laboratory for carrying out the work; and, finally, how easily the project results can be transferred to an interested business unit.

The potential business value of a project is defined in terms of the market share of an existing market that can be captured by the new product, or by the size of a new market that can be developed by the new product, or by the value of new technology that can be sold by the company or transferred to its customers.

After the first tentative list of projects has been established in order of priority, it is "matched" with the existing laboratory human and physical resources to make sure that these resources are well utilised. In fact, creative human resources are the laboratory's most valuable asset, and these should not be wasted by asking researchers to do work outside their disciplines and interests. Also, it is difficult, in a short time, to change the "mix" of available disciplines and equipment, and to hire and fire researchers as is done for labour. Thus, a shift towards new disciplines should be done gradually, avoiding the underutilisation or overloading of the existing resources.

Once the tentative list of prospects has been modified according to the above, the entire "project portfolio" of the R&D laboratory should be balanced, in order to control risk, according to the three types of probabilities listed above.

Technical risk is controlled in two ways: (1) by having a spectrum of projects ranging from low to medium to high technical risk; and (2) by avoiding "bunching" too many projects in the same technology, particularly if the technology could be replaced by a superior technology during the expected lifetime of the new product.

Commercial risk can be controlled by not having "too many eggs in one basket"—that is, by targeting different market segments (e.g., government, capital equipment, consumer, industrial, international) and attacking different competitors, since directly targeting a major competitor may trigger a dangerous counteroffencive and a price war.

Financial risk is controlled by having a majority of small and medium-size projects (in terms of R&D expense), a few large projects, and no projects that, in case of failure, could bankrupt the company. Financial risk, in terms of cash flow, is also controlled by having a spectrum (in time to payoff) of more short and medium-term projects than long-term projects. This type of spectrum is also psychologically important to maintain the credibility of the R&D laboratory in the face of upper-level executives who keep asking "What have you done for me lately?"

By definition, R&D is a risky activity, and there are no "zero-risk" R&D projects, since these would then be engineering projects. While the majority of the projects in an R&D portfolio should be categorized as low-risk, some medium-risk projects are justified, and even a few high-risk projects, provided their expected value is high. In other words, the higher the risk, the higher the expected payoff if the project succeeds.

Finally, project evaluation and selection should be made objectively, in order to develop and maintain a favourable climate for creativity and innovation. Researchers will be naturally disappointed when their projects are not approved. Some may even suspect that other projects were preferred for subjective reasons, such as the "halo" effect (the past track record and prestige of other, more senior, researchers), the reluctance of management to terminate less-deserving projects, and especially political influences to select" pet" projects of executives. If there is a feeling that project selection is not done objectively, many researchers, particularly the junior ones, will lose their enthusiasm and renounce proposing new projects of a high potential value for the company. Eventually, if this situation persists, the laboratory will lose its creativity and concentrate on routine low-risk (but also low-payoff!) or "political" projects, and it will have difficulty in keeping and attracting the best researchers. Therefore, it is desirable that the project evaluation and selection criteria be properly explained and that all researchers be asked to participate in the evaluation process. Also, the final project portfolio should be presented to, and discussed with, all the researchers.

The management of R&D projects basically follows the principles and methods of project management. There is, however, one significant caveat in relation to normal engineering projects: R&D projects are risky, and it is difficult to develop an accurate budget, in terms of technical milestones, costs, and time to completion of the various tasks. Therefore, R&D budgets should be considered initially as tentative, and should be gradually refined as more information becomes available as a result of preliminary work and the learning process. Historically, many R&D projects have exceeded, sometimes with disastrous consequences, the forecasted and budgeted times to completion and funds to be expended. A typical example is the Concorde supersonic aircraft, a high-visibility "national prestige" project of the French and British governments. The original budget was £150 million and 5 years to completion, while the actual expenditures were £1.1 billion and 12 years. As a consequence, the Concorde was a great technical success and a financial disaster! Although the Concorde was still flying in 1999, only the operating expenses were covered, and there was no prospect of recovering the initial investment. Therefore, in R&D, measuring technical progress and completion of milestones is generally more important than measuring expenditures over time.

Finally, termination of projects is a difficult subject because of the political repercussions on the laboratory. Theoretically, a project should be discontinued for one of the following three reasons:

1. There is a change in the environment—for instance, new government regulations, new competitive offerings, or price declines—that make the new product less attractive to the company.
2. Unforeseen technical obstacles are encountered and the laboratory does not have the resources to overcome them.
3. The project falls hopelessly behind schedule and corrective actions are not forthcoming.

Due to organisational inertia, and the fear of antagonizing senior "prima donna" researchers or executives with pet projects, there is often the tendency to let a project continue, hoping for a miraculous breakthrough that seldom happens.

In theory, an optimal number of projects should be initiated and this number should be gradually reduced over time to make room for more deserving projects. Also, the monthly cost of a project is much lower in the early stages than in the later stages, when more personnel and equipment have been committed. Thus, from a financial risk management viewpoint, it is better to waste money on several promising young projects than on a few maturing "dogs" with low payoff and high expense. In practice, in many laboratories it is difficult to start a new project because all the resources have already been committed, and just as difficult to terminate a project, for the reasons given above. Thus, an able and astute R&D manager should continuously evaluate his or her project portfolio in relation to changes in company strategy, should continuously and objectively monitor the progress of each R&D project, and should not hesitate to terminate projects that have lost their value to the company in terms of payoff and probability of success.

In conclusion, by assuring a close coupling with the company's strategic goals and by maintaining close contacts with operations, the laboratory and the R&D function will maintain credibility and strengthen their strategic value for the corporation.

Operational Efficiency

In a business context, operational efficiency can be defined as the ratio between the input to run a business operation and the output gained from the business. When improving operational efficiency, the output to input ratio improves.

Inputs would typically be money (cost), people (headcount) or time/effort. Outputs would typically be money (revenue, margin, cash), new customers, customer loyalty, market differentiation, headcount productivity, innovation, quality, speed & agility, complexity or opportunities.

The terms "operational efficiency", "efficiency" and "productivity" are often used interchangeably. An explanation to the difference between efficiency and (total factor) productivity is found in "An Introduction to Efficiency and Productivity Analysis". To complicate, "operational excellence" which is about continuous improvement - not limited to efficiency - is occasionally used when meaning operational efficiency. From time to time "operating efficiency" is also used with the same meaning as "operational efficiency".

Measuring Operational Efficiency

In order to improve operational efficiency, one has to start by measuring it. Since operational efficiency is about the output to input ratio, it should be measured both on the input and the output side. Quite often, company management is measuring primarily on the input side, e.g. the unit production cost or the man hours required to produce one unit. Even though important, input indicators like the unit production cost should not be seen as sole indicators of operational efficiency. When measuring operational efficiency, a company should define, measure and track a number of performance indicators on both the input and output side. The exact definition of these performance indicators will vary from industry to industry, but typically these categories are covered:

- Input: Operational expenditure (OPEX), capital expenditure (CAPEX), headcount (including headcount of partners)

- Output: Revenue, customer numbers/distribution between segments, quality, growth, customer satisfaction

Comparing Operational Efficiency

If the intention is to compare numbers with others through benchmarking it is important to define, measure and track performance indicators for load and complexity as well. Even within the same industry, customer behaviour might e.g. be significantly different between two markets (or two countries) leading to one company having to assign more resources and cost to handling of customers. Not measuring such load and complexity factors might lead to incorrect conclusions on operational efficiency.

When interpreting the quantitative results of the benchmarking, it is important to consider the strategic differentiation:

"Cost is generated by performing activities, and cost advantage arises from performing particular activities more efficiently than competitors. Similarly, differentiation arises from both the choice of activities and how they are performed."

When qualitatively interpreting the quantitative results of the benchmarking, one has to take the company strategy into consideration - as well as the individual strategies of the other members of the peer group. If not done, quantitative results that are a consequence of strategy, not of inefficiency, can't be eliminated.

One company might have a strategy to differentiate with low price. For that company, it is critical to have low unit production costs and high efficiency in distribution. For another company, differentiating with premium quality, the unit production cost is not that critical (but still important to know, of course). Instead, it will be critical to have satisfied and loyal customers and a high absolute revenue per customer. Actual quality levels will also be key to understand.

Improving Operational Efficiency

When improving operational efficiency, companies have a few alternatives. The most common are:

- Same for less, i.e. same output for less input
- More for same, i.e. more output for same input
- Much more for more, i.e. much more output for more input

It is a common misconception that costs, in absolute terms, are always cut when improving operational efficiency. It is true for the "same for less" alternative, but not for the two other alternatives. It can be operationally efficient to increase cost - as long as the output is increasing more.

One example of a *same for less* alternative is when a manufacturing company reduces its total personnel (and thereby personnel cost) while still producing the same volume of goods. This can e.g. be achieved through centralisation, automation or optimisation of working processes. An example of a *more for same* alternative is a manufacturing company reducing its output of faulty products (and thereby reducing after sales cost) without using more money or resources. This can e.g. be achieved through use of quality management systems, addressing quality in existing training programs for personnel or introduction of higher quality requirements when prolonging subcontractor agreements.

An example of a *much more for more* alternative is when a manufacturing company invests in a new production plant which will enable them to produce products with a higher level of refinement than what could be produced in the old production plants. These products can be sold with a premium that more than compensates for the additional cost. Another example of "much more for more" is when a service company invests in expanding its customer service in order to increase customer satisfaction and customer loyalty.

Cost Externalizing

Cost externalizing is a socio-economical term describing how a business maximizes its profits by off-loading indirect costs and forcing negative effects to a third party.

Business to Society

Fundamentally, cost externalization occurs when a company transfers some of its moral responsibilities as costs to the community directly or as degradation to the environment. For example, railroads and airlines transfer the cost of fuel, noise, and terminal infrastructure to the community. Airlines and auto manufacturers transfer the cost of degraded air quality to the community and the environment. By externalizing to the community or the environment, many true costs become lost in analysis because the true cost is non-quantifiable and neither the community nor the environment have effective advocates to recoup the damages. A major modern theme in the relationship of business to society is the society's ability (or inability) to resist this kind of externalization. In its extreme, society collapses as business realises its profits.

Business to Market

Cost externalizing is one of the steps a company may take to "shape up" or reduce overhead by down sizing a cost centre or an unprofitable department. An example of cost externalizing would be using a global courier service (such as FedEx and UPS) to do all or most of the shipping and logistics work for the company. For a business to take on the responsibilities of worldwide shipping by itself would be too costly. It would be far more sensible to let a third party who specialise in shipping to take care of the task and pay them for it.

B2B Cost Externalization

Cost externalizing in no way should be considered a quick fix. Simply forcing suppliers and service providers to take on more responsibilities and cost is not a healthy externalization of cost. Careful operational forecasting must take place before taking steps towards cost externalization. Otherwise, there is no way to ascertain if cost externalizing would actually lower the operational cost of the company.

To externalize cost, budgeting must also take place. Because the company will be paying out to a third party, the cost would be more clear than when the process took place in-house. This would in turn give a chance for the suppliers and service providers to compete for business and may further reduce cost. Yet in some cases, the reduction in cost may lead to reduction in quality. Because quality is not quantified easily, it may be difficult to measure and compare - especially if the quality for all parties begin to fall, business managers may fail to notice the change in quality. This is one kind of control that a business loses when externalizing cost.

B2C Cost Externalization

Another option is for a company to transfer some of its costs to its customers. For example, reducing staff in a customer service department that handles incoming phone calls will usually increase hold times for customers seeking support. The company reduces its costs by reducing staff, while the customer bears the increased cost of waiting on hold. Thus an expense has been transferred from the company to the customer. This can reduce customer satisfaction, to the point that some customers will be motivated to switch to another company. However if the company can gain a legal monopoly (through, for example, intellectual property laws) the customer has no choice of a competitor available. The customer's only option then is to take it or leave it.

Customers can also absorb some of a company's costs by performing tasks that the company formerly provided. An early example of this was the self-service gas station, followed more recently by self checkout kiosks in grocery stores. This can have less of a negative customer satisfaction impact because some customers actually prefer to help themselves.

As in any business operation, costs externalization has its pros and cons. It is up to the business managers to make the decisions and take advantage of cost externalization.

Price War

Price war is "commercial competition characterized by the repeated cutting of prices below those of competitors". One competitor will lower its price, then others will lower their prices to match. If one of them reduces their price again, a new round of reductions starts. In the short term, price wars are good for buyers, who can take advantage of lower prices. Often they are not good for the companies involved because the lower prices reduce profit margins and can threaten their survival.

In the medium to long term, price wars can be good for the dominant firms in the industry. Typically, the smaller, more marginal, firms cannot compete and must close. The remaining firms absorb the market share of those that have closed. The real losers then, are the marginal firms and their investors. In the long term, the consumer may lose too. With fewer firms in the industry, prices tend to increase, sometimes higher than before the price war started.

Causes

The main reasons that price wars occur are:

- Product differentiation: Some products are, or at least are seen as, commodities. Because there is little to choose between brands, price is the main competing factor.
- Penetration pricing: If a merchant is trying to enter an established market, it may offer lower prices than existing brands.
- Oligopoly: If the industry structure is oligopolistic (that is, has few major competitors), the players will closely monitor each other's prices and be prepared to respond to any price cuts.
- Process optimization: merchants may incline to lower prices rather than shut down or reduce output if they wish to maintain the economy of scale. Similarly, new processes may make it cheaper to make the same product.
- Bankruptcy: Companies near bankruptcy may be forced to reduce their prices to increase sales volume and thereby provide enough liquidity to survive.

- Predatory pricing: A merchant with a healthy bank balance may deliberately price new or existing products in an attempt to topple existing merchants in that market.
- Competitors: A competitor might target a product and attempt to gain market share by selling its alternative at a lower price. Some argue that it is better to introduce a new rival brand instead of trying to match the prices of those already in the market.

Reactions to Price Challenges

The first reaction to a price reduction should always be to consider carefully. Has the competitor decided upon a long-term price reduction? Is this just a short-term promotion? If it is the latter, then the reaction should be that relating to short-term promotional activity, and the optimum response is often simply to ignore the challenge. Too often, price wars have been started because simple promotional activities have been misunderstood as major strategic changes.

But if it seems that it is a long-term move then there are many possible reactions:

- Reduce price: The most obvious, and most popular, reaction is to match the competitor's move. This maintains the status quo (but reduces profits pro rata). If this route is to be chosen it is as well to make the move rapidly and obviously - not least to send signals to the competitor of your intention to fight.
- Maintain price: Another reaction is to hope that the competitor has made a mistake, but if the competitor's action does make inroads into a merchant's share, this can soon mean customers lose confidence and a subsequent a loss of sales.
- Split the market: Branch one product into two, selling one as a premium and another as a basic. This effective tactic was notably used by Heublein, the former owner of the Smirnoff brand of vodka).
- React with other measures - Reducing price is not the only weapon. Other tactics can be used to great effect: improved quality, increased promotion (perhaps to improve the idea of quality).

Avoiding Price Wars

Avoidance is by far the best policy, but it is advice which may not always be taken if the benefits seem attractive to others(which they may also be to competitors).

Price Stickiness

In oligopoly markets prices can become 'sticky' because if the price rises, competitors will not follow the rise. So the merchant will lose its market share to its competitors on lower prices. But if the price falls, other players will merchants will follow suit if they can. At some point, merchants find that they can not gain profit if they cut the price further— so the sticky price remains.

Price stickiness is extremely common among large supermarket chains and prices, especially for commodities, tend not to vary much between them. Many of the supermarkets monitor price changes in other supermarket chains and vary their prices accordingly until they reach the point where any further decrease in their price will affect profits.

Chapter 2

Forms of Collaborative Research

The Triple Helix Concept

The concept of the Triple Helix of university-industry-government relationships initiated in the 1990s by Etzkowitz (1993) and Etzkowitz and Leydesdorff (1995), encompassing elements of precursor works by Lowe (1982) and Sábato and Mackenzi (1982), interprets the shift from a dominating industry-government dyad in the Industrial Society to a growing triadic relationship between university-industry-government in the Knowledge Society.

The Triple Helix thesis is that the potential for innovation and economic development in a Knowledge Society lies in a more prominent role for the university and in the hybridisation of elements from university, industry and government to generate new institutional and social formats for the production, transfer and application of knowledge. This vision encompasses not only the creative destruction that appears as a natural innovation dynamics (Schumpeter, 1942), but also the creative renewal that arises within each of the three institutional spheres of university, industry and government, as well as at their intersections.

Through subsequent development, a significant body of Triple Helix theoretical and empirical research has grown over the last two decades that provides a general framework for exploring complex innovation dynamics and for informing national, regional and international innovation and development policy-making. This substantive body of Triple Helix literature can be broadly seen from two main complementary perspectives:

(i) A (neo) institutional perspective which examines the growing prominence of the university among innovation actors through national and regional case studies (e.g. in Latin America: Mello and Rocha, 2004; Etzkowitz, Mello and Almeida, 2005; Saenz, 2008; Bianco and Viscardi, 2008; Luna and Tirtido, 2008; in Africa: Konde, 2004; Kruss, 2008; Booyens, 2011; in the US: Campbell et al. 2004; Feldman and Desrochers, 2004; Boardman 2009; Wang and Shapira, 2012; in Europe: Klofsten et al. 1999; 2010; Inzelt, 2004; Geuna and Nesta, 2006; Lawton Smith and Bagchi-Sen, 2010; Geuna and Rossi, 2011; Svensson et al. 2012) and through comparative historical analyses (e.g. Etzkowitz, 2002; Furman and MacGarvie, 2009). These studies look at various aspects of the university 'third mission' of commercialization of academic research and involvement in socio-economic development, such as forms, stakeholders, drivers, barriers, benefits and impact, university technology transfer and entrepreneurship, contribution to regional development, government policies aimed to strengthen university-industry links, etc.

The (neo) institutional perspective distinguishes between three main configurations in the positioning of the university, industry and government institutional spheres relative to each other: (i) a *statist* configuration, where government plays the lead role, driving academia and industry, but also limiting their capacity to initiate and develop innovative transformations (e.g. in Russia, China, some Latin American and Eastern Europe countries); (b) a *laissez-faire* configuration, characterised by a limited state intervention in the economy (e.g. the US, some Western Europe countries), with industry as the driving force and the other two spheres acting as ancillary support structures and having limited roles in innovation: university acting mainly as a provider of skilled human capital, and government mainly as a regulator of social and economic mechanisms; and (iii) a *balanced* configuration, specific to the transition to a Knowledge Society, where university and other knowledge institutions act in partnership with industry and government and even take the lead in joint initiatives (Etzkowitz and Leydesdorff 2000). The balanced configuration offers the most important insights for innovation, as the most favourable environments for innovation are created at the intersections of the spheres.

(ii) A (neo) evolutionary perspective, inspired by the theory of social systems of communication (Luhmann, 1975, 1984) and mathematical theory of communication (Shannon, 1948) sees the University, Industry and Government as co-evolving subsets of social systems that interact through an overlay of recursive networks and organisations which reshape their institutional arrangements through reflexive sub-dynamics (e.g. markets and technological innovations) (e.g. Leydesdorff, 1996, 1997, 1999, 2000, 2006, 2008; Leydesdorff and Meyer, 2006; Dolfsma and Leydesdorff, 2009). These interactions are part of two processes of communication and differentiation: *a functional* one, between science and markets, and *an institutional* one, between private and public control at the level of universities, industries and government, which allow various degrees of selective mutual adjustment (Leydesdorff and Etzkowitz, 1996, 1998). In addition, *internal differentiation* within each institutional sphere generates new types of links and structures between the spheres, such as industrial liaison offices in universities or strategic alliances among companies, creating new network integration mechanisms (Leydesdorff and Etzkowitz, 1998). The institutional spheres are also seen as *selection environments*, and the institutional communications between them act as *selection mechanisms*, which may generate new innovation environments and ensure thus the 'regeneration' of the system (Etzkowitz and Leydesdorff, 2000; Leydesdorff, 2000). The interactions between the Triple Helix actors can be measured in terms of probabilistic entropy, which, when negative, suggests a self-organising dynamic that may temporarily be stabilized in the overlay of communications among the carrying agencies (e.g. Leydesdorff, 2003; Leydesdorff, Dolfsma and Van der Panne, 2006). The interaction is also captured by specific indicators (e.g. bibliometrics, patent indicators) that can provide insights on trends and patterns of public-private cooperation, its geographical concentrations and implications (e.g. Kwon et al. 2012; Tijssen 2006, 2012; Azagra-Caro et al., 2010; Leydesdorff and Meyer, 2010).

The Entrepreneurial University is a central concept to the Triple Helix. It takes a pro-active stance in putting knowledge to use and in creating new knowledge. It operates according to an interactive rather than a linear model of innovation. As firms raise their technological level, they engage in higher levels of training and knowledge sharing. Government acts as a public entrepreneur and venture capitalist, in addition to its traditional regulatory role in setting the rules of the game. As universities develop links, they can combine discrete pieces of intellectual property and jointly exploit them. Innovation has expanded from an internal process within and even among firms to an activity that involves institutions not traditionally thought of as having a direct role in innovation such as universities. The academic 'third mission' - involvement in socio-economic development, next to the traditional missions of teaching and research, is most salient in the Enterprenurial University. Collaborative links with the other innovation actors have enhanced the central presence of universities in the production of scientific research over time, disproving former views that increasing diversification of knowledge production loci would diminish the role of universities in the knowledge production process. The Entrepreneurial University also has an enhanced capacity to provide students with new ideas, skills and entrepreneurial talent. Students are not only the new generations of professionals in various scientific disciplines, business, culture etc., but they can also be trained and encouraged to become entrepreneurs and firm founders, contributing to economic growth and job creation in a society that needs such outcomes more than ever. Moreover, entrepreneurial universities are also extending their capabilities of educating individuals to educating organisations, through entrepreneurship and incubation programmes and new training modules at venues such as inter-disciplinary centres, science parks, academic spin-offs, incubators and venture capital firms. Entrepreneurial universities also have an enhanced capacity to generate technology that has changed their position, from a traditional source of human resources and knowledge to a new source of technology generation and transfer. Rather than only serving as a source of new ideas for existing firms, universities are combining their research and teaching capabilities in new formats to become a source of new firm formation, especially in advanced areas of science and technology. Universities increasingly become the source of regional economic development and academic institutions are re-oriented or founded for this purpose.

The concept of Triple Helix Systems of innovation (Ranga and Etzkowitz, 2013) was recently introduced as an analytical framework that synthesises the key features of Triple Helix interactions into an 'innovation system' format, defined according to the systems theory as a set of components, relationships and functions. Among the components of Triple Helix Systems, a distinction is made between: (i) R&D and non-R&D innovators; (ii) "single-sphere" and "multi-sphere" (hybrid) institutions; and (iii) individual and institutional innovators. The relationships between components are synthesised into five main types: technology transfer, collaboration and conflict moderation, collaborative leadership, substitution, and networking. The overall function of Triple Helix systems of knowledge and innovation generation, diffusion and use is realised through a set of activities in the Knowledge, Innovation and Consensus Spaces. This perspective provides an explicit framework for the systemic interaction between Triple Helix actors that was lacking heretofore, and a more fine-grained view of the circulation of knowledge flows and resources within and among the spaces, helping to identify existing blockages or gaps. From a Triple Helix systems perspective, the consolidation of the spaces and the non-linear interactions between them can generate new combinations of knowledge and resources that can advance innovation theory and practice, especially at the regional level.

The Triple Helix: Metaphor, Model, Reality?

The complex system of a Triple Helix depends as a regime of transition on the local trajectories which can be observed (Leydesdorff & Etzkowitz 1996; Etzkowitz & Leydesdorff 1997). One witnesses the institutional dynamics between industries, governments, and universities. The dimensions of government, industry, and higher education tend to be reproduced because they continue to serve different functions. The institutions embody the value systems or the codes of these functions.

New codes of communication are being developed at all the interfaces. For example, science is no longer valued only as a quest for truth, but also from the perspective of utilisation; legal systems are developed with the aim of supporting innovative processes; industries are transformed and restructured both from the perspective of control and from the perspective of adaptation to new technological options. The institutions are involved in the transitions that they cause by their interactions.

Two discussions threaded through the meeting: one empirical, the other normative. The empirical debate raged over the question of whether universites (or the public research sector), government, and industry were sufficient components of a model to explain the emerging trends. Joske Bunders (Free University, Amsterdam) suggested that NGOs (non-governmental organisations) have played a key role in technology transfer, especially in developing countries. In her research on third-world peasants (e.g., Bunders and Broerse 1998), she found that NGO's were able to influence how technology was introduced into their societies through self-organisation and alliances with first-world social movements.

In our opinion, the Triple Helix is mainly a model for analyzing innovation in a knowledge-based economy. This model accounts for the phenomenon of emergence, that is, it helps us to understand how the innovation system is based on expectations. While the complex phenomenon of innovation remains the *explanandum*, different theories provide us with a varitey of *explanans*. More than a single explanation is expected because different perspectives are useful. To take an the evolutionary metaphor, the perspectives can be considered as the "genotypes" that reflect on specific interactions within and among the helices, while the complex dynamics of innovation are "phenotypical," that is, beyond the control of any given perspectives (Langton 1989; Leydesdorff 1998).

In contrast to biological evolution, the "genes" are not given, but constructed in the social, technical, and economic evolution of modern societies with their tendency to transform themselves and their interactions operationally by rearranging their configurations. In a new regime, the system is reconstructed from a set of its own previous states, including the natural environment and society's communal roots. Thus, technology celebrates community as a social achievement, including its ongoing redefinition of "nature" and "culture".

The enterprise is risky. As Marx noted, "alienation" is the dark side of the enlightenment process. The reconstructive transformation of nature can lead to the destruction of resources that are vital to the reproduction of the system. But there is no single "best practice." At theoretical levels, one is able to simplify the reconstruction by taking for example, the national state, the discipline, or the enterprise as a unit of analysis. Analyses of innovations in terms of national systems, major technological waves, or industries, however, fail to understand innovation in terms of the interactive results among these institutionalized spheres. Interaction presumes communication among differently coded value systems, including the risk of potential conflicts.

One example of the transformations implied was presented to the conference audience by Lucio Biggiero, with his analysis of the Italian Districts from an evolutionary perspective. The Italian Districts have been widely studied because of their economic potential. Biggiero (1998) proposes to study them as hyper-networks: because of the multitude of formal and informal links between agents in these networks, niches can be maintained with extremely high problem-solving capacities. A crucial factor is the maintenance of trust in cross-institutional relations in the face of potential conflicts (Ferraro & Borroi 1998).

Many of us may recognise the best of our own institutions as hyper-networks. While one complains about the disappearance of reliable structures, the fluidities enable us to solve problems and also to approach problems from a new angle. Most changes, of course, are not innovative in the economically relevant sense of the term. The recombinations provide the variation. The Internet has taught us to play with options as variation that enables us to envisage what actually occurs as one possible event among many possible occurrences. As we proceed in this "virtual reality," the emerging structure begins to feed back on our "real" relations. This experience is prototypical for the regime change the world is nowadays experiencing. The virtual dimension does not dissolve the "real" one, yet it changes our perspective on it (Nowak and Grantham 1998).

The hyper-network reveals new recombinations as feasible and meaningful. But one has to be able to follow up locally on these global options. One important step, however, is to recognise the specificity of the closed shop in which one tends to live. Whether this is a "national system", the problems on the agenda from a current crisis, the framework of an established discipline, or the fight for recognition of a specific transfer agency, there is always a world beyond. By envisaging new dimensions to the problem, one enlarges one's analytical scope.

"Global" versus "Local"

Future developments are expected to be the outcomes of changes in the local contingencies and their relevant environments. Global developments induce local dynamics, and local recombinations constitute the variation for higher-order systems. The contextual changes can be perceived reflexively from the perspective of local institutions. The markets and the laboratories select by using their respective codes, that is, in terms of prices and performance. "The local" and "the global" are thus important specifications for using a Triple Helix model.

In addition to their direct policy relevance (for example, for reasons of evaluation), case studies inform us about new recombinations and emerging institutional structures. These innovations reflect and anticipate on adaptation to knowledge-intensive developments. How are the contingencies communicated and optimalized so that local advantages can be exploited as in niches? These issues couple the Triple Helix model to policy agendas as in the case of regional development, university-based incubator activities and SMEs, the local organisation of new departments which cross institutional boundaries, etc.

The institutional dynamics are analyzed in terms of the coupling which they provide to global developments. In many parts of the world, a continuous "disorganisation" of existing institutional boundaries has been signalled (Turpin & Garrett-Jones 1997). While from a local perspective, this may sometimes be felt as discouraging, theorizing provides us with heuristics for assessing the multitude of possibilities that the dynamics generate. Here the evolutionary dimension of the model steps in: the disturbances generate variation which tests the existing lock-ins for other potentially emerging recombinations.

What precisely is evolving in these interactions? Authors from economics have tended to take the firm or the industry as their implied unit of analysis (Andersen 1994). Historians have often focused on technologies or on the development of the university as an indicator of developments in the knowledge infrastructure. All these units are continuously developing within a larger system; borderlines are transgressed and coevolutions are generated in the various processes of mutual shapings. This dynamics becomes complex when a trilateral overlay of interactions among the recurrent bilateral interactions provides options for even more complex forms of stabilization. Globalization or "the transition to Mode 2" are thus a consequence of increasing network relations, not a cause (Leydesdorff 1997).

First, the recursive operation of the institutions has allowed for the stabilization of mutual interactions between institutions (e.g., corporations) and technologies along trajectories (Nelson 1994). The implied trade-offs allow for accommodation to options emerging from fuzzy processes at the interfaces (Dosi 1982). The multinational corporation, for example, has deliberately exploited the differences among national systems. Additionally, a diversified corporation is to a certain extent able to capitalize on differences in the life-cycles among technologies (Abernathy & Utterback 1978). The state can analogously be locked into technologies, as in the case of energy policies (McKelvey 1997), or the state and the economy can be locked into each other, as in the Soviet system.

When the levels of control in a third dimension are distributed, options at other levels may prevail either in the international arena or locally in a given region. For example, a network at the European level provides all the partners with options that cannot be grasped at the respective national levels. Taking the example of the Airbus development in civil aviation, Koen Frenken (INRA, Grenoble) explained in his paper how the addition of another layer to Kauffman's (1993) NK-models enables us to understand why the European dimension allowed for innovation in this industry. The existing lock-ins in the respective national systems could be both maintained and recombined.

The new layers of networking induce adaptation mechanisms within the carrying units. An academic revolution is one of the consequences: most universities nowadays use their R&D potential for economic as well as scientific functions. Internally, the transfer of resources within the university from one function to another is to be legitimated in terms of positive feedbacks (Etzkowitz 1994). The new functions require additional codes of communication, to be developed in an intermediary layer of S&T policy networks (Rip & Van der Meulen 1996). Inventions of "rules of thumb" that allow for flexible applications may help to solve conflicts of interest in the public sector and develop standard practices, particularly in relation to intellectual property rights. In other cases, formalization and even legislation may be needed to secure a new environment (Berneman & Denis 1998).

Corporations which previously had to develop a technostructure within their organisations (Galbraith 1967), have now developed an interface with public institutions in response to the new regulatory regimes of environmental and other (knowledge-intensive) legislation. Randolph Guschl, Director of Corporate Technology Transfer at DuPont Central R&D, noted that DuPont's expenditure on external technology resources increased from US$20 MM in 1993 to over US$45 MM in 1995, and this budget is still increasing. Another DuPont representative gave an example of R&D outsourcing to academic researchers in India. Instead of the company having to carry the entire cost of a group internally, an external group can integrate work for DuPont into a portfolio of related projects, with lower personnel and infrastructure costs.

Frances Via (Director for Contract Research, AKZO-Nobel Corporation, U.S.A.) supported the DuPont thesis with examples of how corporations are able to meet a business need faster, more cheaply, and with a better technology by leveraging external technology sources. As Guschl noted, "There are better ways to find partners than to go back to your thesis advisor of twenty years ago." DuPont asks its scientists to come with three options before making a commitment to an external supplier. This increased focus on identifying potential research providers reflects changes in the corporation, from internally producing its own R&D to drawing more on external sources. It also reflected in a new focus on licensing and spinning out internally developed technology deemed irrelevant to existing or projected business goals.

A Regime of Transitions

Knowledge-intensity induces differentiation between a strategic level (a discourse about the questions "what and why?") and an operational level ("how?") in the organisations involved (Chandler 1962; Galbraith & Nathanson 1978). Both levels can be made relevant for specific forms of collaboration. The dynamics of the uncertainties involved, however, do not allow for rigidly fixed boundaries. Participants at one level of networking can use collaborations or boundaries at other levels as resources. Conflicts have to be addressed and elaborated into (perhaps provisional) codifications.

The established systems try to retain their contributions by reproducing themselves. Thus, the network is expected to contain tendencies toward both integration and differentiation. Whereas each co-evolution exhibits a tendency towards "mutual shaping" and thus stability along a trajectory, the complex dynamics of a Triple Helix allows for reshaping of the trajectories on which the next-order system recursively has to build.

The capacity of relevant participants to handle the complexity of the implied communications, is then the evolving unit. Adelaide Baeta discussed the learning capacity of technology transfer in the Brazilian context (Baeta 1998). Herbert Fusfeld, former President of the Industrial Research Institute (IRI) and Director Emeritus of the Centre for Science and Technology Policy at Rensselaer Polytechnic Institute, noted how the meaning of technology transfer has evolved, from how R&D results are moved from central laboratories of companies to their operating divisions, from developed to developing countries, and from outside the company into the company.

Not only the substance of the communications develop, but also their codes. By translating between codes, translators communicate reflexively about communications at the interfaces. While heretofore institutional and functional differentiations have tended to correspond as in a division of labour, one now may use the one differentiation to reorganise the other. The coordination mechanisms of society have thus become further differentiated. Strategic communications open new windows by combining perspectives, while the institutional dynamics adapt selectively, as the retention mechanism. When three uncertainties operate upon each other, as among markets, sciences, and control, new combinations enable the survival of niches which are superior to the 'natural' fits, yet unexpectedly and from a global perspective. Niche management and human capital management are core objectives of this complex dynamics (Tong 1996).

More than any other technology, the Internet has been paradigmatic for a global transition in the communication structure beyond the control of corporations and/or national governments. From this perspective, "national systems of innovation" are still relevant, but only as one dynamic among other subdynamics of the complex system. "User interfaces" and "networks of innovation" can be relevant for the further development of a regional university, but so are the traditional disciplines. The different interfaces codify along other axes. The one dynamic replaces the other only to a certain extent and perhaps only provisionally; otherwise, the new dimensions of communication constitute additional layers (Leydesdorff & Van den Besselaar 1997).

The emerging mix of opportunities are continuously assessed, and agreements and disagreements about the best guesses can then be codified and communicated. In this knowledge-intensive enterprise one is able to restructure continuously the future location of research. A theoretically informed exchange of examples and ideas is needed, since further learning requires reaching beyond established boundaries among domains. Manabu Eto (MITI, Japan), for example, reported on a major conclusion of an evaluation study of collaborative projects in Japan: too much competition among otherwise equivalent partners in one of the dimensions can be a disturbing factor in the collaboration (Eto 1998). One needs differences to create new perspectives. Each partner, for example, has to be forced to explain what s/he means when using jargon and abbreviations.

Models and Policies of Innovation

Among the participants we observed an increasing consensus that there is no single "best practice." Common themes, such as differences in funding mechanisms and their structuring effects on exchange mechanisms, brought a wide range of interests among delegates into focus in plenary sessions, while the rest of the conference was mainly organised in parallel streams. The focus, however, was all the time on "innovation" and the knowledge infrastructure, and not on specific industries, a technology, or institutional reform. What can be learned about innovation when comparing across industries, across technologies, across nations? How can one disentangle intellectually the complexities of the interactions involved?

The Brazilian Technology Agency (FINEPE) and the State Science Agency of Rio de Janiero (FABERJ), represented by their scientific directors, have invited "Triple Helix III: Relations Among Social, Economic, and Scientific Development" to Rio de Janiero in April 2000, to be preceded by a regional meeting in 1999. This outcome was among the consequences of a plenary discussion where policy models and theoretical models were confronted.

Angela Uller, director of COPPETEC at the Federal University of Rio de Janeiro, explained how the unit has become involved in community work. Residents of low-income "favelas" are invited to the university to assist in organising cooperatives, taking a new role in the formation of low-tech service businesses. The industrial relations arm of the university, utilising the interface skills gained by linking academic researchers to industry, brings these resources to bear in a creative way to address social problems, going well beyond its original official mission. The example has since become a model for a Brazilian national program.

In this same panel, Rikard Stankievicz (Lund University, Sweden) and Richard Hull (UMIST, Manchester, UK) discussed evolutionary and network models for understanding the implied changes in the concept of engineering sciences in these new social contexts, the different role of the state and local governments in organising such niches, etc. Jean-Eric Aubert (OECD, Paris) intervened from the audience with a discussion of socio-cultural differences among nations and world regions that set the scene for the possibility of creating bridges between academic puzzle-solving and social problem-solving. Analyses at the level of the social system can thus be helpful in understanding the boundaries that one may seek to overcome.

Is Technology a Celebration of Community?

A special session organised by the New York Academy of Sciences in New York City focused on the potential for high-tech development in the metropolitan region. At the meeting, James Hayward, President and CEO of Collaborative Laboratories Inc., submitted that "technology is a celebration of community." The multicultural environment of the metropolitan area makes it urgent to study communities as the social constructions needed to move technologies forward. Community as the basis of communication can no longer be taken for granted. As far as one may be able to communicate across otherwise dividing lines, one is able to find new solutions to old problems, and thus to improve on modes of production in terms of using resources (including human capital) in a more sustainable way.

The social shaping of technology has increasingly become an optimalization problem given dynamic market constraints: how can niches be sustained in which technologies can be nourished as a communal goal? How can human capital be made available at the right place and the right time given the complexities of the dynamics involved? What is the role of universities, of industry, of local governments, and of large research facilities in localizing inputs made available by higher-order dynamics such as global changes, intergovernmental organisations, technological developments, and multi-national corporations?

The Triple Helix thesis implies that the paradigm of research in innovation studies has definitively incorporated a network mode including uncertain relations with a plurality of environments. The helices contain communication processes which select on the interactive dynamics perceived at their borders using their respective codes to provide the new information with specific meanings. The different codes can be shared at the interfaces, and sometimes a transient arrangement can be institutionalized. Niches for knowledge-intensive industries are thus created and sustained.

From the evolutionary perspective, R&D and invention can be considered as institutionalized sources of variation, that is, as purposeful attempts at reflexive reconstruction. This variation is selected on market places on the basis of different systems of innovation. Markets may be local or global, and innovation systems may be public or private, regional or transnational. This complex system can no longer be fully understood from a single angle, since each perspective tends to stabilize another reflection. The systems under study are interactive and therefore transient and understandable only in terms of fluxes.

This "Mode 2" of innovation networks (cf. Gibbons *et al.* 1994) resounds with Marx's (1848) grandiose vision of modern capitalism as a system in which "all that is solid melts into air" (Berman 1982). It deviates, however, from Marx's vision in shifting the emphasis from the concreteness of industry to the elusiveness of communication networks which can be understood only reflexively. The helices are differently combined in a phase space of possibilities, in which the systems that have previously occurred provide the trajectories on which participants will have to build when constructing their innovations.

Path-dependent trajectories are expected to collide continuously, allowing for the creation of new dynamics. Following alternation between paths, a new synthesis may emerge if a next-order level of communication can be sustained. For example, contemporary science policy in the State of Rio de Janiero was found to be an amalgam of contrasting themes derived from competing interest groups and ideologies rooted in historic, economic, and geopolitical differences (Etzkowitz *et al.* 1998b). The awareness among the participants of the evolving complexities has geared this system into the knowledge-intensive mode. The emerging order cannot be observed directly, yet it can be inferred on the basis of reflexive observations. The new direction focuses on the future while being rooted in the past.

Innovation is initially the result of a local interaction between scientific invention, economic diffusion, and political power. Innovation systems are expected to develop further on the basis of reflexive translations. The transformations challenge the analytical understanding as they transform the conditions of the emerging achievements. In other words: what you see is not what you get. Central concepts have to be reformulated: what counts is not the accumulation of past performance, but the resourcefulness of these assets in relation to further developments. Where industries have matured or major disciplines have been established, the question has shifted toward the issue of how to recombine on the basis of existing combinations into new configurations better equipped to meet the exigencies of tomorrow (cf. Tobias and Birrer 1998).

The local instantiations, that is, the case studies, are needed for making the inferences about reorganisation possible. Observations heuristically guide further research questions. No answers can be provided unless one is willing to accept an expectation as an answer. By reorganising on the basis of new information, one makes the institutions more informed and thus more knowledge-intensive. Furthermore, the expectation of a complex dynamics enables us to improve our understanding of path-dependency and thus perhaps to achieve a competitive vantage point. The competitive vantage point is a necessary, but not a sufficient condition for a next advantage.

The Triple Helix is not meant to mesh the different communications together into the grey semblance of a compromise, but to allow for the reflexive fine-tuning of communications with different value systems in the background. Communications are also expressions of diverse institutional traditions and manifold interests. The thematically focused opening of the communication from a variety of perspectives promotes creativity, enables us to access an increasingly knowledge-intensive economy, and thus to celebrate innovation as a vital human possibility.

Innovation

Innovation is a new idea, device or process. Innovation can be viewed as the application of better solutions that meet new requirements, inarticulated needs, or existing market needs. This is accomplished through more effective products, processes, services, technologies, or ideas that are readily available to markets, governments and society. The term innovation can be defined as something original and, as a consequence, new, that "breaks into" the market or society.

While a novel device is often described as an innovation, in economics, management science, and other fields of practice and analysis innovation is generally considered to be a process that brings together various novel ideas in a way that they have an impact on society.

Innovation differs from invention in that innovation refers to the use of a better and, as a result, novel idea or method, whereas invention refers more directly to the creation of the idea or method itself. Innovation differs from improvement in that innovation refers to the notion of doing something different rather than doing the same thing better.

Innovation Economics

Innovation economics is a growing economic doctrine that reformulates conventional economics theory so that knowledge, technology, entrepreneurship, and innovation are positioned at the centre of the model rather than seen as independent forces that are largely unaffected by policy. Innovation economics is based on two fundamental tenets: that the central goal of economic policy should be to spur higher productivity through greater innovation, and that markets relying on input resources and price signals alone will not always be as effective in spurring higher productivity, and thereby economic growth.

This is in contrast to the two other conventional economic doctrines, neoclassical economics and Keynesian economics.

Historical Origins

If Adam Smith is the patron saint of classical economics and Keynes of Keynesian economics, it is Joseph Schumpeter who is the patron saint of innovation economics, especially with his classic 1942 book *Capitalism, Socialism and Democracy*. Writing around the same time as Keynes, Schumpeter had a decidedly different take on the economy and on economics. For Schumpeter it was evolving institutions, entrepreneurs, and technological change that were at the heart of economic growth. He argued that creative destruction is crucial in capitalism.

But it is only within the last 15 years that a theory and narrative of economic growth focused on innovation that was grounded in

Schumpeter's ideas has emerged. Innovation economics attempted to answer the fundamental problem in the puzzle of total factor productivity growth. Continual growth of output could no longer be explained only in increase of inputs used in the production process as understood in industrialization. Hence, innovation economics focused on a theory of economic creativity that would impact the theory of the firm and organisation decision-making. Hovering between heterodox economics that emphasized the fragility of conventional assumptions and orthodox economics that ignored the fragility of such assumptions, innovation economics aims for joint didactics between the two. As such, it enlarges the Schumpeterian analyses of new technological system by incorporating new ideas of information and communication technology in the global economy.

Indeed, a new theory and narrative of economic growth focused on innovation has emerged in the last decade. Innovation economics emerges on the wage of other schools of thoughts in economics, including new institutional economics, new growth theory, endogenous growth theory, evolutionary economics, neo-Schumpeterian economics—provides an economic framework that explains and helps support growth in today's knowledge economy.

Leading theorists of innovation economics include both formal economists, as well as management theorists, technology policy experts, and others. These include Paul Romer, Elhanan Helpman, W. Brian Arthur, Robert Axtell, Richard R. Nelson, Richard Lipsey, Michael Porter, Christopher Freeman, Igor Yegorov.

Theory

Innovation economists believe that what primarily drives economic growth in today's knowledge-based economy is not capital accumulation, as claimed by neoclassicalism asserts, but innovative capacity spurred by appropriable knowledge and technological externalities. Economics growth in innovation economics is the end-product of knowledge (tacit vs. codified); regimes and policies allowing for entrepreneurship and innovation (i.e., R&D expenditures, permits, licenses); technological spillovers and externalities between collaborative firms; and systems of innovation that create innovative environments (i.e., clusters, agglomerations, metropolitan areas).

In 1970, economist Milton Friedman said in the *New York Times* that a business's sole purpose is to generate profits for their shareholders and companies that pursued other missions would be less competitive, resulting in fewer benefits to owners, employees, and society. Yet data over the past several decades shows that while profits matter, good firms supply far more, particularly in bringing innovation to the market. This fosters economic growth, employment gains, and other society-wide benefits. Business school professor David Ahlstrom asserts: "the main goal of business is to develop new and innovative goods and services that generate economic growth while delivering benefits to society."

In contrast to neoclassical economics, innovation economics offer differing perspectives on main focus, reasons for economic growth, and the assumptions of context between economic actors:

Economic thought	*Focus*	*Growth*	*Context*
Neoclassical	Market price signals in using scarce resources	Productive factor accumulation (capital, labor)	Individuals and firms behaving in vacuum
Innovation	Innovative capacity to create more effective processes, products, business models	Knowledge/technology (R&D, patents)	Institutions of research, government, society

Despite the differences in economic thought, both perspectives are based on the same core premise: the foundation of all economic growth is the optimization of the utilisation of factors and the measure of success is how well the factor utilisation is optimized. Whatever the factors, it nonetheless leads to the same situation of special endowments, varying relative prices, and production processes. So while, the two differ in theoretical concepts, innovation economics can find fertile ground in mainstream economics, rather than remain in diametric contention.

Evidence

Empirical evidence worldwide points to a positive link between technological innovation and economic performance. The drive of biotech firms in Germany was due to the R&D subsidies to joint projects, network partners, and close cognitive distance of collaborative partners within a cluster. These factors increased patent performance in the biotech industry. Additionally, innovation capacity explains much of the GDP growth in India and China between 1981–2004 but especially in the 1990s. Their development of a National Innovation System through heavy investment of R&D expenditures and personnel, patents, and high-tech/service exports strengthened their innovation capacity. By linking the science sector with the business sector, establishing incentives for innovative activities, and balancing the import of technology and indigenous R&D effort, both countries experienced rapid economic growth in recent decades. Also, the Council of Foreign

Relations asserted that since the end of the 1970s, the U.S. has gained a disproportionate share of the world's wealth through their aggressive pursuit of technological change, demonstrating that technological innovation is a central catalyst of steady economic performance. Concisely, evidence shows that innovation contributes to steady economic growth and rise in per capita income.

However, some empirical studies investigating the innovation-performance-link lead to rather mixed results and indicate that the relationship be more subtle and complex than commonly assumed. In particular, the relationship between innovativeness and performance seems to differ in intensity and significance across empirical contexts, environmental circumstances, and conceptual dimensions.

All of the above has taken place in an era of data constraint, as identified by Zvi Griliches twenty years ago. Because the primary domain of innovation is commerce the key data resides there; continually out of campus reach in reports hidden within factories, corporate offices and technical centres. This recusal still stymies progress today. Recent attempts at data transference have led, not least, to the 'positive link' (above) being upgraded to exact algebra between R&D productivity and GDP allowing prediction from one to the other. This is pending further disclosure from commercial sources but several pertinent documents are already available.

Geography

While innovation is important, it is not a happenstance occurrence as a natural harbor or natural resources are, but a deliberate, concerted effort of markets, institutions, policymakers, and effect use of geographic space. In global economic restructuring, location has a become key element in establishing competitive advantage as regions focus on their unique assets to spur innovation (i.e., information technology in Silicon Valley, CA; digital media in Seoul, South Korea). Even more, thriving metropolitan economies that carry multiple clusters (i.e., Tokyo, Chicago, London) essentially fuel national economies through their pools of human capital, innovation, quality places, and infrastructure. Cities become "innovative spaces" and "cradles of creativity" as drivers of innovation. They become essential to the system of innovation through the supply side: ready, available, abundant capital and labor; good infrastructure for productive activities, and diversified production structures that spawn synergies and hence innovation. In addition they grow due to the demand side: diverse population of varying occupations, ideas, skills; high and differentiated level of consumer demand; and constant recreation of urban order especially infrastructure of streets, water systems, energy, and transportation.

Organisations

In the organisational context, innovation may be linked to positive changes in efficiency, productivity, quality, competitiveness, and market share. However, recent research findings highlight the complementary role of organisational culture in enabling organisations to translate innovative activity into tangible performance improvements. Organisations can also improve profits and performance by providing work groups opportunities and resources to innovate, in addition to employee's core job tasks. Peter Drucker wrote that "Innovation is the specific function of entrepreneurship, whether in an existing business, a public service institution, or a new venture started by a lone individual in the family kitchen. It is the means by which the entrepreneur either creates new wealth-producing resources or endows existing resources with enhanced potential for creating wealth." In the organisational context, innovation may be linked to positive changes in efficiency, productivity, quality, competitiveness, market share, and others. However, recent research findings highlight the complementary role of organisational culture in enabling organisations to translate innovative activity into tangible performance improvements.

According to Clayton Christensen "Disruptive Innovation" is the key to future success in business. The organisation requires a proper structure in order to retain competitive advantage. It is necessary to create and nurture an environment of innovation. Executives and managers need to break away from traditional ways of thinking and use change to their advantage. It is a time of risk but even greater opportunity. The world of work is changing with the increase in the use of technology and both companies and businesses are becoming increasingly competitive. Companies will have to downsize and re-engineer their operations to remain competitive. This will impact on employment as businesses will be forced to reduce the number of people employed while accomplishing the same amount of work if not more.

All organisations can innovate, including for example hospitals, universities, and local governments. For instance, former Mayor Martin O'Malley pushed the City of Baltimore to use CitiStat, a performance-measurement data and management system that allows city officials to maintain statistics on crime trends to condition of potholes. This system aids in better evaluation of policies and procedures with accountability and efficiency in terms of time and money. In its first year, CitiStat saved the city $13.2 million. Even mass transit systems have innovated with hybrid bus fleets to real-time tracking at bus stands. In addition, the growing use of mobile data terminals in vehicles that serves as communication hubs between vehicles and control centre automatically send data on location, passenger counts, engine performance, mileage and other information. This tool helps to deliver and manage transportation systems.

Still other innovative strategies include hospitals digitizing medical information in electronic medical records. For example, the U.S. Department of Housing and Urban Development's HOPE VI initiatives turned severely distressed public housing in urban areas into revitalized, mixed-income environments; the Harlem Children's Zone used a community-based approach to educate local area children; and the Environmental Protection Agency's brownfield grants facilitates turning over brownfields for environmental protection, green spaces, community and commercial development.

Sources of Innovation

There are several sources of innovation. It can occur as a result of a focus effort by a range of different agents, by chance, or as a result of a major system failure.

According to Peter F. Drucker the general sources of innovations are different changes in industry structure, in market structure, in local and global demographics, in human perception, mood and meaning, in the amount of already available scientific knowledge, etc.

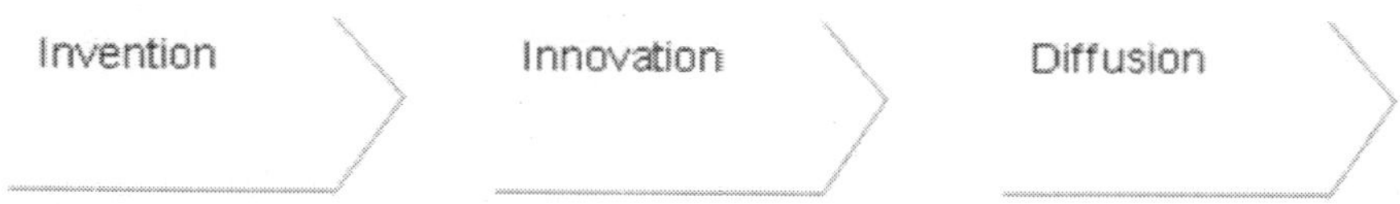

Figure: *Original model of three phases of the process of Technological Change*

In the simplest linear model of innovation the traditionally recognised source is *manufacturer innovation*. This is where an agent (person or business) innovates in order to sell the innovation.

Another source of innovation, only now becoming widely recognised, is *end-user innovation*. This is where an agent (person or company) develops an innovation for their own (personal or in-house) use because existing products do not meet their needs. MIT economist Eric von Hippel has identified end-user innovation as, by far, the most important and critical in his classic book on the subject, *Sources of Innovation*.

The robotics engineer Joseph F. Engelberger asserts that innovations require only three things:

1. A recognised need,
2. Competent people with relevant technology, and
3. Financial support.

However, innovation processes usually involve: identifying customer needs, macro and meso trends, developing competences, and finding financial support.

The Kline chain-linked model of innovation places emphasis on potential market needs as drivers of the innovation process, and describes the complex and often iterative feedback loops between marketing, design, manufacturing, and R&D.

Innovation by businesses is achieved in many ways, with much attention now given to formal research and development (R&D) for "breakthrough innovations". R&D help spur on patents and other scientific innovations that leads to productive growth in such areas as industry, medicine, engineering, and government. Yet, innovations can be developed by less formal on-the-job modifications of practice, through exchange and combination of professional experience and by many other routes. The more radical and revolutionary innovations tend to emerge from R&D, while more incremental innovations may emerge from practice – but there are many exceptions to each of these trends. Information technology and changing business processes and management style can produce a work climate favourable to innovation. For example, the software tool company Atlassian conducts quarterly "ShipIt Days" in which employees may work on anything related to the company's products. Google employees work on their own projects for 20% of their time (known as Innovation Time Off). Both companies cite these bottom-up processes as major sources for new products and features.

An important innovation factor includes customers buying products or using services. As a result, firms may incorporate users in focus groups (user centred approach), work closely with so called lead users (lead user approach) or users might adapt their products themselves. The lead user method focuses on idea generation based on leading users to develop breakthrough innovations. U-STIR, a project to innovate Europe's surface transportation system, employs such workshops. Regarding this user innovation, a great deal of innovation is done by those actually implementing and using technologies and products as part of their normal activities. In most of the times user innovators have some personal record motivating them. Sometimes user-innovators may become entrepreneurs, selling their product, they may choose to trade their innovation in exchange for other innovations, or they may be adopted by their suppliers. Nowadays, they may also choose to freely reveal their innovations, using methods like open source. In such networks of innovation the users or communities of users can further develop technologies and reinvent their social meaning.

Goals/Failures

Programs of organisational innovation are typically tightly linked to organisational goals and objectives, to the business plan, and to market competitive positioning. One driver for innovation programs in corporations is to achieve growth objectives. As Davila et al. (2006) notes, "Companies cannot grow through cost reduction and reengineering alone... Innovation is the key element in providing aggressive top-line growth, and for increasing bottom-line results".

One survey across a large number of manufacturing and services organisations found, ranked in decreasing order of popularity, that systematic programs of organisational innovation are most frequently driven by: Improved quality, Creation of new markets, Extension of the product range, Reduced labour costs, Improved production processes, Reduced materials, Reduced environmental damage, Replacement of products/services, Reduced energy consumption, Conformance to regulations. These goals vary between improvements to products, processes and services and dispel a popular myth that innovation deals mainly with new product development. Most of the goals could apply to any organisation be it a manufacturing facility, marketing firm, hospital or local government. Whether innovation goals are successfully achieved or otherwise depends greatly on the environment prevailing in the firm.

Conversely, failure can develop in programs of innovations. The causes of failure have been widely researched and can vary considerably. Some causes will be external to the organisation and outside its influence of control. Others will be internal and ultimately within the control of the organisation. Internal causes of failure can be divided into causes associated with the cultural infrastructure and causes associated with the innovation process itself. Common causes of failure within the innovation process in most organisations can be distilled into five types: Poor goal definition, Poor alignment of actions to goals, Poor participation in teams, Poor monitoring of results, Poor communication and access to information.

Diffusion of Innovations

Diffusion of innovations is a theory that seeks to explain how, why, and at what rate new ideas and technology spread through cultures. Everett Rogers, a professor of communication studies, popularized the theory in his book *Diffusion of Innovations*; the book was first published in 1962, and is now in its fifth edition (2003). Rogers argues that diffusion is the process by which an innovation is communicated through certain channels over time among the participants in a social system. The origins of the diffusion of innovations theory are varied and span multiple disciplines.

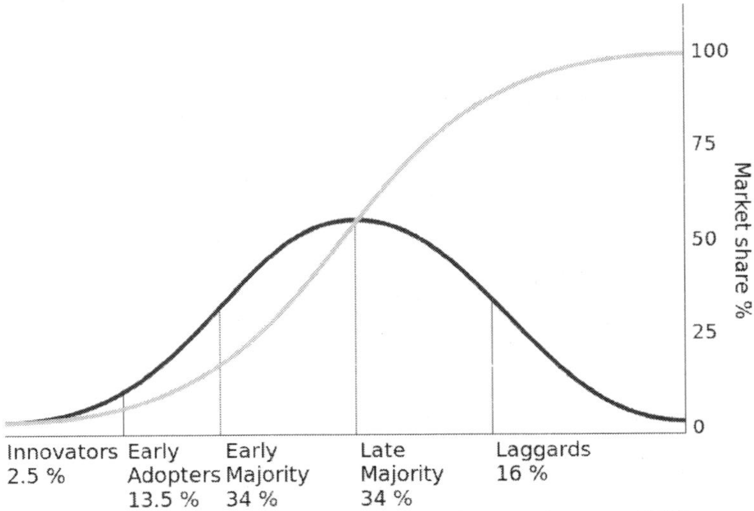

Figure: *The diffusion of innovations according to Rogers. With successive groups of consumers adopting the new technology (shown in blue), its market share (yellow) will eventually reach the saturation level. In mathematics the S curve is known as the logistic function. The curve is broken into sections of adopters.*

Rogers proposes that four main elements influence the spread of a new idea: the innovation itself, communication channels, time, and a social system. This process relies heavily on human capital. The innovation must be widely adopted in order to self-sustain. Within the rate of adoption, there is a point at which an innovation reaches critical mass. The categories of adopters are: innovators, early adopters, early majority, late majority, and laggards. Diffusion manifests itself in different ways in various cultures and fields and is highly subject to the type of adopters and innovation-decision process.

History

The concept of diffusion was first studied by the French sociologist Gabriel Tarde in late 19th century and by German and Austrian anthropologists such as Friedrich Ratzel and Leo Frobenius. The study of diffusion of innovations took off in the subfield of rural sociology in the midwestern United States midwest in the 1920s and 1930s. Agriculture technology was advancing rapidly, and researchers started to examine how independent farmers were adopting hybrid seeds, equipment, and techniques. A study of the adoption of hybrid corn seed in Iowa by Ryan and Gross (1943) solidified the prior work on diffusion into a distinct paradigm that would be cited consistently in the future. Since its start in rural sociology, Diffusion of Innovations has been applied to numerous contexts, including medical sociology, communications, marketing, development studies, health promotion, organisational studies, knowledge management, and complexity studies, with a particularly large impact on the use of medicines, medical techniques, and health communications. In organisational studies, its basic epidemiological or internal-influence form was formulated by H. Earl Pemberton, who provided examples of institutional diffusion such as postage stamps and standardized school ethics codes.

In 1962 Everett Rogers, a professor of rural sociology, published his seminal work: *Diffusion of Innovations*. Rogers synthesized research from over 508 diffusion studies across the fields that initially influenced the theory: anthropology, early sociology, rural sociology, education, industrial sociology and medical sociology. Using his synthesis, Rogers produced a theory of the adoption of innovations among individuals and organisations. *Diffusion of Innovations* and Rogers' later books are among the most often cited in diffusion research. His methodologies are closely followed in recent diffusion research, even as the field has expanded into, and been influenced by, other methodological disciplines such as social network analysis and communication.

Elements

***Table:** The key elements in diffusion research are:*

Element	*Definition*
Innovation	Innovations are a broad category, relative to the current knowledge of the analyzed unit. Any idea, practice, or object that is perceived as new by an individual or other unit of adoption could be considered an innovation available for study.
Adopters	Adopters are the minimal unit of analysis. In most studies, adopters are individuals, but can also be organizations (businesses, schools, hospitals, etc.), clusters within social networks, or countries.
Communication channels	Diffusion, by definition, takes place among people or organizations. Communication channels allow the transfer of information from one unit to the other. Communication patterns or capabilities must be established between parties as a minimum for diffusion to occur.
Time	The passage of time is necessary for innovations to be adopted; they are rarely adopted instantaneously. In fact, in the Ryan and Gross (1943) study on hybrid corn adoption, adoption occurred over more than ten years, and most farmers only dedicated a fraction on their fields to the new corn in the first years after adoption.
Social system	The social system is the combination of external influences (mass media, organizational or governmental mandates) and internal influences (strong and weak social relationships, distance from opinion leaders. There are many roles in a social system, and their combination represents the total influences on a potential adopter.

Characteristics of Innovations

Studies have explored many characteristics of innovations. Meta-reviews have identified several characteristics that are common among most studies. These are in line with the characteristics that Rogers initially cited in his reviews.

Potential adopters evaluate an innovation on its relative advantage (the perceived efficiencies gained by the innovation relative to current tools or procedures), its compatibility with the pre-existing system, its complexity or difficulty to learn, its trialability or testability, its potential for reinvention (using the tool for initially unintended purposes), and its observed effects. These qualities interact and are judged as a whole. For example, an innovation might be extremely complex, reducing its likelihood to be adopted and diffused, but it might be very compatible with a large advantage relative to current tools. Even with this high learning curve, potential adopters might adopt the innovation anyway.

Studies also identify other characteristics of innovations, but these are not as common as the ones that Rogers lists above. The fuzziness of the boundaries of the innovation can impact its adoption. Specifically, innovations with a small core and large periphery are easier to adopt. Innovations that are less risky are easier to adopt as the potential loss from failed integration is lower. Innovations that are disruptive to routine tasks, even when they bring a large relative advantage, might not be adopted because of added instability. Likewise, innovations that make tasks easier are likely to be adopted. Closely related to relative complexity, knowledge requirements are the ability barrier to use presented by the difficulty to use the innovation. Even when there are high knowledge requirements, support from prior adopters or other sources can increase the chances for adoption.

Characteristics of Individual Adopters

Like innovations, adopters have been determined to have traits that affect their likelihood to adopt an innovation. A bevy of individual personality traits have been explored for their impacts on adoption, but with little agreement. Ability and motivation, which vary on situation unlike personality traits, have a large impact on a potential adopter's likelihood to adopt an innovation. Unsurprisingly, potential adopters who have are motivated to adopt an innovation are likely to make the adjustments needed to adopt it. Motivation can be impacted by the meaning that an innovation holds; innovations can have symbolic value that encourage (or discourage) adoption. First proposed by Ryan and Gross (1943), the overall connectedness of a potential adopter to the broad community represented by a city. Potential adopters who frequent metropolitan areas are more likely to adopt an innovation. Finally, potential adopters who have the power or agency to create change, particularly in organisations, are more likely to adopt an innovation than someone with less power over his choices.

Characteristics of Organisations

Organisations face more complex adoption possibilities because organisations are both the aggregate of its individuals and its own system with a set of procedures and norms. Three organisational characteristics match well with the individual characteristics above: tension for change (motivation and ability), innovation-system fit (compatibility), and assessment of implications (observability). Organisations can feel pressured by a tension for change. If the organisation's situation is untenable, it will be motivated to adopt an innovation to change its fortunes. This tension often plays out among its individual members. Innovations that match the organisation's pre-existing system require fewer coincidental changes and are easy to assess are more likely to be adopted. The wider environment of the organisation, often an industry, community, or economy, exerts pressures on the organisation, too. Where an innovation is diffusing through the organisation's environment for any reason, the organisation is more likely to adopt it. Innovations that are intentionally spread, including by political mandate or directive, are also likely to diffuse quickly.

Process

Diffusion occurs through a five–step decision-making process. It occurs through a series of communication channels over a period of time among the members of a similar social system. Ryan and Gross first identified adoption as a process in 1943. Rogers' five stages (steps): awareness, interest, evaluation, trial, and adoption are integral to this theory. An individual might reject an innovation at any time during or after the adoption process. Abrahamson examined this process critically by posing questions such as: How do technically inefficient innovations diffuse and what impedes technically efficient innovations from catching on? Abrahamson makes suggestions for how organisational scientists can more comprehensively evaluate the spread of innovations. In later editions of *Diffusion of Innovation*, Rogers changes his terminology of the five stages to: knowledge, persuasion, decision, implementation, and confirmation. However, the descriptions of the categories have remained similar throughout the editions.

Five stages of the adoption process	
Stage	***Definition***
Knowledge	The individual is first exposed to an innovation, but lacks information about the innovation. During this stage the individual has not yet been inspired to find out more information about the innovation.
Persuasion	The individual is interested in the innovation and actively seeks related information/details.
Decision	The individual takes the concept of the change and weighs the advantages/disadvantages of using the innovation and decides whether to adopt or reject the innovation. Due to the individualistic nature of this stage, Rogers notes that it is the most difficult stage on which to acquire empirical evidence.[11]
Implementation	The individual employs the innovation to a varying degree depending on the situation. During this stage the individual also determines the usefulness of the innovation and may search for further information about it.
Confirmation	The individual finalizes his/her decision to continue using the innovation. This stage is both intrapersonal (may cause cognitive dissonance) and interpersonal, confirmation the group has made the right decision.

Decisions

Two factors determine what type a particular decision is:

- Whether the decision is made freely and implemented voluntarily
- Who makes the decision.

Based on these considerations, three types of innovation-decisions have been identified.

Type	***Definition***
Optional Innovation-Decision	made by an individual who is in some way distinguished from others.
Collective Innovation-Decision	made collectively by all participants.
Authority Innovation-Decision	made for the entire social system by individuals in positions of influence or power.

Rate of Adoption

The rate of adoption is defined as the relative speed at which participants adopt an innovation. Rate is usually measured by the length of time required for a certain percentage of the members of a social system to adopt an innovation. The rates of adoption for innovations are determined by an individual's adopter category. In general, individuals who first adopt an innovation require a shorter adoption period (adoption process) when compared to late adopters.

Within the adoption curve at some point the innovation reaches critical mass. This is when the number of individual adopters ensures that the innovation is self-sustaining. Illustrating how an innovation reaches critical mass,

Adoption Strategies

Rogers outlines several strategies in order to help an innovation reach this stage, including when an innovation adopted by a highly respected individual within a social network and creating an instinctive desire for a specific innovation. Another strategy includes injecting an innovation into a group of individuals who would readily use said technology, as well as providing positive reactions and benefits for early adopters.

Diffusion vs Adoption

Adoption is an individual process detailing the series of stages one undergoes from first hearing about a product to finally adopting it. Diffusion signifies a group phenomena, which suggests how an innovation spreads.

Adopter Categories

Rogers defines an adopter category as a classification of individuals within a social system on the basis of innovativeness. In the book *Diffusion of Innovations*, Rogers suggests a total of five categories of adopters in order to standardize the usage of adopter categories in diffusion research. The adoption of an innovation follows an S curve when plotted over a length of time. The categories of adopters are: innovators, early adopters, early majority, late majority and laggards. In addition to the gatekeepers and opinion leaders who exist within a given community, change agents may come from outside the community. Change agents bring innovations to new communities– first through the gatekeepers, then through the opinion leaders, and so on through the community.

Adopter category	*Definition*
Innovators	Innovators are willing to take risks, have the highest social status, have financial liquidity, are social and have closest contact to scientific sources and interaction with other innovators. Their risk tolerance allows them to adopt technologies that may ultimately fail. Financial resources help absorb these failures.
Early adopters	These individuals have the highest degree of opinion leadership among the adopter categories. Early adopters have a higher social status, financial liquidity, advanced education and are more socially forward than late adopters. They are more discreet in adoption choices than innovators. They use judicious choice of adoption to help them maintain a central communication position.
Early Majority	They adopt an innovation after a varying degree of time that is significantly longer than the innovators and early adopters. Early Majority have above average social status, contact with early adopters and seldom hold positions of opinion leadership in a system (Rogers 1962, p. 283)
Late Majority	They adopt an innovation after the average participant. These individuals approach an innovation with a high degree of skepticism and after the majority of society has adopted the innovation. Late Majority are typically skeptical about an innovation, have below average social status, little financial liquidity, in contact with others in late majority and early majority and little opinion leadership.
Laggards	They are the last to adopt an innovation. Unlike some of the previous categories, individuals in this category show little to no opinion leadership. These individuals typically have an aversion to change-agents. Laggards typically tend to be focused on "traditions", lowest social status, lowest financial liquidity, oldest among adopters, and in contact with only family and close friends.
Leapfroggers	When resistors upgrade they often skip several generations in order to reach the most recent technologies.

Failed Diffusion

Failed diffusion does not mean that the technology was adopted by no one. Rather, failed diffusion often refers to diffusion that does not reach or approach 100% adoption due to its own weaknesses, competition from other innovations, or simply a lack of awareness. From a social networks perspective, a failed diffusion might be widely adopted within certain clusters but fail to make an impact on more distantly related people. Networks that are over-connected might suffer from a rigidity that prevents the changes an innovation might bring, as well.

For example, Rogers discussed a situation in Peru involving the implementation of boiling drinking water to improve health and wellness levels in the village of Los Molinas. The residents had no knowledge of the link between sanitation and illness. The campaign worked with the villagers to try to teach them to boil water, burn their garbage, install latrines and report cases of illness to local health agencies. In Los Molinas, a stigma was linked to boiled water as something that only the "unwell" consumed, and thus, the idea of healthy residents boiling water prior to consumption was frowned upon. The two-year educational campaign was considered to be largely unsuccessful. This failure exemplified the importance of the roles of the communication channels that are involved in such a campaign for social change. An examination of diffusion in El Salvador determined that there can be more than one social network at play as innovations are communicated. One network carries information and the other carries influence. While people might hear of an innovation's uses, in Rogers' Los Molinas sanitation case, a network of influence and status prevented adoption.

Heterophily and Communication Channels

Lazarsfeld and Merton first called attention to the principles of homophily and its opposite, heterophily. Using their definition, Rogers defines homophily as "the degree to which pairs of individuals who interact are similar in certain attributes, such as beliefs, education, social status, and the like". When given the choice, individuals usually choose to interact with someone similar to themselves. Homophilous individuals engage in more effective communication because their similarities lead to greater knowledge gain as well as attitude or behaviour change. As a result, homophilous people tend to promote diffusion among each other. However, diffusion requires a certain degree of heterophily to introduce new ideas into a relationship; if two individuals are identical, no diffusion occurs because there is no new information to exchange. Therefore, an ideal situation would involve potential adopters who are homophilous in every way, except in knowledge of the innovation.

Promotion of healthy behaviour provides an example of the balance required of homophily and heterophily. People tend to be close to others of similar health status. As a result, people with unhealthy behaviours like smoking and obesity are less likely to encounter information and behaviours that encourage good health. This presents a critical challenge for health communications, as ties between heterophilous people are relatively weaker, harder to create, and harder to maintain. Developing heterophilous ties to unhealthy communities can increase the effectiveness of the diffusion of good health behaviours. Once one previously homophilous tie adopts the behaviour or innovation, the other members of that group are more likely to adopt it, too.

The Role of Social Systems

Opinion Leaders

Not all individuals exert an equal amount of influence over others. In this sense opinion leaders are influential in spreading either positive or negative information about an innovation. Rogers relies on the ideas of Katz & Lazarsfeld and the two-step flow theory in developing his ideas on the influence of opinion leaders.

Opinion leaders have the most influence during the evaluation stage of the innovation-decision process and on late adopters. In addition opinion leaders typically have greater exposure to the mass media, more cosmopolitan, greater contact with change agents, more social experience and exposure, higher socioeconomic status, and are more innovative than others.

Research was done in the early 1950s at the University of Chicago attempting to assess the cost-effectiveness of broadcast advertising on the diffusion of new products and services. The findings were that opinion leadership tended to be organised into a hierarchy within a society, with each level in the hierarchy having most influence over other members in the same level, and on those in the next level below it. The lowest levels were generally larger in numbers and tended to coincide with various demographic attributes that might be targeted by mass advertising. However, it found that direct word of mouth and example were far more influential than broadcast messages, which were only effective if they reinforced the direct influences. This led to the conclusion that advertising was best targeted, if possible, on those next in line to adopt, and not on those not yet reached by the chain of influence. Other research relating the concept to public choice theory finds that the hierarchy of influence for innovations need not, and likely does not, coincide with hierarchies of official, political, or economic status. Elites are often not innovators, and innovations may have to be introduced by outsiders and propagated up a hierarchy to the top decision makers.

Electronic Communication Social Networks

Prior to the introduction of the Internet, it was argued that social networks had a crucial role in the diffusion of innovation particularly tacit knowledge in the book The IRG Solution – hierarchical incompetence and how to overcome it. The book argued that the widespread adoption of computer networks of individuals would lead to much better diffusion of innovations, with greater understanding of their possible shortcomings and the identification of needed innovations that would not have otherwise occurred – the relevance paradox. The social model proposed by Ryan and Gross is expanded by Valente who uses social networks as a basis for adopter categorization instead of solely relying on the system-level analysis used by Ryan and Gross. Valente also looks at an individual's personal network, which is a different application than the organisational perspective espoused by many other scholars.

Recent research by Wear shows, that particularly in regional and rural areas, significantly more innovation takes place in communities which have stronger inter-personal networks.

Organisations

Innovations are often adopted by organisations through two types of innovation-decisions: collective innovation decisions and authority innovation decisions. The collective decision occurs when adoption is by consensus. The authority decision occurs by adoption among very few individuals with high positions of power within an organisation. Unlike the optional innovation decision process, these decision processes only occur within an organisation or hierarchical group. Within an organisation certain individuals are termed "champions" who stand behind an innovation and break through opposition. The champion plays a very similar role as the champion used within the efficiency business model Six Sigma. The process contains five stages that are slightly similar to the innovation-decision process that individuals undertake. These stages are: agenda-setting, matching, redefining/ restructuring, clarifying and routinizing.

Extensions of the Theory

Policy

Diffusion of Innovations has been applied beyond its original domains. In the case of political science and administration, policy diffusion focuses on how institutional innovations are adopted by other institutions, at the local, state, or country level. An alternative term is 'policy transfer' where the focus is more on the agents of diffusion and the diffusion of policy knowledge, such as in the work of Diane Stone. Specifically, policy transfer can be defined as "knowledge about how policies administrative arrangements, institutions, and ideas in one political setting (past or present) is used in the development of policies, administrative arrangements, institutions, and ideas in another political setting".

The first interests with regards to policy diffusion were focused in time variation or state lottery adoption, but more recently interest has shifted towards mechanisms (emulation, learning and coercion) or in channels of diffusion where researchers find that regulatory agency creation is transmitted by country and sector channels. At the local level, examining popular city-level policies make it easy to find patterns in diffusion through measuring public awareness. At the international level, economic policies have been thought to transfer among countries according to local politicians' learning of successes and failures elsewhere and outside mandates made by global financial organisations. As a group of countries succeed with a set of policies, others follow, as exemplified by the deregulation and liberalization across the developing world after the successes of the Asian Tigers. The reintroduction of regulations in the early 2000s also shows this learning process, which would fit under the stages of knowledge and decision, can be seen as lessons learned by following China's successful growth.

Technology

Peres, Muller and Mahajan suggested that diffusion is "the process of the market penetration of new products and services that is driven by social influences, which include all interdependencies among consumers that affect various market players with or without their explicit knowledge".

Eveland evaluated diffusion from a phenomenological view, stating, "Technology is information, and exists only to the degree that people can put it into practice and use it to achieve values"

Diffusion of existing technologies has been measured using "S curves". These technologies include radio, television, VCR, cable, flush toilet, clothes washer, refrigerator, home ownership, air conditioning, dishwasher, electrified households, telephone, cordless phone, cellular phone, per capita airline miles, personal computer and the Internet. This data can act as a predictor for future innovations.

Diffusion curves for infrastructure reveal contrasts in the diffusion process of personal technologies versus infrastructure.

Consequences of Adoption

Both positive and negative outcomes are possible when an individual or organisation chooses to adopt a particular innovation. Rogers states that this area needs further research because of the biased positive attitude that is associated with innovation. Rogers lists three categories for consequences: desirable vs. undesirable, direct vs. indirect, and anticipated vs. unanticipated. In contrast Wejnert details two categories: public vs. private and benefits vs. costs.

Public versus Private

Public consequences comprise the impact of an innovation on those other than the actor, while private consequences refer to the impact on the actor. Public consequences usually involve collective actors, such as countries, states, organisations or social movements. The results are usually concerned with issues of societal well-being. Private consequences usually involve individuals or small collective entities, such as a community. The innovations are usually concerned with the improvement of quality of life or the reform of organisational or social structures.

Benefits versus Costs

The benefits of an innovation obviously are the positive consequences, while the costs are the negative. Costs may be monetary or nonmonetary, direct or indirect. Direct costs are usually related to financial uncertainty and the economic state of the actor. Indirect costs are more difficult to identify. An example would be the need to buy a new kind of pesticide to use innovative seeds. Indirect costs may also be social, such as social conflict caused by innovation. Marketers are particularly interested in the diffusion process as it determines the success or failure of a new product. It is quite important for a marketer to understand the diffusion process so as to ensure proper management of the spread of a new product or service.

Mathematical Treatment

The diffusion of an innovation typically follows an S shaped curve which often resembles a logistic function. Mathematical programming models such as the S-D model apply the diffusion of innovations theory to real data problems.

Complex Systems Models

Complex network models can also be used to investigate the spread of innovations among individuals connected to each other by a network of peer-to-peer influences, such as in a physical community or neighbourhood.

Such models represent a system of individuals as *nodes* in a network (or graph). The interactions that link these individuals are represented by the edges of the network and can be based on the probability or strength of social connections. In the dynamics of such models, each node is assigned a current state, indicating whether or not the individual has adopted the innovation, and model equations describe the evolution of these states over time.

In threshold models the uptake of technologies is determined by the balance of two factors: the (perceived) usefulness (sometimes called utility) of the innovation to the individual as well as barriers to adoption, such as cost. The multiple parameters that influence decisions to adopt, both individual and socially motivated, can be represented by such models as a series of nodes and connections that represent real relationships. Borrowing from social network analysis, each node is an innovator, an adopter, or a potential adopter. Potential adopters have a threshold, which is a fraction of his neighbours who adopt the innovation that must be reached before he will adopt. Over time, each potential adopter views his neighbours and decides whether he should adopt based on the technologies they are using. When the effect of each individual node is analyzed along with its influence over the entire network, the expected level of adoption was seen to depend on the number of initial adopters and the network's structure and properties. Two factors emerge as important to successful spread of the innovation: the number of connections of nodes with their neighbours and the presence of a high degree of common connections in the network (quantified by the clustering coefficient). These models are particularly good at showing at showing the impact of opinion leaders relative to others. Computer models are often used to investigate this balance between the social aspects of diffusion and perceived intrinsic benefit to the individuals.

Criticism

Because there are more than four thousand articles across many disciplines published on Diffusion of Innovations, with a vast majority written after Rogers created a systematic theory, there have been few widely adopted changes to the theory. Although each study applies the theory in slightly different ways, this lack of cohesion has left the theory stagnant and difficult to apply with consistency to new problems.

Diffusion is difficult to quantify because humans and human networks are complex. It is extremely difficult, if not impossible, to measure what exactly causes adoption of an innovation. This is important, particularly in healthcare. Those encouraging adoption of health behaviours or new medical technologies need to be aware of the many forces acting on an individual and his or her decision to adopt a new behaviour or technology. Diffusion theories can never account for all variables, and therefore might miss critical predictors of adoption. This variety of variables has also led to inconsistent results in research, reducing heuristic value.

Rogers placed the contributions and criticisms of diffusion research into four categories: pro-innovation bias, individual-blame bias, recall problem, and issues of equality. The pro-innovation bias, in particular, implies that all innovation is positive and that all innovations should be adopted. Cultural traditions and beliefs can be consumer by another culture's through diffusion, which can impose significant costs on a group of people. The one-way information flow, from sender to receiver, is another weakness of this theory. The message sender has a goal to persuade the receiver, and there is little to no reverse flow. The person implementing the change controls the direction and outcome of the campaign. In some cases, this is the best approach, but other cases require a more participatory approach. In complex environments where the adopter is receiving information from many sources and is returning feedback to the sender, a one-way model is insufficient and multiple communication flows need to be examined.

Measures

There are two different types of measures for innovation: the organisational level and the political level.

Organisational Level

The measure of innovation at the organisational level relates to individuals, team-level assessments, and private companies from the smallest to the largest. Measure of innovation for organisations can be conducted by surveys, workshops, consultants, or internal benchmarking. There is today no established general way to measure organisational innovation. Corporate measurements are generally structured around balanced scorecards which cover several aspects of innovation such as business measures related to finances, innovation process efficiency, employees' contribution and motivation, as well benefits for customers. Measured values will vary widely between businesses, covering for example new product revenue, spending in R&D, time to market, customer and employee perception & satisfaction, number of patents, additional sales resulting from past innovations.

Political Level

For the political level, measures of innovation are more focused on a country or region competitive advantage through innovation. In this context, organisational capabilities can be evaluated through various evaluation frameworks, such as those of the European Foundation for Quality Management. The OECD Oslo Manual (1995) suggests standard guidelines on measuring technological product and process innovation. Some people consider the Oslo Manual complementary to the Frascati Manual from 1963. The new Oslo manual from 2005 takes a wider perspective to innovation, and includes marketing and organisational innovation. These standards are used for example in the European Community Innovation Surveys.

Other ways of measuring innovation have traditionally been expenditure, for example, investment in R&D (Research and Development) as percentage of GNP (Gross National Product). Whether this is a good measurement of innovation has been widely discussed and the Oslo Manual has incorporated some of the critique against earlier methods of measuring. The traditional methods of measuring still inform many policy decisions. The EU Lisbon Strategy has set as a goal that their average expenditure on R&D should be 3% of GDP.

Indicators

Many scholars claim that there is a great bias towards the "science and technology mode" (S&T-mode or STI-mode), while the "learning by doing, using and interacting mode" (DUI-mode) is widely ignored. For an example, that means you can have the better high tech or software, but there are also crucial learning tasks important for innovation. But these measurements and research are rarely done.

A common industry view (unsupported by empirical evidence) is that comparative cost-effectiveness research (CER) is a form of price control which, by reducing returns to industry, limits R&D expenditure, stifles future innovation and compromises new products access to markets. Some academics claim the CER is a valuable value-based measure of innovation which accords truly significant advances in therapy (those that provide "health gain") higher prices than free market mechanisms. Such value-based pricing has been viewed as a means of indicating to industry the type of innovation that should be rewarded from the public purse. The Australian academic Thomas Alured Faunce has developed the case that national comparative cost-effectiveness assessment systems should be viewed as measuring "health innovation" as an evidence-based concept distinct from valuing innovation through the operation of competitive markets (a method which requires strong anti-trust laws to be effective) on the basis that both methods of assessing innovation in pharmaceuticals are mentioned in annex 2C.1 of the AUSFTA.

Rate of Innovation

Several indexes exist that attempt to measure innovation include:

- The Innovation Index, developed by the Indiana Business Research Centre, to measure innovation capacity at the county or regional level in the United States.
- The State Technology and Science Index, developed by the Milken Institute is a U.S.-wide benchmark to measure the science and technology capabilities that furnish high paying jobs based around key components.
- The Oslo Manual is focused on North America, Europe, and other rich economies.
- The Bogota Manual, similar to the above, focuses on Latin America and the Caribbean countries.
- The Creative Class developed by Richard Florida
- The Innovation Capacity Index (ICI) published by a large number of international professors working in a collaborative fashion. The top scorers of ICI 2009–2010 being: 1. Sweden 82.2; 2. Finland 77.8; and 3. United States 77.5.
- The Global Innovation Index is a global index measuring the level of innovation of a country, produced jointly by The Boston Consulting Group (BCG), the National Association of Manufacturers (NAM), and The Manufacturing Institute (MI), the NAM's nonpartisan research affiliate. NAM describes it as the "largest and most comprehensive global index of its kind".
- The INSEAD Global Innovation Index
- The INSEAD Innovation Efficacy Index
- The NYCEDC Innovation Index

The Management Innovation Index - Model for Managing Intangibility of Organisational Creativity: Management Innovation

Index A peer reviewed article can be found on the Management Innovation Index in Model for Managing Intangibility of Organisational Creativity: Management Innovation Index

Global Innovation Index

This international innovation index is one of many research studies that try to build a ranking of countries related to innovation. Other indexes are the Innovations Indicator, Innovation Union Scoreboard, EIU Innovation Ranking, BCG International Innovation Index, Global Competitiveness Report, World Competitiveness Scoreboard, ITIF Index. The Global Innovation Index looks at both the business outcomes of innovation and government's ability to encourage and support innovation through public policy. The study comprised a survey of more than 1,000 senior executives from NAM member companies across all industries; in-depth interviews with 30 of the executives; and a comparison of the "innovation friendliness" of 110 countries and all 50 U.S. states. The findings are published in the report, "The Global Innovation Index 2013".

The report discusses not only country performance but also what companies are doing and should be doing to spur innovation. It looks at new policy indicators for innovation, including tax incentives and policies for immigration, education and intellectual property.

Slowing of Innovation

Jonathan Huebner, a physicist working at the Pentagon's Naval Air Warfare Centre, argued on the basis of both U.S. patents and world technological breakthroughs, per capita, that the rate of human technological innovation peaked in 1873 and has been slowing ever since. In his article, he asked "Will the level of technology reach a maximum and then decline as in the Dark Ages?" In later comments to *New Scientist* magazine, Huebner clarified that while he believed that we will reach a rate of innovation in 2024 equivalent to that of the Dark Ages, he was not predicting the reoccurrence of the Dark Ages themselves.

His Paper Received Some Mainstream News Coverage at the Time

The claim has been met with criticism by John Smart, founder of the Acceleration Studies Foundation, who asserted that research by technological singularity researcher Ray Kurzweil and others showed a "clear trend of acceleration, not deceleration" when it came to innovations. The foundation issued a reply to Huebner in the pages of the journal his article was published in, citing the existence of Second

Life and eHarmony as proof of accelerating innovation; Huebner also replied to this. However, in 2010, Joseph A. Tainter, Deborah Strumsky, and José Lobo confirmed Huebner's findings using U.S. Patent Office data.

Government Policies

Given the noticeable effects on efficiency, quality of life, and productive growth, innovation is a key factor in society and economy. Consequently, policymakers have long worked to develop environments that will foster innovation and its resulting positive benefits, from funding Research and Development to supporting regulatory change, funding the development of innovation clusters, and using public purchasing and standardisation to 'pull' innovation through.

For instance, experts are advocating that the U.S. federal government launch a National Infrastructure Foundation, a nimble, collaborative strategic intervention organisation that will house innovations programs from fragmented silos under one entity, inform federal officials on innovation performance metrics, strengthen industry-university partnerships, and support innovation economic development initiatives, especially to strengthen regional clusters. Because clusters are the geographic incubators of innovative products and processes, a cluster development grant program would also be targeted for implementation. By focusing on innovating in such areas as precision manufacturing, information technology, and clean energy, other areas of national concern would be tackled including government debt, carbon footprint, and oil dependence. The U.S. Economic Development Administration understand this reality in their continued Regional Innovation Clusters initiative. In addition, federal grants in R&D, a crucial driver of innovation and productive growth, should be expanded to levels similar to Japan, Finland, South Korea, and Switzerland in order to stay globally competitive. Also, such grants should be better procured to metropolitan areas, the essential engines of the American economy.

Many countries recognise the importance of research and development as well as innovation including Japan's Ministry of Education, Culture, Sports, Science and Technology (MEXT); Germany's Federal Ministry of Education and Research; and the Ministry of Science and Technology in the People's Republic of China [1]. Furthermore, Russia's innovation programme is the Medvedev modernisation programme which aims at creating a diversified economy based on high technology and innovation. Also, the Government of Western Australia has established a number of innovation incentives for government departments. Landgate was the first Western

Australian government agency to establish its Innovation Program. The Cairns Region established the Tropical Innovation Awards in 2010 open to all businesses in Australia. The 2011 Awards were extended to include participants from all Tropical Zone Countries.

Accounting for Research and Development Activity

In general, research and development (R&D) activities are conducted by specialised units or centres belonging to a company, or can be outsourced to contract research organisations, universities, or state agencies . In the context of commerce, research and development normally refers to future-oriented, long-term activities in science or technology, using similar techniques to scientific research but directed toward desired outcomes and with broad forecasts of commercial yield.

Cycle of Research and Development, from "Research and Evaluation on Education in Science and Engineering (REESE), Program Solicitation NSF 09-601"

In the United States, a typical ratio of research and development for an industrial company is about 3.5% of revenues. A high technology company such as a computer manufacturer might spend 7%. Although Allergan (a biotech company) tops the spending table with 43.4% investment, anything over 15% is remarkable and usually gains a reputation for being a high technology company. Companies in this category include pharmaceutical companies such as Merck & Co. (14.1%) or Novartis (15.1%), and engineering companies like Ericsson (24.9%). Such companies are often seen as credit risks because their spending ratios are so unusual.

Research and development costs are the costs incurred in a planned search for new knowledge and in translating such knowledge into new products or processes. Prior to 1975, businesses often capitalized research and development costs as intangible assets when future benefits were expected from their incurrence. Due to the difficulty of determining the costs applicable to future benefits, many companies expensed all such costs as incurred. Other companies capitalized those costs that related to proven products and expensed the rest as incurred.

As a result of these varied accounting practices, in 1974 the Financial Accounting Standards Board in Statement No. 2 ruled that firms must expense all research and development costs when incurred, unless they were directly reimbursable by government agencies and others. Immediate expensing is justified on the following grounds:

1. The amount of costs applicable to the future cannot be measured with any high degree of precision

2. Doubt exists as to whether any future benefits will be received
3. Even if benefits are expected, they cannot be measured

Research and development costs thus no longer appear as intangible assets on the balance sheet. The Board applies the same line of reasoning to other costs associated with internally generated intangible assets, such as the internal costs of developing a patent.

R&D as an Administrative Cost

Administrative costs are non-manufacturing costs that include the costs of top administrative functions and various staff departments such as accounting, data processing, and personnel. Executive salaries, clerical salaries, office expenses, office rent, donations, research and development costs, and legal costs are also administrative costs. As with selling costs, all organisations have administrative costs.

R&D Management

R&D management is the discipline of designing and leading R&D processes, managing R&D organisations, and ensuring smooth transfer of new know-how and technology to other groups or departments involved in innovation.

Definitions

R&D management can be defined as where the tasks of innovation management (i.e., creating and commercializing inventions) meet the tasks of technology management (i.e., external and internal creation and retention of technological know-how). It covers activities such as basic research, fundamental research, technology development, advanced development, concept development, new product development, process development, prototyping, R&D portfolio management, technology transfer, etc., but generally is not considered to include technology licensing, innovation management, IP management, corporate venturing, incubation, etc. as those are sufficiently independent activities that can be carried out without the presence of a R&D function in a firm.

Management Models

Few dedicated management models for R&D exist. Among the more popularized ones are Arthur D. Little's Third generation R&D management, the Development funnel, the Phase–gate model All these models are concerned with improving R&D performance and result productivity, managing R&D as a process, and providing the R&D function with an environment in which the inherent technological and market uncertainties can be managed.

The Path to Developing Successful New Products a joint research by MIT & McKinsey & Co. points out three key practices that can play critical role in R&D Management: Talk to the customer, Nurture a project culture, Keep it focused.

Innovation Management

Innovation management is the management of innovation processes. It refers both to product and organisational innovation. Innovation management includes a set of tools that allow managers and engineers to cooperate with a common understanding of processes and goals. Innovation management allows the organisation to respond to external or internal opportunities, and use its creativity to introduce new ideas, processes or products. It is not relegated to R&D; it involves workers at every level in contributing creatively to a company's product development, manufacturing and marketing.

By utilising innovation management tools, management can trigger and deploy the creative capabilities of the work force for the continuous development of a company. Common tools include brainstorming, virtual prototyping, product lifecycle management, idea management, TRIZ, Phase–gate model, project management, product line planning and portfolio management. The process can be viewed as an evolutionary integration of organisation, technology and market by iterating series of activities: search, select, implement and capture.

Innovation processes can either be *pushed* or *pulled* through development. A *pushed* process is based on existing or newly invented technology, that the organisation has access to, and tries to find profitable applications for.

A *pulled* process is based on finding areas where customers needs are not met, and then find solutions to those needs. To succeed with either method, an understanding of both the market and the technical problems are needed. By creating multi-functional development teams, containing both engineers and marketers, both dimensions can be solved.

The product lifecycle of products is getting shorter because of increased competition. This forces companies to reduce the time to market. Innovation managers must therefore decrease development time, without sacrificing quality or meeting the needs of the market.

Definition

In a survey of literature on innovation, Edison et al. found over 40 definitions. They also performed an industrial survey to capture how is innovation defined in the software industry. After analysis of the existing definitions whether these definitions comprehensively cover all the dimensions of innovation, they found the following definition to be the most complete: *"Innovation is: production or adoption, assimilation, and exploitation of a value-added novelty in economic and social spheres; renewal and enlargement of products, services, and markets; development of new methods of production; and establishment of new management systems. It is both a process and an outcome."*. This definition was given by Crossan and Apaydin and it builds on the OECD manual's definition.

Edison et al. also found two interesting dimensions of innovation including: degree of novelty (i.e. whether an innovation is new to the firm, new to the market, new to the industry, and new to the world) and type of innovation (whether it is process or product/service innovation).

The pioneer of innovation management was the Austrian economist Joseph Schumpeter, working during the 1930s, who identified innovation as a significant factor in economic growth. His book *"Capitalism, Socialism and Democracy"* first fully developed the concept of creative destruction.

Innovation management helps an organisation grasp an opportunity and use it to create and introduce new ideas, processes, or products industriously. Creativity is the basis of innovation management; the end goal is a change in services or business process. Innovative ideas are the result of two consecutive steps, *imitation* and *invention.*

By utilising innovation management tools, management can trigger and deploy the creative capabilities of the work force for the continuous development of a company. Common tools include brainstorming, virtual prototyping, product lifecycle management, idea management, TRIZ, Phase–gate model, project management, product line planning and portfolio management. The process can be viewed as an evolutionary integration of organisation, technology, and market, by iterating series of activities: search, select, implement and capture.

Innovation processes can either be *pushed* or *pulled* through development. A *pushed* process is based on existing or newly invented technology that the organisation has access to. The goal is to find profitable applications for the already-existing technology. A *pulled* process, by contrast, is based on finding areas where customers' needs are not met and finding solutions to those needs. To succeed with either method, an understanding of both the market and the technical problems are needed. By creating multi-functional development teams, containing both engineers and marketers, both dimensions can be solved.

Innovation, although not sufficient, is a necessary prerequisite for the continued survival and development of enterprises. The most direct way of business innovation is technological innovation and institutional innovation. Management innovation, however, plays a significant role in promoting technological and institutional innovation.

The goal of innovation management within a company is to cultivate a suitable environment to encourage innovation. The suitable environment would help the firms get more cooperation projects, even 'the take-off platform for business ventures'. Senior management's support is crucial to successful innovation; clear direction, endorsement, and support are essential to innovation pursuits.

Managing Complex Innovation

Innovation is a change that outperforms a previous practice. To lead or sustain with innovations, managers need to concentrate heavily on the innovation network, which requires deep understanding of the complexity of innovation. Collaboration is an important source of innovation. Innovations are increasingly brought to the market by networks of firms, selected according to their comparative advantages, and operating in a coordinated manner.

When a technology goes through a major transformation phase and yields a successful innovation, it becomes a great learning experience, not only for the parent industry but other industries as well. Big innovations are generally the outcome of intra- and interdisciplinary networking among technological sectors, along with combination of implicit and explicit knowledge. Networking is required, but network integration is the key to success for complex innovation. Social economic zones, technology corridors, free trade agreements, and technology clusters are some of the ways to encourage organisational networking and cross-functional innovations.

Enhancing Business through Joint Venture

Trade and the motive of traders is not the constant for all the types of market prevailing globally. The developing countries has different trade strategy where as the developed countries has also acquired superior strategy for their dynamic growth. The measuring scale i.e. economy of a nation clearly explains the growth of trade in a particular nation. Trade practices are no more similar for all the players prevailing in the market in the same way driving workforce for fulfilling their need is also not a constant one. Globalization and the stiff competition have challenged every organisation to adapt unique business model for existence and growth in the future. In the days of globalization, no economy can stand alone and immune from the developments in the abroad sector. India is, therefore, legitimately affected by what happens in the rest of the world. The international transmission effect is speedier, more substantial and more sustained than over before. International economic relations between India and other countries have been working through trade, payments, technology transfer, joint ventures and the like. The commodity-composition and the country-composition of India's exports to reflect the volume, value and direction of our foreign trade.

Joint Venture companies are the most ideal form of corporate entities for Doing Business in India. The companies incorporated in India, even with up to cent percentage foreign equity, are treated the same as domestic companies. A Joint Venture may be any of the business entities existing in India.

Why Companies Go for Joint Venture

The reasons behind forming a joint venture include business expansion, development of new products or moving into new markets, particularly overseas. One companies business may have strong potential for growth and the entrepreneur may have innovative ideas and products. However, a joint venture could be a successful integration of business for:

- More resources
- Greater capacity
- Increased technical expertise
- Access to established markets and distribution channels

Entering into a joint venture is a major decision for an organisation.

Important Factors to be Considered before a Joint Venture is Formed

- Screening of prospective partners
- Joint development of a detailed business plan and shortlisting a set of prospective partners based on their contribution to developing a business plan
- Availability of appreciated or depreciated property being contributed to the joint venture; by misunderstanding the significance of appreciated property, companies can fundamentally weaken the economics of the deal for themselves and their partners. Special allocations of income, gain, loss or

deduction to be made among the partners compensation to the members that provide services.

- Due diligence - checking the credentials of the other party ("trust and verify" - trust the information you receive from the prospective partner, but it's good business practice to verify the facts through interviews with third parties)
- Development of an exit strategy and terms of dissolution of the joint venture
- Most appropriate structure (e.g. most joint ventures involving fast growing companies are structured as strategic corporate partnerships)
- Availability of appreciated or depreciated property being contributed to the joint venture; by misunderstanding the significance of appreciated property, companies can fundamentally weaken the economics of the deal for themselves and their partners.
- Special allocations of income, gain, loss or deduction to be made among the partners
- Compensation to the members that provide services

Joint Venture Business Advantages

Businesses of any size can use joint ventures to strengthen long-term relationships or to collaborate on short-term projects. A successful joint venture gives rise to following benefits:

- Combining complementary R&D or technology:
- Provide companies with the opportunity to obtain new capacity and expertise
- Efficient commercialization of a technology or business concept
- Developing or acquiring marketing or distribution expertise
- Sharing of scientists or professionals with unique skills- The complexity of the knowledge to be transferred is a key factor in determining the contractual relationship between the partners. One or more participants may seek to learn more about a relatively new product market activity. This might concern all aspects of the activity or a limited segment like R&D, production, marketing or product servicing.
- Allow companies to enter into related businesses or new geographic markets or obtain new technological knowledge
- Have a relatively short life span (5-7 years) and therefore do not represent a long-term commitment

- Improving access to financial resources for both partners: - financial resources increases because when to parties undertake economic activity together then they share expenses this leads to more access to each others financial sources .Financial support, or sharing of economic risk- It reduces the risks in a number of ways as the activities can be expanded with smaller investment outlays than if financed independently. A small firm with a new product idea that involves high risk and requires relatively large amounts of investment capital may form a joint venture with a large firm. The larger firm might be able to carry the financial risks and be interested in becoming involved in a new business activity that promises growth and profitability. In addition, the larger firm might thereby gain experience in the new area of activity that may represent the opportunity for a major new business thrust in the future.
- Proper utilisation of resources- Resources are inputs into a firm's production process, such as capital, equipment, the skills of individual employees, patents, finance, and talented managers. Resources are either tangible or intangible in nature. With increasing effectiveness, the set of resources available to the firm tends to become larger. Individual resources may not yield to a competitive advantage. It is through the synergistic combination and integration of sets of resources that competitive advantages are formed.
- Acceleration of revenue growth
- Ability to increase profit margins
- Expansion to new domestic markets and international markets- It also helps in expanding the firm's operations into foreign countries. The local partners contribute in the form of specialised knowledge about local conditions, which are essential to the success of the venture.
- New product development
- Higher rate of profit and more control over the operations.
- Sharing of risk and ability to combine the local in-depth knowledge with a foreign partner with know-how in technology or process.
- Tax advantages are a significant factor in many joint ventures.
- A joint venture can also be very flexible. For example, a joint venture can have a limited life span and only cover part of what company needs, thus limiting the commitment for both parties and the business' exposure.

- Market conditions require initial long-term build-up of contacts or creation of demand, e.g. China

The Disadvantages of Joint Venture

Partnering with another business can be complex. It takes time and effort to build the right relationship. Problems are likely to arise if:

- The objectives of the venture are not 100 per cent clear and communicated to everyone involved
- The partners have different objectives for the joint venture
- Varied organisational structures may lead to less efficient decision-making
- There is an imbalance in levels of expertise, investment or assets brought into the venture by the different partners
- Cultural difference: Different cultures and management styles result in poor integration and co-operation
- The partners don't provide sufficient leadership and support in the early stages
- High level of commitment of staff and management
- Time consuming (especially where a new venture is involved)
- Political risks in the country where the joint venture is based
- Working in a different legal and commercial system

Success in a joint venture depends on thorough research and analysis of aims and objectives. This should be followed up with effective communication of the business plan to everyone involved.

A joint venture may be subjected to several difficulties. As circumstances change, the contract might be too inflexible to permit the required adjustments to be made. The basic reasons for failure of a joint venture are:-

- Inadequate preplanning for the joint venture.
- Cultural differences
- Poor integration process
- The hoped-for technology never developed.
- Agreements could not be reached on alternative approaches to solving the basic objectives of the joint venture.
- People with expertise in one company refused to share knowledge with their counterparts in the joint venture.
- Parent companies are unable to share control or compromise on difficult issues.

Reason Behind Joint Venture Failures

Joint venture breakdowns, for example, are often accompanied by a lack of partner rapport. This lack of rapport can take either of two forms. Often there are allegations of interference in each others activities and even of outright cheating. In fact, even in joint ventures that ultimately succeed such allegations abound. In a few cases, however, exactly the reverse happens with a severe lack of communication between the partner firms. An important reason behind joint venture failures is the lack of frequent consultations between partners. While disagreements among partners can be caused by many factors, one oft mentioned point of contention is the supply of inputs by the parent firms to the joint venture. One of the most serious problems with a partnership arises when one or more parties supply the venture with product or services. The supply of inputs is one of the factors that lead to conflicts among the parent firms. In fact, such opportunistic behaviour is an important manifestation of the control problems that make joint ventures problematic to manage. One way to mitigate such opportunistic behaviour would be to monitor the activities of the partner firms. In fact one of the key features behind joint venture success is to monitor the progress of the alliance on a regular basis. With monitoring of course, it is easy to see why allegations of cheating and interference may arise.

Chapter 3

Research and Development

Consortia

Research and development (R&D) consortia are formed by manufacturing companies, often with the support of government, for the purpose of conducting shared research on new technologies for the benefit of the consortium's member companies. Government-supported R&D consortia *(kumaia)* have been common in Japan since the 1960s, and now number more than 200. In the United States, however, the formation of industry specific R&D consortia was hindered by antitrust laws that penalized cooperation among competitors until Congress passed the National Cooperative Research Act of 1984 (NCRA). In 1993 the NCRA was amended to include cooperative production and redesignated the National Cooperative Research and Production Act of 1993 (NCRPA). These legislative acts reflected a new technology policy aimed at reducing governmental obstacles to the commercialization of new technology.

Under the NCRPA, firms within an industry may form consortia to conduct "precompetitive" research. Precompetitive research is research that is considered generic to the development of multiple products of basic value to all participants. By forming R&D consortia, manufacturing firms can avoid duplicating basic research tasks and share the results more cost effectively. As a result they are able to compete more effectively in the global marketplace.

Research and development consortia are required by the NCRPA to register with the U.S. Department of Justice, which recorded more than 600 new consortia from 1985 to 1996. While the NCRPA does not provide exemption from antitrust laws, it limits the damages that may be assessed if an antitrust violation occurs. Where antitrust laws provide for triple damages to be assessed, the NCRPA limits liability to single damages. In addition, any alleged antitrust violations would be judged under a rule of reason standard, rather than assuming they were illegal per se. In the years since NCRPA was passed, however, no antitrust proceedings have been brought against registered consortia.

Research and development consortia can provide member companies with many benefits. They are formed to share expenses and resources and to pool talent and expertise. Consortia that are formed in the United States to compete globally are eligible for government funding. The most common type of consortia are horizontal, consisting of competing firms within an industry. Vertical consortia include firms ranging from materials suppliers to finished product manufacturers.

Companies form research and development consortia for different reasons. Among the reasons cited are market pressures, international competition, the increased pace of new product development, cutbacks in corporate research and development budgets, and shared concerns about meeting new regulatory or safety requirements. According to a survey conducted in 1993 by the *Economist* magazine, the three reasons most commonly cited were to gain access to a market, to exploit complimentary technologies, and to reduce the time taken for innovation.

Following the passage of the NCRA, research and development consortia were most frequently formed in the electronics, semiconductor, and pharmaceutical industries. In the chemical industry, companies more frequently entered into dual-company alliances rather than multicompany consortia.

Research and development consortia have been successful in spurring innovation. SEMATECH, a Texas-based consortia of major semiconductor manufacturers founded in 1987, has had dramatic success in helping its member companies regain dominant market shares in the international semiconductor equipment and silicon-chip markets. Another consortia, the U.S. Council for Automotive Research (USCAR), was formed to accelerate technological innovation among the major automobile manufacturers.

After manufacturing companies have agreed to form a consortium and have registered with the U.S. Department of Justice, they then assign personnel and budget funds to it. Joint research is usually conducted at a single specified site. Under the NCRPA, the research must be precompetitive, concerning areas generic to the products of each member company. As the consortium develops new technologies and improves on existing ones, individual companies may begin to apply those technologies to their own products. At a certain point, the companies may agree to dissolve the consortium to focus on their own applications.

Research and development consortia may consist exclusively of companies from a single nation, or they may be international in scope. Japan's Ministry of International Trade and Industry (MITI), which supports and directs R&D consortia in Japan, began opening some of its R&D consortia to foreign companies in 1990. In the European Union, U.S. companies are allowed to participate in publicly supported R&D consortia. In the United States, consortia that receive government funds are limited to domestic companies.

In the United States, joint ventures between private industry and federal laboratories offer similar research sharing and development opportunities as R&D consortia. Called Cooperative Research and Development Agreements (CRADAs), they are becoming more commonplace as federal laboratories refocus their efforts away from Cold War defence projects to help domestic industries develop new technologies.

Cross-Licensing

A cross-licensing agreement is a contract between two or more parties where each party grants rights to their intellectual property to the other parties.

Patent Law

In patent law, a cross-licensing agreement is an agreement according to which two or more parties grant a license to each other for the exploitation of the subject-matter claimed in one or more of the patents each owns. Usually, this type of agreement happens between two parties in order to avoid litigation or to settle an infringement dispute. Very often, the patents that each party owns covers different essential aspects of a given commercial product. Thus by cross licensing, each party maintains their freedom to bring the commercial product to market. The term "cross licensing" implies that neither party pays monetary royalties to the other party, although this may be the case.

For example, Microsoft and JVC entered into a cross license agreement in January 2008. Each party, therefore, is able to practice the inventions covered by the patents included in the agreement. This benefits competition by allowing each more freedom to design products covered by the others patents without provoking a patent infringement lawsuit.

Parties that enter into cross-licensing agreements must be careful not to violate antitrust laws and regulations. This can easily become a complex issue, involving (as far as the European Union is concerned) Art. 101 and 102 of the Treaty on the Functioning of the European Union (TFEU), previously Art. 81 and 82 of the EC Treaty, (abuse of dominant position, etc.) as well as licensing directives, cartels, etc.

Some companies file patent applications primarily to be able to cross license the resulting patents, as opposed to trying to stop a competitor from bringing a product to market. In the early 1990s, for example, Taiwanese original design manufacturers, such as Hon Hai, rapidly increased their patent filings after their US competitors brought patent infringement lawsuits against them. They used the patents to cross license.

One of the limitations of cross licensing is that it is ineffective against patent holding companies. The primary business of a patent holding company is to license patents in exchange for a monetary royalty. Thus, they have no need for rights to practice other companies' patents. These companies are often referred to pejoratively as patent trolls.

The economics literature has shown that firms with high capital intensities are more likely to strike a cross-licensing deal.

Non Patent Law

Other non-patent intellectual property such as copyright and trademark can also be cross-licensed. For example, a literary work and an anthology that includes that literary work may be cross-licensed between two publishers. A cross-license for computer software may involve a combination of patent, copyright, and trademark licensing.

Contract Research Organisation

A contract research organisation (CRO) is an organisation that provides support to the pharmaceutical, biotechnology, and medical device industries in the form of research services outsourced on a contract basis. A CRO may provide such services as biopharmaceutical development, biologic assay development, commercialization, preclinical research, clinical research, clinical trials management, and pharmacovigilance. CROs also support foundations, research institutions, and universities, in addition to governmental organisations (such as the NIH, EMEA, etc.).

Many CROs specifically provide clinical-study and clinical-trial support for drugs and/or medical devices. CROs range from large, international full-service organisations to small, niche speciality groups.

CROs that specialise in clinical-trials services can offer their clients the expertise of moving a new drug or device from its conception to FDA/EMA marketing approval, without the drug sponsor having to maintain a staff for these services.

Regulatory Aspects

Specifically pertaining to CROs providing clinical-trials services, the International Conference on Harmonisation of technical requirements for registration of pharmaceuticals for human use (ICH-GCP) (E6 1.20) defines a Contract Research Organisation (CRO) as: "A person or an organisation (commercial, academic, or other) contracted by the sponsor to perform one or more of a sponsor's trial-related duties and functions."

- (5.2.1) A sponsor may transfer any or all of the sponsor's trial-related duties and functions to a CRO, but the ultimate responsibility for the quality and integrity of the trial data always resides with the sponsor. The CRO should implement quality assurance and quality control.
- (5.2.2) Any trial-related duty and function that is transferred to and assumed by a CRO should be specified in writing.
- (5.2.3) Any trial-related duties and functions not specifically transferred to and assumed by a CRO are retained by the sponsor.
- (5.2.4) All references to a sponsor in this guideline also apply to a CRO to the extent that a CRO has assumed the trial-related duties and functions of a sponsor.

In spite of this statement of principles, at least one publicly traded biopharmaceutical company that makes use of CROs has stated in investor filings:

Due to our reliance on third party contract research organisations to conduct our clinical trials, we are unable to directly control the timing, conduct, expense and quality of our clinical trials.

Market Size and Growth

A significant portion of R&D budgets are spent on outsourcing services (domestic and/or international) offered by the CRO industry, approximately $15 billion in 2007. This figure is expected to grow at 15% over the next seven years and should increase further with the broadening of the spectrum of services outsourced to cover the entire value chain. As outsourced services in developing countries such as China and India move up the value chain to cover phase 1/2 trials, the total contracts value may increase to $20 billion by 2010. Furthermore, certain therapeutic areas within pharmaceutical development are due for an even greater rate of growth, namely the oncology class, expected to see continued growth of upwards of 21% over the next few years due to the large target market, strong unmet medical need, and overwhelming number of drugs currently in development (667 for cancer vs. 252 for CNS disorders, 206 for cadiovascular disorders, and 186 for infections).

An increasing number of clinical trials are run by CROs; the amount spent on CRO-run research increased from $1.6 billion in 1994 to $7.6 billion in 2004. Over the same time period, the share of clinical trials run at academic medical centres dropped from 63% to 26%. As one author put it:

What began as small specialised boutique firms offering narrowly targeted outsourcing services to pharmaceutical clients have come to dominate drug development and clinical trial management.

There are over 1,100 CROs in the world, despite continued trends toward consolidation (many CROs are being acquired in recent times or others go out of business). It is a very fragmented industry with the top 10 controlling 56.1% of the market in 2008 and down to 55% in 2009. One estimate had the size of the market set to reach $24 billion in 2010 and set to grow at a rate of 8.5% through 2015.

The largest CROs, according to Industry Standard Research, are Quintiles, Parexel, Covance, Pharmaceutical Product Development (PPD), Icon, INC Research, inVentiv Health inc, and BTS Research.

According to an article in September 2013, the merger of PRA International and ReSearch Pharmaceutical Services (RPS) made the newly named PRA Health Sciences the fourth-largest CRO.

What are R&D Systems

Research and development, better known as R&D, plays a major part in advancing technology in nearly every type of industrial pursuit. R&D systems are organisations that may be private or public, part of a company or separate entities that perform guided experimentation geared toward inventing or discovering new ideas and finding practical means of application. R&D systems are common in electronics, biomedics, and pharmaceuticals, but may also be used to study consumer or financial trends.

Technology moves exceedingly fast, especially at the commercial level. Companies that have produced one innovative product, such as a computer, must put out more and more advanced versions of the product in order to keep a constant flow of business. R&D systems are often the means used to keep up with consumer demand for improvements; by constantly testing new theories, creating improved designs, and trying new techniques, R&D systems can help fuel the next generation of nearly every available product.

The actual process of R&D systems may be frustrating to those who expect research to follow a business model. Unfortunately, with the most dedicated workers, the best equipment, and the largest budget, advances can still not be simply willed to occur, nor can scientists promise results from an experiment. This can lead to a business vs. science catch-22, where R&D experiments can't get funding unless they promise results, but scientists can't be sure if there are going to be positive results until the experiments are run. Some believe that this leads to the corruption of pure science, as scientists are forced into the uncomfortable and often unethical position of having to guarantee results without any data.

Some R&D systems work towards specific goals, which can be as large as improving chemotherapy success, or as small as making letter keys on keyboards more durable. Others have broader perspectives on a large subject, such as the development of new types of alternative energy plants. Large or small, narrow or wide, most R&D systems follow a constantly revolving cycle. Developments or improvements are theorized, designed, tested, and implemented. Once the product or idea is implemented, the cycle begins all over again, using the knowledge gained in the last development process to fuel the next research period.

R&D systems may be privately owned or funded by the government. Some private companies qualify for government grants, since development is generally seen to be beneficial for the general population even if it starts as a proprietary concept. Universities commonly have R&D groups that contribute to various programs and projects on campus. Since trade secrets are a major part of the commercial realm, many large corporations own and operate R&D systems that are exclusively devoted to the technology and development needs of the company.

What are the Different Research and Development Costs?

Research and development (R&D) costs are investments in the future by a company or an entire nation. Combined, these two segments of the economy — corporations and government — account for most of the research and development advancements around the world. Companies in industries including pharmaceutical and technology usually earmark a percentage of their profits for research and development costs. These funds are used to develop and upgrade products and services. A government applies research and development to improvements in standard of living, space programs, national security, and government policies, and costs depend on economic growth in the country.

Most companies spend a minimal percentage of profits on research and development costs, but pharmaceutical and technology corporations tend to spend more. In pharmacy, it often takes many years and a great deal of money to introduce a single new drug to the market, and still there are no guarantees that a drug will be approved by regulators. Also, patent protection on blockbuster drugs runs out, making it possible for rivals to create generic versions of the same medicine. In order to continually develop new drugs, pharmaceutical companies employ thousands of people and spend huge amounts of money each year on research and development.

Technology developed by software and semiconductor companies becomes obsolete more quickly than in most other industries, making technology a giant in research and development spending. Since technology can be adopted universally, technology companies sometimes outsource research and development tasks offshore to other countries to save on costs. China and India have highly developed technology industries. It is less costly for some US-based global technology companies to outsource research and development tasks, especially to India, which commands lower wages than China.

Governments spend money on research and development to improve social welfare in a nation. In the US, major contractors hired by the Department of Defence spend billions of US Dollars annually on defence procurement. These contractors are permitted to report reasonable research and development costs as indirect expenses, and therefore recoup a large percentage of those costs.

Depending on the accounting standard that a country adheres to, research and development costs are accounted for differently around the world. In the US, where Generally Accepted Accounting Standards (GAAP) are the norm, any reasonable costs associated with research and development are accounted for as an expense when incurred. The standards for countries using International Financial Reporting Standards (IFRS) are more stringent. Companies based in countries using IFRS cannot report an intangible asset, for instance a software license, as a research and development expense unless certain criteria are met.

What is the R&D Process

As researchers narrow down ideas suggested during the earliest phase, they may also conduct market research to learn about how well an idea will be accepted by the public or by potential clients. Using this information, ideas with potential are singled out, and the R&D process moves into the next phase, which involves bringing those ideas to life. At this stage, product developers start figuring out how the idea can be executed, and they work on prototypes. As the R&D process continues, prototypes become more and more sophisticated, and designers start thinking about issues like mass production, identification of problems with the prototype, and so forth.

With something approaching a final product, the R&D process branches out. Branches of the company concerned with regulatory issues start exploring the regulations which could impact the product and the tests which the product may need to pass in order to sell, as in the case of pharmaceuticals which need to be taken through clinical trials. Advertising departments, meanwhile, start to think about advertising campaigns, branding, and product naming so that the company can experience a successful product roll out. The company also thinks about issues like pricing, distribution, and so forth.

The culmination of the R&D process ideally involves the introduction of a product to the public. However, many roadblocks can be encountered along the way; ideas may be taken quite far through development before being abandoned, and many ideas are quickly cut at the start of the process. Most companies want to encourage R&D innovation, so they support input from employees at all stages of the process, under the assumption that everyone may have a good idea which could benefit the company.

What is R&D Technology

Research and Development (R&D) technology is the practical application of knowledge, gained through systematic and methodical research, that allows a company to bring to market new and innovative products that they can exploit for commercial advantage. Utilisation of the technical knowledge acquired during the research phase can be used for a specific purpose, to introduce new products or processes to the market through production and engineering techniques. It can also be used to improve existing products so as to increase a business's existing market share.

In order to stay competitive in a rapidly evolving marketplace and meet the changing preferences and expectations of consumers, new product design and development is often a critical factor in the survival of a company. In industries that are constantly evolving due to continuous technological advancements, such as computer hardware and software, businesses must continually revise their design and range of product offerings in order to stay competitive. R&D technology is one way companies seek to maintain their competitive edge.

The funding source for most consumer-oriented companies' R&D technology efforts comes from their retained earnings. These companies forego short-term profit in order to maximize long term gain by acquiring a dominant market share for their products that successfully incorporate leading technological advantages. One of the attributes of a high tech company is the amount it spends on technology development. Pharmaceutical companies, for example, typically spend 15% of their revenues on average for research and development facilities in the hope that continuous research will lead to new patents being issued for some of their drugs in the development stages.

Some corporations focus their R&D technology efforts on recombining or experimenting with old ideas in new ways to see how existing technologies in one product market could lead to breakthrough innovations in another separate market. Often, innovative products introduced into the market have resulted from assessing consumer demand and then incorporating existing technology into a new product in a new and novel way. An early and exemplary practitioner of this type of research for commercial product development was Thomas Edison.

Many of Edison's inventions that met with commercial success were ideas that were borrowed from existing patents of other scientists or from inventions that others had created. Edison was able to constantly innovate because he how to adapt and improve existing technologies. This put him ahead of his competitors, who could not yet envision such innovations.

Similarly, the concept underlying the computer mouse first appeared in Xerox's Palo Alto R&D technology research facility in the 1970s. These devices didn't become well-known until later, however. It was the founders of Apple computer, ten years later, who successfully incorporated this idea as an integral aspect of the user interface of the first Macintosh computers.

What is Research and Development?

Research and development, often called R&D, is a phrase that means different things in different applications. In the world of business, it's the phase in a product's life that might be considered the product's "conception." That is, basic science must exist to support the product's viability, and if the science is lacking, it must be discovered; this is considered the *research* phase. If the science exists, then turning it into a useful product is the *development* phase. Further terminology refinements might call it *engineering* to refine production so that the product can be made for a cost that appeals to consumers.

R&D is an investment in a company's future. Companies that do not spend sufficiently in this phase are often said to be "eating the seed corn" — that is, when their current product lines become outdated and overtaken by their competitors, they will not have viable successors in the pipeline. How much is reasonable to spend on research and development is highly dependent both on the technology area and how fast the market is moving. It might be enough to spend 2% of company revenue, not profit, in a fairly sedate market, but to keep up in rapidly changing markets, companies should expect to spend 15% or more, just to keep up with the rest of the pack.

There is considerable debate over which is the "R" and which is the "D" in R&D. Traditionally, *research* was broken into *basic research* and *applied research*, with basic research delving into basic scientific principles and applied research looking for ways to use the basic science to better human lives. More recently, there is very little truly basic research being done in the corporate world; it is mainly the province of academia, often with corporate or government funding support.

Older standards hold that *research* looked at least five to ten years into the future, and *development* one to five years, but those time frames have shortened as the speed of technology has increased. It is always difficult, in times of tight money, to justify spending significant sums on something that may not yield returns for another ten to 15 years, if ever. Spending on research and development is vital to continued growth and prosperity, however, both for a company and for a country.

R&D Collaboration: The Process, Risks and Checkpoints

As research and development (R&D) collaboration becomes increasingly used in large international enterprises, it is of growing importance to have the related business processes, procedures, supportive materials, information security, controls, information systems and risk management in order. This article shows positive and negative aspects of R&D collaboration, discusses the various categories of R&D collaboration, gives general checkpoints for the R&D collaboration process management and examines some of the risks and information security issues involved in R&D collaboration.

R&D Collaboration or Not?

In R&D there are cases when it may be favourable for a large enterprise to collaborate with a company, university or some other organisation or consortia. In the case of an IT enterprise in today's business world, while the importance of R&D cannot be emphasized enough, it is not economically justified to carry out R&D alone on the hundreds of R&D fields in IT.

To successfully achieve R&D collaboration, the organisation must manage the many business processes, risks, controls and all the other issues involved. If an enterprise does not manage these issues, the collaboration may bring many drawbacks including significant economic losses to the enterprise, inefficient R&D collaboration, missed deadlines, wrongly used resources, damages to the brand, missed business opportunities and information security breaches. R&D collaboration usually starts with small projects and then, when mutual trust increases, the collaboration may deepen. This possible development process may take several years.

Positive Aspects of R&D Collaboration Include:

- It is useful when it is not possible or reasonable, for resource, economic or competence reasons, to complete all the R&D work internally.
- There is an increased flexibility in resourcing, competence development and technology focus.
- Knowledge can be purchased with ease and quickness.
- It provides freedom for internal resources to concentrate on more strategic tasks in product development.
- It provides ease and reliability by having a central figure responsible for R&D collaboration.
- In some cases, it provides a more accurate prediction of project costs.

Negative Aspects of R&D Collaboration include

- Generally speaking and mainly for security reasons, areas that are of significant strategic importance should not be subcontracted.
- There are risks involved in relying too heavily on one collaborator, especially in strategic R&D.
- Many concerns arise when using subcontracting, such as what will be subcontracted and to whom, why subcontractors will be used, what the expected results are, and how the results will be linked to and integrated into the whole work.

- There is a risk that the collaborator's level of information security, risk awareness and risk management is not adequate.
- There is a possibility of communications issues/problems due to differences in corporate and national cultures.
- The organisation may lose the opportunity to gain important strategic knowledge that may be necessary in the future.
- A project might be more difficult to manage with the addition of collaborators.

Categories of R&D Collaboration

In large enterprises in the business area of IT, there are a number of categories and subcategories of R&D collaboration. The various categories demand that strategy selections be undertaken for finding the most suitable form of collaboration for a project. The decision-making process may be long, troublesome and time-demanding. Actually, there are as many strategy selections as there are collaborators. The R&D collaboration categories include, but are not limited to:

- University sponsoring/cooperation:
- Thesis works—Thesis works of a single person, such as a master's, diploma or doctorate thesis, are typical examples of this category. An example of this would be engineering students who, at the end of their studies, may write their diploma work for a research laboratory in a large enterprise.
- Sponsored research—A sponsored research model can be used when a university is doing high-quality research on research fields that are of interest to the enterprise, but where the applications of the research are not yet clear enough for other approaches. One can, for example, support the university's activities by donating resources to buy important research equipment.
- University with a research consortium—This category typically is funded when there is clear added value in conducting the research as a consortium. The added value may come from the cooperation inside the consortium and/or from aggregating critical R&D resources. There are many types of consortia, e.g., a collaboration project where there are a university, the enterprise, two companies functioning as subcontractors and a national research institution. The management of large consortia may be especially complicated.

- University professor—University professors can be financed if they are the clear key researchers of the area in question. In this category, professors can get resources through their university for doing research on an area of their expertise.
- Specific institution, faculty or university institute—For example, a research institution receives financial resources from a large enterprise for doing research on a specific topic/module. In the majority of such cases, a university has done excellent research on the topic over a long period of time. In these cases, universities typically are active in marketing their work to an enterprise to get additional funding and top-class guidance in helping them find the industrial relevance for their research. Sometimes an enterprise recruits researchers from such projects and tries to give a positive impact to the level of education as a result of country or specific strategic business reasons.
- A company as R&D collaborator:
- Large collaboration project—An example of this is an enterprise having a multimillion-dollar R&D project with a collaborator. Using companies in R&D may be challenging because they may lack some competencies. Therefore, companies in R&D mostly are used for specific research where more straightforward tasks already have been identified. However, this is case-specific to a high degree.
- Resource hiring or subcontracting from a company—Resource hiring is a rather straightforward extension of an enterprise's own resources. It is used in cases where tasks are defined and can be given to an external person having the necessary skills. The skills hired typically are based on old working cooperations/relationships. The business relations can be domestic/international, onsite or offshore.
- Module, design or unit—A part (module/design/unit) of the working total is ordered from an R&D collaborator. These mostly are fixed-price subcontracting projects. The part is delivered, tested and then integrated into the whole product.
- International resource hiring—Generally speaking, this category has become increasingly used in many large organisations during the last few years. A specific challenge to international resource hiring cases is that it may be difficult to verify that ethical principles required and demanded by the enterprise are followed. For example, a resource hiring company placed in country A, renting personnel from country B to an

enterprise in country C, may provide a cost/benefit to the enterprise hiring the resource. However, a possible drawback is that it might be difficult to ensure that this arrangement fulfills the employment/employee regulations in all the involved countries, that appropriate ethical principles are followed in respect to the employees and that the enterprise's values are fully understood and followed.

- Special variants of R&D collaboration:

  This third category of R&D collaboration deals with categories that are "especially special," such as the external (i.e., nonenterprise) person who has made an invention and contacts the enterprise, hoping to sell the invention or subcontract it. In this category, there also is the R&D collaborator working for a unit in an enterprise, but in another department's project and facilities.

- Collaborator's subcontractor—This also includes any subcontractors of the R&D collaborators (who also may have their own subcontractors). The key business rule is to check and assess topics such as confidentiality, security, contractual requirements, third-party intellectual property rights (IPR) principles, product liability, assessments of the collaborator/ subcontractor and warranties. One also has to be careful that collaborators and their subcontractors do not get the opportunity to participate in internal discussions where they might get patentable ideas. This aspect has to be considered in all subcontracting categories, but this is a case-specific issue. Information security is naturally of special importance in this category. However, this is case-specific, as there may exist tight collaboration, more of partnership. In partnership, a deep and long-term collaboration is in question, where the driving forces behind the partnership are the carefully mapped-out benefits for both parties and mutual trust. Further, in this category it is of especially great importance to achieve a win-win situation.

- *Ad hoc* R&D subcontracting—R&D subcontracting *ad hoc* would be necessary in a case where, for example, the project is at risk of being late, the researchers are sick and, with the existing resources, the project will not remain on schedule. This kind of *ad hoc* R&D subcontracting is mostly done on an hourly basis. In such cases, the use of existing collaborators (i.e., those already in use by another unit/department within the organisation) is recommended to keep up existing timetables until a new suitable and reliable collaborator can be found if necessary.

- Alliance or cooperation forum—Although this is a tight form of collaboration, it is looser than a joint venture. This type of alliance may create a natural potential collaborator and subcontractor base for all the interested and participating companies and may speed up technology take-up and ramp-up of global developer communities, as well as facilitate global standardization of (future) core technologies.
- International R&D projects—Examples are projects financed by the European Union (EU). EU-financed projects in R&D and in the area of IT are large, usually have several participants and run in several European countries. The participants mostly are universities, enterprises, research institutions, collaborators and interest organisations. EU projects usually have specific contractual obligations that must be considered and included in the collaboration legal agreements.

General Checkpoints for R&D Collaboration

For an R&D collaboration project, it is necessary to have a large number of checkpoints (a list of items to complete) for before, during and after the project's completion. The following are some possible checkpoints:

- Identifying the project entity where R&D collaboration is needed
- Defining the parts that can be subcontracted
- Defining the parts that must not be subcontracted
- Identifying all the partnership alternatives and combinations of products or services that might meet the project's needs
- Completing a thorough audit and assessment of the collaborator, including finances, IS, security, personnel, product(s), strategy, processes and ownership of the company
- Taking into account the collaborator's overall technology strategy
- Maintaining financial controls in the project and the collaboration project
- Checking the various types of billing, such as hour-based and module-based
- Ensuring that the external person signs the nondisclosure agreement (NDA), which is completed by the project manager
- Surveying for, assessing and finding the most suitable collaborator

- Completing time scales, which should be detailed in the project plan
- Setting and following realistic and achievable quality standards
- Completing the selection based on technical and business reasons
- Checking the giving out and management of accesses to information and information systems
- Completing the contract drafting process, including proposal request, NDA and the contents of the contract. When a contract draft has been made and the collaborator's comments received, the enterprise has to, with regard to the comments from the other party, decide which proposed changes are acceptable or unacceptable. For large collaborators with which an enterprise has a long-term cooperative agreement, it may be advantageous to make a memorandum of understanding (MoU). An MoU is a mutual understanding by the parties to do something together in the future.
- Making the final decision whether to use the collaborator in question
- Completing negotiations and contract signings, including practical arrangements, such as the location to sign the contract, who will sign the contract and the rights to sign it
- Setting project checkpoints, including the financial situation of a project
- Setting up a project and collaboration project library, which includes minutes, materials, change requests, reports, plans, etc.
- Setting reporting procedures internally and externally
- Remembering that mutual respect and commitment are crucial for successful R&D collaboration
- Taking into account that a large enterprise may have to advise and support the collaborator and help it to develop and grow
- Continuing to manage the collaboration project
- Testing the deliverables
- Carrying out the R&D collaboration in a legal and ethical way with full respect to all involved parties, countries, companies, employees, organisations, legislations, ethical principles and cultures

- Following up, which includes questioning if the project's good and bad points have been recognised, documented and communicated in a constructive manner, both internally and with the collaborator
- Storing the project and R&D collaboration project's materials in a secure and systematic way for security, audit trail and legal reasons

Managing the Risks in R&D Collaboration

In risk management (RM) there are a number of alternative methods to deal with the risks, such as risk avoidance, risk control, risk transfer, risk monitoring and risk acceptance. The most important thing is to recognise the risks and choose a way to deal with them. In R&D collaboration, there likely are a few thousand risks because of the magnitude and interdisciplinary nature of the area in question. R&D collaboration involves areas such as finance, sourcing, legal, tax, intellectual property rights, contract management, project management, planning, security, information systems, controls, risk management, engineering, human resources, quality and reporting. Further, the risks in R&D collaboration are not only a question of risks in the collaboration itself but also, among others, the general risks in the business environment. There should be replacement strategies, procedures and plans if something should go wrong with the collaborator and the cooperation. There is no such thing as a typical, standard R&D collaboration case, but every single project has its specific risks and checkpoints. In a large enterprise there may be simultaneously running, globally, thousands of collaboration projects. Further, the collaboration itself also is a process, as it usually starts from a small project with the collaborator. Then, as the mutual respect, confidence, resources and processes become stronger, the amount of collaboration can increase to a large scale where the collaborator is a trusted partner and strongly involved in the enterprise's activities.

Below are, from a General (Non-Case-Specific) Point of View, Some of the Risks and Information Security Issues in R&D Collaboration:

- There is a risk if there is inadequate communication between the enterprise and collaborator. One reason for this may be differences in corporate cultures.
- Inadequate reporting procedures can constitute risks, as a subcontractor may not use the same tools (for project management, reporting, etc.) as an enterprise.

- Multiple changes to what was agreed to with the collaborator originally may bring problems. This is especially problematic if changes are left undocumented or documentation is done carelessly.
- A problematic issue can be inadequate communication and identification of risks in the project before its commencement.
- A lack of awareness among the steering group and project group of the importance of risk management is indeed a risk. Additionally, a steering group should have meetings regularly for, among other reasons, checking that budgets, timetables and quality requirements are kept.
- Especially in global multisite and transdivisional projects, there may arise additional specific issues and risks to be considered, such as in reporting, management, resourcing, contract management, IS security, personnel security, cultural issues, travelling security and insurance.
- If information systems security has been constructed so that it slows down the work progress, a project can be delayed. Security is there for supporting business.
- Selecting the wrong R&D collaborator and/or not following up with an existing one can bring significant problems to the project. This is especially urgent if quality, budgets and time scales are not kept.
- Too much dependence on one R&D collaborator can, in some very specific cases, constitute risks.
- Risk may exist if there is inadequate personal communication between the organisation and the collaborator.
- In today's world there is a risk that an enterprise is the target of industrial espionage. For example, there is a risk that collaborators may be used to get access to the enterprise's information, such as breakthrough R&D results.
- A collaborator who wants to get rid off all responsibilities (cash in and run away) when a project is over may constitute a severe risk, as this may show that the collaborator has weak or no confidence in what has been delivered.
- The risk exists that R&D collaborators will, against a legal agreement, start their own business based on the research results. If so, legal measures have to be taken.
- Making amendments to the contract without contacting legal authorities can, for example, lead to disputes between an

enterprise and a collaborator in a worst-case scenario regarding intellectual property rights.

- For legal and contract reasons, among others, there always should be an audit trail.
- If there are no or inadequate quality requirements, there is a risk that the product will be of low quality. Because of this, a systematic quality control process is important.
- If the wrong module is subcontracted, i.e., the one the enterprise should do by itself, there is a risk with inadequate in-house knowledge.
- Too much or inadequate monitoring of an R&D collaborator's work may slow down the performance of work.
- Before acceptance, a delivered product always should be thoroughly tested, and possible reclamations should be completed in a written form.
- Having unknowingly received "rookies" (e.g., recent university graduates) from a collaborator may, in the worst case, delay a project.
- Not completing a follow-up of the collaboration project may lead to similar problems and risks in the next comparable collaboration project.
- Ignorance of risks, information security, processes, subprocesses, policies and supporting materials always is a risk.
- And finally, the largest risk of all is not knowing what the enterprise (as the client) wants from the R&D collaboration project.

Conclusion

The number of business processes, risks and information security issues is indeed large in R&D collaboration. To manage those issues, an enterprise must have a systematic, modelled, up-to-date and flexible approach to the R&D collaboration. The management of these issues may be resource-demanding, but very necessary for managing the many risks and maintaining the efficiency in collaboration. In today's business environment, it is of growing importance to have well-working, efficient, reliable and secure R&D collaboration. There is no large global enterprise using IT that can isolate itself from the world and complete all R&D work by itself.

Protecting Know-How and Trade Secrets in Collaborative R&D Relationships

The number of collaborative R&D relationships is increasing rapidly. Central to these relationships is the need to share proprietary intellectual assets. Equally important is the need to protect that information from unintended use. This article describes legal and non-legal methods firms use to protect intellectual assets. Legal methods include crafting a series of agreements and linking the agreements to the activities of the collaboration. Non-legal methods include ensuring employees in both firms understand what information MUST be shared with the partner, MAY be shared with the partner and MUST NEVER be shared with the partner. Training also includes a clear understanding of each firms' rights-to-use the disclosed information.

Key Concepts

Collaboration agreements, non disclosure agreements, joint development agreements, trade secrets, know-how, intellectual asset management, collaborative R&D, licensing, licenses, encumbrances, proprietary information, intellectual asset training

Technology is the currency of the new millennium. Firms that develop and/or acquire proprietary positions in leading edge technologies create a solid foundation for growth. However, the days when one firm internally creates all of the technology it needs to compete in the market place are over. Even simple products contain a bewildering number of sophisticated technologies as customers demand capabilities only dreamed about a few years ago.

To gain access to this technology a company can (a) develop the technology internally (b) obtain it from outside parties via license/ purchase or (c) jointly develop the technology with an external firm. This article focuses on the third possibility, developing technology through a joint development agreement. Specifically, we will describe the issues and identify industry practices surrounding protecting the firm's intellectual assets (IA) during interactions with outside parties.

The number of collaborative research and development agreements is increasing rapidly. Industrial Research Institute member firms are engaging small high technology companies, Federal Laboratories, Universities, international firms and competitors in ways not dreamed of just five years ago. Central to these collaborations is the need to share proprietary intellectual assets to meet the objectives of the collaboration. Equally important is the need to protect that information from unintended use.

The nature of intangible assets such as know how and trade secrets is a barrier to their protection. They are easily shared, travel effortlessly in peoples' minds, and resist being categorized into neat little piles labelled proprietary and non-proprietary knowledge. To complicate matters further, know-how is fun to talk about. Business and technical people are naturally drawn into discussions of how a particular technology works, or the reasons why one technology will outperform another in the marketplace. While these conversations are interesting, employees may inappropriately divulge proprietary information. In this article we will not distinguish between "know how", which is information or skills required to do something useful, or "trade secrets", which are valuable information the firm takes specific actions to protect. In particular there are statutory definitions of "trade secrets" that are not especially relevant to this discussion. The real issue is protecting proprietary information, i.e., valuable knowledge a firm wishes to protect from unintended use.

What is a Trade Secret?

In general a trade secret is information of value to a business that gives some advantage to the business and that the business keeps secret. This notion is a bit vague and a precise, uniform definition is not possible. The term 'trade secret' is defined in various federal and state statutes (e.g., The Uniform Trade Secrets Act, the Illinois Trade Secrets Act) and by legal associations (e.g., The Restatement of the Law Third, Unfair Competition by the American Law Institute). If a company's information meets a statutory definition there are specific protections that can be claimed. To avoid these details, we choose to use the term know-how in this paper, and are referring to proprietary information that a company views as valuable.

To understand how firms successfully share proprietary information in collaborative relationships, interviews were conducted with over twenty representatives of IRI companies. Participants represented a cross section of industry sectors including life sciences, consumer products, oil & gas, chemicals, materials, federal laboratories, control systems, defence/aerospace, electronics and academia. Each was selected because of his/her central role in protecting IA and their organisation's extensive experience in licensing and using collaborative research agreements to meet technology commercialization goals.

The results of this study fall into four general areas: (1) Collaborations require a series of agreements (2) Issues in Non - Disclosure Agreements (3) Issues in Joint Development agreements and (4) Organisational issues that effect intellectual asset protection.

Collaborations Require a Series of Agreements

The reality of the collaborative process is that different legal agreements build on one another as the collaboration moves through various phases. The Non-Disclosure Agreement (NDA) is normally the first agreement in the series. It may be followed by an agreement covering development of new technology such as a collaborative research agreement, a joint development agreement, or an agreement to purchase developments from one of the parties. If the collaboration is successful, they are followed by agreements that enable the operation of a business such as purchase agreements, joint marketing agreements, and various types of licenses to assure each party has the necessary rights to operate their business. Figure 1 follows the process from the exploration period that ends with a signed joint development agreement, to the collaboration period that ends with a signed commercialization agreement. In each stage, specific people carry out specific activities under the appropriate agreements. The limits of each agreement, and an understanding of which agreements have and have not been signed, is a critical piece of information that guides the actions of technical and business staff. Employees' ability to protect proprietary information is maximized when the legal agreements are in phase with the collaboration's operational activities. Too often, these agreements get out of phase. For example, when operational managers see agreements as "boiler plate" or "legal stuff", they press on with development while negotiations are underway but before an agreement is in place. These actions open up both firms to risk. Better to form an effective link between legal/business staff and technical staff that allows the firms' to collaborate under well crafted agreements.

Issues in Non- Disclosure Agreement

The first line of defence for protecting proprietary information is the Non-Disclosure Agreement (NDA). Also known as the Confidential Disclosure Agreement (CDA), this document allows employees from different firms to share proprietary information; typically technical capabilities, application requirements and business models. This information can be extremely valuable. The hope is that the companies can combine capabilities, or match the capability of one with a need of the other, to create significant business value. These early discussions include information about the marketplace, the specific technical needs, and resources or capabilities that each firm requires to meet the need. These discussions are sensitive and should be held under a NDA.

Experienced technical and business staff understand that an NDA creates an opportunity, not an obligation to share information. These men and women temper its use by applying a large dose of common sense. They take time to understand the purpose of the disclosure and only describe enough information to meet that purpose. It is vital that employees from both firms understand what information is covered, and what information is not covered under the agreement. Neither side wants to be unnecessarily polluted with proprietary information of the other at this early date. Before the joint development agreement is in place, either firm may break off discussions and collaborate with another. Thus, the goal is to provide the disclosee with just enough information to allow them to make the next go-no go decision. This may require a series of meetings with each meeting exposing more and more details within the areas identified in the NDA.

While Table depicted earlier, identifies the major conditions NDAs must cover, three key issues require special attention:

1. what confidential information is being disclosed
2. each firm's rights to use the disclosed information
3. the timing of confidentiality (both the disclosure and confidentiality period).

Firms avoid misunderstandings when the NDA clearly and accurately identifies the information each party will disclose under the agreement. Writing the description is a balancing act. It must be broad enough to allow each potential partner to evaluate the other's intellectual assets (IA) and make a go/no-go decision to enter joint development negotiations. However, it must be narrow enough so that only that subset of the firm's science base, relevant to the potential collaboration, is disclosed.

Once the parties understand what information will, and will not be disclosed, they must agree on each firms "rights to use" the information. The goal is to prevent misuse by either party by clearly stating the purpose of the disclosure. An example is helpful here. A common clause in NDAs state that each party can only use the information for the purpose of evaluating the technology or for discussions related to establishing a potential business relationship. Another common clause is to enable the parties to coordinate in preparing a joint response to a solicitation. These clauses protect the disclosing party from unintended use. They also place a burden on the disclosee to think through its freedom to operate after the disclosure. For example, will the disclosee be able to exit discussions with this firm, and enter into discussions with the firm's competitor, given the nature of the disclosure? This is a realistic scenario given that the firms are exploring a potential collaboration and have not entered into a joint development agreement. After assessing the disclosed information, either party may decide to terminate discussions and search for a better partner.

This scenario is particularly troublesome for large firms. They are seen as "deep pockets" by small entrepreneurial and venture capital based firms. If any large firm business unit introduces a similar technology into the market, the small firm may feel that its proprietary knowledge was used, or that they stimulated the large firm to invent. It is hard for large technology-based firms to deal with this issue when they have multiple projects, in similar technical areas, proceeding simultaneously in diverse business units, often in different markets and countries.

The time periods specified in NDAs are information management tools. The first is the disclosure period. It states the specific dates during which the disclosure will take place. Information disclosed outside that time period is not covered by the agreement. The confidentiality period is the length of time the information must be protected. It is common to see three year, five year, or in some cases perpetual confidentiality periods. As a general rule, the discloser seeks longer confidentiality periods while the disclosee seeks shorter periods. This reflects each sides desire to minimize risk. Interestingly, the real risk has less to do with time, and more to do with managing information in a modern organisation. As people transfer to other departments, leave the company, and simply forget what information was disclosed under NDA versus disclosed publicly, the risk of an improper disclosure increases.

Table 1 – Key Components of a Non – Disclosure Agreement

A well-crafted NDA includes statements that describe:

- The identity of the parties
- The purpose of the discussion and/or a description of the potential collaboration
- Whether the agreements is a one-way or two-way disclosure of information
- The rights of each party to use the disclosed information
- What information is protected and what information falls outside the scope of the agreement (i.e., was in the public domain, already in the receiving parties possession, subsequently disclosed by a third party not under the obligation of confidentiality)
- How information will be protected by each party during discussions and returned upon completion of the discussions
- That the agreement does, or does not, create an obligation between the companies (i.e., grant a right, license or commitment to enter into any other agreement)

- The definition of confidential information (i.e., anything marked confidential or verbal information followed up in 30 days by a written description marked confidential)
- Whether or not the agreement can be assigned
- A process for exchanging the information (meetings and discussions are best followed up in writing)
- Governing law.
- An entire agreement clause
- Timing (both the disclosure and confidentiality period)

How Much Protection does an NDA Actually Provide?

It is safe to say that thousands of NDAs are signed each month. However, the number of NDA disputes that actually go to court each year is very small. The number of disputes that result in dollar awards sufficient to cover the expense of litigation, and the associated organisational costs, is even smaller. This might lead to the conclusion that NDAs provide true protection in only a small number of very high value, very egregious cases. However, the reality of NDAs is that they serve two valuable functions. First, they raise awareness in the minds of both firms' employees about the proprietary nature of the information being shared. Second, they protect the patent rights of the disclosing party. In many parts of the world, once an invention is publicly divulged, the right to file for patent protection is forfeited. When the disclosure takes place under confidentiality, the patent filing rights are preserved.

Potential Misuse of an NDA

The most common misuse stems from the enthusiasm of technical staff, not malicious intent. Comforted by the fact that a NDA is in-place and the negotiating teams are hard at work on a JDA, the two firms' technical staffs begin brainstorming in ways that lead to invention. While no-one wants to stifle innovation in a collaborative relationship, if an invention is jointly created by members of both firms without an agreement in place, that invention is considered a joint invention. Under United States law joint inventorship results in joint ownership. Either partner can do whatever it wants with their patent rights, without the consent of the other joint owner. This includes licensing or selling their ownership interest to anyone they wish including the partner's chief competitor. Joint ownership may, or may not maximize the value of the innovation for either firm. Better for both firms to negotiate how intellectual property developed during the course of the agreement will be allocated between the parties and write that agreement into the JDA. Absent that contract, any jointly developed patent defaults to joint ownership with few restrictions on how it can be used.

"Joint Ownership – the International Perspective"

Collaborations with foreign firms introduce some wrinkles for United States firms that are used to dealing with the United States' system of allocating and protecting IA rights. One example is the default method of handling jointly owned patentable IA. In the United States the usual practice is allow any one of the owners to use or license the patent without accounting to, or requiring the consent of, the other owner. In most of the world, a patent co-owner is allowed some consideration unless the agreement specifically states otherwise. This could require the co-owner's approval prior to commercialization or the sharing of financial returns. Another common concern with certain countries is the lack of a proven track record in the courts that demonstrates IA rights are enforceable. Local legal counsel should be consulted about the risks related to enforcing patent rights against infringers, protecting IA against misappropriation, pirating and collecting fees and royalties.

Issues in Joint Development Agreements

Anyone familiar with collaborative research understands the complexity of structuring and negotiating an agreement. While a complete discussion of JDA terms and conditions is outside the scope of this article2, Table 2 contains a list of key components that must be considered in every JDA. We will go into detail on three of them as they relate to protecting tacit knowledge:

1. Developing a clear description of the joint development
2. Bounding the agreement
3. Defining each firm's rights to use both background and foreground IA.

Developing a clear description of the joint development is difficult because each firm is good at what it does, but not so good at what the partner does. Therefore, it's hard to assess each others skills and capabilities, and ensure that the firms' combined resources are sufficient to carry out the development. The result is uncertainty when writing the Statement of Work.

Good Statements of Work carefully and completely describe the obligations of the parties including, what each party will do separately and what the parties will do together. However, since collaborative agreements often target projects at the edge of both firms' capabilities, the outcome is uncertain. The worst case scenario is when employees in both firms carry out their responsibilities but the end result is lacking because the initial plan was incomplete. While there is no sure cure for this situation, a well-crafted Statement of Work minimizes the risk. Part of crafting the agreement is ensuring that each side has access and rights to the specific know-how needed to carry out their roles (and joint roles).

The second challenge is bounding the agreement. Boundaries are a clear statement of the scope of the alliance. Inside the boundaries, the firms are allied. They will play by a set of rules defined by the alliance agreement. Outside the boundaries, the firms are not allied, and a different set of rules will apply. Boundaries are determined by translating each firm's business and technical intents into a set of statements that determine the scope of the alliance. The scope is often determined by asking each firm to describe its business and technical intent along four dimensions; technologies, markets, products and geographies.

Severe problems arise when boundaries are not clearly defined. Take the example of two firms collaborating to develop one or more products, under an agreement in which the firms agree on significant restrictions on the use of each other's background intellectual property. The management of Company A views the product boundaries of the collaboration as the circle on the left in Figure, while the management of Company B believes the product boundaries are represented by the circle on the right. The first product being cooperatively developed is in the overlapping area, which both firms agree it is inside the boundaries. Now suppose Company B uses Company A's background intellectual property in a different product represented by Point 1. Company B believes that such use is allowed under terms of the alliance agreement that permits use of the partner's background intellectual property in products within the boundaries. But Company A does not recognise the product represented by Point 1 as inside the boundaries, and is angered since the alliance agreement does not permit the use of each other's background intellectual property outside the boundaries. Company A's managers react badly since they view Company B's behaviour as a deliberate violation of that agreement. Managers in Company B do not understand Company A's reaction because they believe Point 1 is within the boundaries. Actual disputes can be more complex than this example, since the dimensions of boundaries can encompass not only products, but also underlying technology, classes of applications or customers, or geographical regions. To avoid this arguments, which sometimes stem from genuine misunderstandings, it is essential that prospective alliance partners carefully define the boundaries as part of the negotiation.

The third challenge is defining each firm's rights to use background and foreground intellectual assets. For any collaborative research agreement to succeed, each partner must have the necessary background rights from the other (and possibly from third parties) to carry out its roles in the alliance. Furthermore, the agreement must allocate foreground rights between the collaborators in a mutually satisfactory way. Our interviewees are careful to outline the rights each firm has to the background of the other, and the jointly developed foreground under three conditions; inside the boundaries of the collaboration, outside the boundaries, and upon termination of the agreement. These rights extend to all types of intellectual assets, not just patents.

Key Components of a Joint Development Agreement:

- Clear Understanding of Value Proposition from both firms' perspective
- Description of relationship
- Statement of Work
- Funding and Costs
- Boundaries of the agreement
- Each firms rights to use Background intellectual assets inside/ outside the boundaries and upon termination
- Each firms rights to use foreground intellectual assets inside/ outside the boundaries and upon termination
- Which partner(s) are responsible for third party relationships
- What rights do third parties have to the partners' intellectual assets
- License terms (if a licensing agreement)
- Supply terms (if a supply agreement)
- Governance
- Protection of confidential Information
- Term and termination clause
- Governing Law
- Assign ability
- Indemnifications, warranties, and disclaimers
- Compliance Issues (export etc)

Organisational Issues

NDAs and JDAs are documents that provide legal protection to intellectual assets. These documents are most effective when they are supported by specific organisational actions. One action is to ensure

that both firms will provide the quantity and quality of resources (including know-how) needed to make the collaboration a success. There is a subtle but critical insight related to this issue. Every research collaboration is really "three collaborations in one". The first is the alliance between Company A and Company B. The second is the internal alliance among key groups inside Company A. The third is that same internal alliance inside Company B. If any of these internal groups do not understand the agreement, or fail to coordinate their resources with those of the other internal groups, problems arise. For example, if one group in Company A's internal alliance is out of phase with the others, and does not provide the appropriate quantity or quality of resources/information; the entire relationship may be at risk.

Experienced companies deal with this issue by assigning members of all key groups to the planning and negotiating team. This ensures effective communication of the agreement, as well as buy-in of key stakeholders. The best teams involve members from every group that will provide critical resources to the collaboration during implementation, and members from key corporate groups that have decision making authority (i.e., finance, tax, IP).

Tracking the Portfolio of Licenses and Collaborative Agreements

Companies maximize the value of their IA portfolio by entering into a wide variety of licensing and collaborative agreements. Tracking these agreements is an onerous task, especially when exclusivity is granted. Exclusivity is the third rail of collaborative agreements. Large technology-intense firms shy away from exclusivity because tracking the myriad of constraints increases exponentially with the number of signed exclusive agreements. The problem of tracking patents is trivial compared to tracking note book entries and know-how never captured on paper. Few firms have a neural net powerful enough to track exclusivity in all its forms. Furthermore each asset can be exclusively licensed in terms of field of use, time, based on continued payments, and geography. The use of exclusive agreements is particularly burdensome in JDAs because managers must ensure that potential jointly developed foreground is not constrained by exclusively licensed background in either partner.

Having outlined the negative impacts of exclusivity, there is one overriding positive impact. Exclusive agreements can unlock real value. There are potential partners that will only collaborate on an exclusive basis. Some firms can only maximize the relationship's value when they receive exclusive rights. It is easy to lose sight of the market place impact of exclusive relationship when focusing on tracking. It may be worth the investment to acquire a sophisticated commercial tracking tool and remain focused on value creation.

These tracking tools can pay for themselves during JDA negotiations. A common challenge during joint development negotiations is tracking each firm's IA needs as those needs unfold. During early negotiations the parties may discuss the need to grant each other background rights that are not encumbered in either firm. As negotiations continue, the parties may add requirements that sweep in additional IP that is encumbered. To deal with this challenge, one interviewee conducts three (3) intellectual asset checks during negotiations. The first occurs during early discussions. That IA check informs the internal team and the potential partner of any IA encumbrances that impacts the current vision of the collaboration. A second check occurs midway through negotiations and checks for encumbrances on any additional intellectual assets the collaboration requires. The final check occurs prior to signing the agreement. This last check is particularly is important because large swings in each firm's negotiating positions often occur at the end of negotiations. Those swings may have an important impact on IA needs.

Training Employees to Protect Intellectual Assets through Their Every Day Behaviours.

Well crafted NDAs and JDAs are a necessary but not sufficient condition to protect intellectual assets. An equally important line of defence is a technical staff that understands how IAs create value for the firm, and knows how/when to share them.

Taking employees through a well constructed intellectual asset training program breaths life into everything outlined above. Management takes a giant step forward when it creates an environment in which every member of business and technical staff understand more than just the principles, but the rigors of protecting IA. While most technology managers believe their staff is well versed in this area, they may be overconfident. Take this simple test. Ask five technologists to answer the following question, "What are our firm's proprietary intellectual assets as they relate to this collaboration?" The alignment or lack of alignment of the responses is a useful indicator. Intellectual asset training is an organisational protection mechanism that augments the legal protections of the NDA and JDA. At a minimum, this training must clearly outline to team members what intellectual assets they:

1. must share with the partner
2. may share with the partner
3. must never share with the partner.

When technical staff understands these limits, they monitor their own behaviour.

Protecting Your Know-How in University Relationships

The university culture of open sharing is both a leverage point and a barrier to industrial collaboration. From a leverage point perspective, university researchers nurture the leading edge thinking that results in future products. From a barrier perspective, university researchers share information vigorously. When dealing with universities, leading firms use all the techniques outlined in this article and take two additional steps to protect their commercial interests. First, they clearly outline the university's rights to disclose the results of the collaboration at conferences and in academic journals. Second, they ensure that every academic colleague working on the project, including graduate students, understand the terms of the agreement(s). Most graduate students have little or no experience with contracts such as non-disclosure agreements. While the university should describe the obligations of the agreement to its personnel, the corporate partner is well advised to ensure each university employee understands these obligations.

Educating your employees solves half the problem. The other half is ensuring that the partner's employees are equally sensitive to IA protection. Do the partner's employees know how to protect your IA? Do they know which disclosed material is sensitive and which is not? Apart from the assurances in the contract, behavioural training ensures that employees in the partner firm understand the basic principles of IA management and how they apply to this particular collaboration. The collaboration's kick off meeting is an important intervention point. It may be one of the few times that all of the collaborators are together at the same time. Leading companies use this opportunity to ensure that team members from both firms come to a common understanding of what will be shared, and how the shared information will be protected.

Third party involvement is another aspect of protecting know-how that deserves management attention. Most research collaborations include one or more consultants, contract employees, and/or third party companies. The concern goes beyond what is written in the NDA concerning third parties. The concern goes to the third party's understanding of what is proprietary, and a clear understanding of their responsibility to protect that information. Again, training employees to identify and protect proprietary information is key. This is particularly important in university relationships. Universities have a culture of open sharing. Graduate students must produce a thesis that is publishable. They are encouraged to share intellectual assets, not protect them. These students will work in their chosen field, and may work for your competitor. Their continuing responsibility to protect your firm's IA upon graduation is an important discussion topic.

Conclusion

This discussion highlights the two-fold challenge of protecting intellectual assets. From a legal/contractual perspective, nothing substitutes for a series of well-crafted legal agreements such as a Non-Disclosure Agreement and a Joint Development Agreement. These documents contain the intellectual asset terms and conditions each side must abide by during the collaboration. They also ensure that collaborating researchers have the necessary rights to carry out the collaboration and take the fruits of the work into the marketplace.

From the human behaviour perspective, firms must ensure that collaborating researchers have an understanding of the relevant terms of the contract, including what information must and must not be shared. While this sounds straightforward, it is not. The real challenge with protecting intellectual assets is that they are both "leaky" and "sticky". They leak out of the organisation with every visit of an outsider, and they stick in the minds of anyone who hears them. It takes one nanosecond for the person who just learned interesting information to convince themselves that they always knew that information, and therefore have a right to use it. Providing training to members of both firms, with a specific focus on protecting sensitive information during the course of the collaboration, pays enormous dividends.

Collaborative R&D: How Effective is It?

R&D collaboration is widespread in the U.S. economy of the 1990s. Literally hundreds of agreements now link the R&D efforts of U.S. firms, and other collaborative agreements involve both U.S. and non-U.S. firms. Collaboration between U.S. universities and industry also has grown significantly since the early 1980s-hundreds of industry-university research centres have been established, and industry's share of U.S. university research funding has doubled during this period, albeit to a relatively modest 7 percent. Collaboration between industrial firms and the U.S. national laboratories has grown as well during this period, with the negotiation of hundreds of agreements for cooperative R&D.

R&D collaboration has been widely touted as a new phenomenon and a potent means to enhance economic returns from public R&D programs and improve U.S. industrial competitiveness. In fact, collaborative R&D projects have a long history in U.S. science and technology policy. Major collaborative initiatives in pharmaceuticals manufacture, petrochemicals, synthetic rubber, and atomic weapons were launched during World War II, and the National Advisory Committee on Aeronautics, founded in 1915 and absorbed into NASA in 1958, made important contributions to commercial and military aircraft design throughout its existence. Similarly, university-industry research collaboration was well established in the U.S. economy of the 1920s and 1930s and contributed to the development of the academic discipline of chemical engineering, transforming the U.S. chemicals industry.

A single minded industry "vision" can conserve resources, but it may be ill advised in the earliest stages of development.

There is no doubt that collaborative R&D has made and will continue to make important contributions to the technological and economic well-being of U.S. citizens. But in considering the roles and contributions of collaboration, we must focus on the objectives of collaborative programs, rather than treating R&D collaboration as a "good thing" in and of itself. Collaborative R&D can yield positive payoffs, but it is not without risks. Moreover, R&D collaboration covers a diverse array programs, projects, and institutional actors. No single recipe for project design, program policies, or evaluation applies to all of these disparate entities.

In short, R&D collaboration is a means, not an end. Moreover, the dearth of systematic analysis and evaluation of existing federal policies toward collaboration hampers efforts to match the design of collaborative programs to the needs of different firms, industries, or sectors. A review of U.S. experience reveals a number of useful lessons and highlights several areas where more study is needed.

Policy Evolution

Since the mid-1970s, federal policy has encouraged collaboration among many different institutional actors in the U.S. R&D system.

One of the earliest initiatives in this area was the University-Industry Cooperative Research program of the National Science Foundation (NSF), which began in the 1970s to provide partial funding to university research programs enlisting industrial firms as participants in collaborative research activities. The NSF efforts were expanded during the 1980s to support the creation of Engineering Research Centres, and other NSF programs now encourage financial contributions from industry as a condition for awarding research funds to academic institutions. Moreover, the NSF model has been emulated by other federal agencies in requiring greater cost-sharing from institutional or industry sources in competitive research grant programs. The NSF and other federal initiatives were associated with the establishment of more than 500 university-industry research centres during the 1980s.

R&D collaboration between industrial firms and universities received another impetus from the Bayh-Dole Act, passed in 1980 and amended in 1986, which rationalized and simplified federal policy toward the patenting and licensing by nonprofit institutions of the results of publicly funded research. The Bayh-Dole Act has been credited with significant expansion in the number of universities operating offices to support the patenting, licensing, and transfer to industrial firms of university research results. These offices and the legislation have also provided incentives for industrial firms to form collaborative R&D relationships with universities.

The Bayh-Dole Act, the Stevenson-Wydler Act of 1980, and the Technology Transfer Act of 1986 also created new mechanisms for R&D collaboration between industrial firms and federal laboratories through the mechanism of the Cooperative Research and Development Agreement (CRADA). Under the terms of a CRADA, federal laboratories are empowered to cooperate in R&D with private firms and may assign private firms the rights to any intellectual property resulting from the joint work; the federal government retains a nonexclusive license to the intellectual property. The XXXXXX XXXXXX Act [Which Act?] was amended in 1989 to allow contractor-operated federal laboratories to participate in CRADAs. Federal agencies and research laboratories have signed hundreds of CRADAs since the late 1980s; between 1989 and 1995, the Department of Energy (DOE) alone signed more than 1,000 CRADAs. The 1996 Technology Transfer Improvements and Advancement Act strengthened the rights of industrial firms to exclusively license patents resulting from CRADAs.

Federal antitrust policy toward collaborative R&D also was revised considerably during the early 1980s. Through much of the 1960s and 1970s, federal antitrust policy was hostile toward R&D collaboration among industrial firms. The Carter administration's review of federal policies toward industrial innovation resulted in a new enforcement posture by the Justice Department, embodied in guidelines issued in 1980 that were less hostile toward such collaboration. In 1984, the passage of the National Cooperative Research Act (NCRA) created a statutory "safe harbor" from treble damages in private antitrust suits for firms registering their collaborative ventures with the Justice Department. The NCRA was amended to incorporate collaborative ventures in production in 1993. During the period from 1985 through 1994, U.S. firms formed 575 "research joint ventures," the majority of which focused on process R&D. Interestingly, Justice Department data on filings under the NCRA since the passage of the 1993 amendments report the formation of only three joint production ventures.

Finally, the federal government began under the Reagan administration to provide financial support to R&D consortia in selected technologies and industries. The most celebrated example of this policy shift is SEMATECH, the semiconductor industry R&D consortium established in 1987 with funding from the federal government (until 1996), industry, and the state of Texas. Since 1987, the Advanced Technology Program, established under the Bush administration, has provided matching funds for a number of industry-led R&D consortia, some of which involve universities or federal laboratories as participants. More recent programs such as the Technology Reinvestment Program and the Project for a New Generation of Vehicles have drawn on funding from other federal agencies to supplement industry financial contributions for the support of industry-led R&D consortia.

Although the federal policy has shifted dramatically in the past 20 years and spawned a diverse array of collaborative arrangements, surprisingly little effort has been devoted to evaluation of any one of the legislative or administrative initiatives noted above. For example, how should one interpret the evidence on the small number of production joint ventures filed with the Justice Department since 1993? A broader assessment of the consistency and effects of these policies as a whole is needed. Recognising the number of such initiatives implemented in a relatively short period of time, their occasionally inconsistent structure, and their potentially far-reaching effects, this comprehensive assessment should precede additional legislation or other policy initiatives.

Benefits and Risks

A brief discussion of the potential benefits and risks of R&D collaboration is useful to assess the design and implementation of specific collaborative programs. The economics literature identifies three broad classes of benefits from R&D collaboration among industrial firms: (1) enabling member firms to capture "knowledge spillovers" that otherwise are lost to the firm investing in the R&D that gives rise to them, (2) reducing duplication among member firms' R&D investments, and (3) supporting the exploitation of scale economies in R&D. This group of (theoretical) benefits has been supplemented by others in more recent discussions of policy that often address other forms of collaboration: (1) accelerating the commercialization of new technologies, (2) facilitating and accelerating the transfer of research results from universities or public laboratories to industry, (3) supporting access by industrial firms to the R&D capabilities of federal research facilities, and (4) supporting the creation of a common technological "vision" within an industry that can guide R&D and related investments by public and private entities.

This is a long list of goals for any policy instrument. Moreover, many of these goals deal with issues of technology development and commercialization rather than scientific research. Although a sharp separation between scientific research and technology development is unwarranted on empirical and conceptual grounds, the fact remains that collaboration in "R" raises different issues and poses different challenges than does collaboration in "D" or in R&D.

Broad patents and restrictive licenses on publicly funded collaborative R&D should be discouraged. The benefits of collaborative R&D that economists have cited in theoretical work are difficult to measure. More important, however, they imply guidelines for the design of R&D collaboration that may conflict with other goals of public R&D policy. The hypothesized ability of industry-led consortia to internalize knowledge spillovers, for example, is one reason to expect them to support more fundamental, long-range research. Nonetheless, most industry-led consortia, including SEMATECH, support R&D with a relatively short time horizon of three to five years. In addition, most industry-led R&D consortia seek to protect jointly created intellectual property. Yet protection of the results of collaborative R&D may limit the broader diffusion and exploitation of these results that would increase the social returns from these investments. When industry-led consortia receive public financial support, this dilemma is sharper still.

A similar tension may appear in collaborations between U.S. universities and industrial firms, especially those centred around the licensing of university research results. In fact, university research has long been transferred to industrial enterprises through a large number of mechanisms, including the training of graduates, publication of scientific papers, faculty consulting, and faculty-founded startup firms. Efforts by universities to obtain strong formal protection of this intellectual property or restrictive licensing terms may reduce knowledge transfer from the university, with potentially serious economic consequences. There is no compelling evidence of such effects as yet, but detailed study of this issue has only begun.

Reduced duplication among the R&D strategies of member firms in consortia and other forms of R&D collaboration is another theoretical benefit that may be overstated. The experience of participants in industry-led consortia, collaborations between federal laboratories and industry, and university-industry collaborations all suggest that some intrafirm R&D investment is essential if the results of the R&D performed in the collaborative venue are to be absorbed and applied by participating firms. In other words, some level of in-house duplication of the R&D performed externally is necessary to realise the returns from collaborative R&D.

The other goals of R&D collaboration that are noted above raise difficult issues. For example, the reduction of duplicative R&D programs within collaborating firms and the development by an industry of a common technological vision both imply some reduction in the diversity of scientific or technological avenues explored by research performers. Since one of the hallmarks of technology development, especially in its earliest stages, is pervasive uncertainty about future developments, the elimination of such diversity introduces some risk of collective myopia. One may overlook promising avenues for future research or even bypass opportunities for commercial technology development. A single-minded industry vision can conserve resources, but it may be risky or even ill-advised when one is in the earliest stages of development of a new area of science or technology. After all, the postwar United States has been effective in spawning new technology-intensive industries precisely because of the ability of the U.S. market and financial system to support the exploration of many competing, and often conflicting, views of the likely future path of development of breakthroughs such as the integrated circuit, the laser, or recombinant DNA techniques.

Managing R&D collaboration between industrial firms and universities or federal laboratories is difficult, and problems of implementation and management frequently hamper the realisation of other goals of such collaboration. Collaborative R&D may accelerate the transfer of research results from these public R&D performers to industry, but the devil is in the details. The sheer complexity of the management requirements for R&D collaborations, especially those involving many firms and more than one university or laboratory, may slow technology transfer. In addition, the costs of such transfer-including the maintenance by participating firms of parallel R&D efforts in-house and/or the rotation of staff to an offsite R&D facility-may exceed the resources of smaller firms. In some cases, the effectiveness of CRADAs between federal labcratories and university-industry collaborations has been impeded by negotiations over intellectual property rights, regardless of the actual importance of such rights, in order to conform with the statutory and administrative requirements of such collaborations.

A Beginning at Differentiation

At the risk of oversimplifying a very complex phenomenon, one can single out three categories of R&D collaboration as especially important: (1) industry-led consortia, which may or may not receive public funds; (2) collaborations between universities and industry; and (3) collaborations between industry and federal laboratories, often supported through CRADAs. These forms of collaboration have received direct encouragement, and in some cases financial support, from federal policy in the past 20 years. In addition to the variety of collaborative mechanisms, there is considerable variation among technology classes in the types of policies or organisational structures that will support effective R&D performance and dissemination.

Industry-led consortia. As noted earlier, these undertakings rarely focus on long-range research. Indeed, many consortia in the United States pursue activities that more closely resemble technology adoption than technology creation. SEMATECH, for example, has devoted considerable effort to the development of performance standards for new manufacturing equipment. These efforts are hardly long-range R&D, but they can aid equipment firms' sales of these products and SEMATECH members' adoption of new manufacturing technologies. Industry consortia also do not eliminate duplication in the R&D programs of participants because of the requirements for in-house investments in R&D and related activities to support inward transfer and application of collaborative R&D results. The need for these investments means that small firms may find it difficult to exploit the results of consortia R&D, and particular attention must be devoted to their needs. Consortia may aid in the formation of an industry-wide vision of future directions for technological innovation, but such consensus views are not always reliable, especially when technologies are relatively immature and the direction of their future development highly uncertain. Such visions can be overtaken by unexpected scientific or technological developments. Some of these features of "best practice" that have been identified with the SEMATECH experience, especially the need for flexibility in agenda-setting and adaptation, may be difficult to reconcile with the requirements of public oversight and evaluation of publicly funded programs. Moreover, the SEMATECH experience suggests that collaborative R&D alone is insufficient to overcome weaknesses in manufacturing quality, marketing, or other aspects of management. Indeed, in its efforts to strengthen smaller equipment suppliers, SEMATECH supplemented R&D with outreach and education (mainly in the equipment and materials industries) in areas such as quality management and financial management.

Effective industry university relationships differ considerably among different industries, academic disciplines, and research areas.

University-industry collaborations. Collaborative research involving industry and universities has a long history. A combination of growing R&D costs within academia and industry, along with the supportive federal legislation and policy shifts described above, have given considerable impetus to university-industry collaboration during the past 20 years. Industry now accounts for roughly 7 percent of academic R&D spending in the United States, the number of university-industry research centres has grown, and university patenting and licensing have expanded significantly since 1980. As in the case of SEMATECH, recent experience supports several observations about the effectiveness of these collaborations for industrial, academic, and national goals and welfare:

Little evidence is available about the ability of these collaborative R&D ventures to support long-term research. Cohen et al. (1994) found that most university-industry engineering research centres tended to focus on relatively near-term research problems and issues faced by industry. Other undertakings, however, such as the MARCO initiative sponsored by SEMATECH, are intended to underwrite long-range R&D efforts. University-industry collaboration thus may be able to support long-range R&D more effectively than industry-led consortia.

Preliminary evidence indicates that the Bayh-Dole Act has had little effect on the characteristics of the invention disclosures from faculty. Bayh-Dole did cause many other universities to enter into patenting and licensing activities. In addition, data from the University of California, which was active in patenting and licensing before the passage of the bill, suggest that the number of annual invention disclosures began to grow more rapidly and shifted to include a larger proportion of biomedical inventions before, rather than after, the passage of this law. These findings are preliminary, however, and a broader evaluation of the effects of the Bayh-Dole Act is long overdue.

Effective industry-university relationships differ considerably among different industries, academic disciplines, and research areas. In biomedical research, for example, individual patents have considerable strength and therefore potentially great commercial value. Licensing relationships covering intellectual property "deliverables" thus have been quite effective. In other areas, however, such as chemical engineering or semiconductors, the goals of industry-university collaborations, and the vehicles that are best suited to their support, differ considerably. Firms in these industries often are less concerned with obtaining title to specific pieces of intellectual property than with seeking "windows" on new developments at the scientific frontier and access to high-quality graduates (who are themselves effective vehicles for the transfer of academic research results to industry). For firms with these objectives, extensive requirements for specification and negotiation of the disposition of intellectual property rights from collaborative research may impede such collaboration. The design of university-industry relationships should be responsive to such differences among fields of research.

Excessive emphasis on the protection by universities of the intellectual property resulting from collaborative ventures, especially when combined with restrictive licensing terms, may have a chilling effect on other channels of transfer, restricting the diffusion of research results and conceivably reducing the social returns from university research. Unbalanced policies, such as restrictions on publication, raise particular dangers for graduate education, which is a central mission of the modern university and an important channel for university-industry interaction and technology transfer.

Management of industry-university relationships should be informed by more realistic expectations among both industry executives and university administrators on means and ends. In many cases, universities may be better advised to focus their management of such relationships and any associated intellectual property on the establishment or strengthening of research relationships, rather than attempting to maximize licensing and royalty income.

As is true of industry-led consortia, industrial participants in collaborative R&D projects with universities must invest in mechanisms to support the inward transfer and absorption of R&D results. The requirements for such absorptive capacity mean that university-industry collaborations may prove less beneficial or feasible for small firms with insufficient internal resources to undertake such investments.

Collaborations between federal laboratories and industry. Our recent examination of a small sample of CRADAs between a large DOE nuclear weapons laboratory and a diverse group of industrial firms suggests the following preliminary observations concerning this type of R&D collaboration:

Cultural differences matter. All of the firms participating in these CRADAs agreed that this DOE laboratory had unique capabilities, facilities, and equipment that in many cases could not be duplicated elsewhere. Nevertheless, their contrasting backgrounds meant that laboratory and firm researchers had different approaches to project management that occasionally conflicted. Moreover, the limited familiarity of many laboratory personnel with the needs of potential commercial users of these firms' technologies meant that collaboration in areas distant from the laboratory's historic missions was more difficult and often less successful.

The focus of many CRADAs on specification of intellectual property (IP) rights often served as an obstacle to the timely negotiation of the terms of these ventures. In a majority of the cases we reviewed, the participating firms were not particularly interested in patenting the results of their projects. The importance of formal IP rights differs among technological fields, but the emphasis in many CRADAs on intellectual property rights may be misplaced, and alternative vehicles for collaboration may be better suited to the support of such collaboration. As with university-industry collaboration, no single instrument will serve to support collaboration in all technologies or research fields. Laboratory and firm management needs to devote more effort to selecting projects for collaboration and must improve the fit between the project and the specific vehicle for such collaboration.

Most of the CRADAs reviewed in our study were concerned with near-term R&D or technology development. Participating firms frequently found it difficult to manage the transition from development to production without some continuing support from DOE personnel. Yet the terms of many of these CRADAs made a more gradual handoff very difficult.

As in other types of R&D collaboration, significant investments by participating firms to support inward transfer and application of the results of CRADAs were indispensable. Firms that found CRADAs to be especially beneficial had invested heavily in this relationship, including significant personnel rotation, travel, and communications.

Along with the small size of their budgets, the costs of these investments made CRADAs involving small firms difficult to manage.

Who Pays?

The case for public funding of collaborative R&D resembles the case for public funding of R&D more generally. This case is strongest where there is a high social return from collaborative R&D activities, and the gap between private and social returns is such that without public funding, the work would not be undertaken. But these arguments for public funding of collaborative R&D raise two important challenges to the design of such projects:

What is the appropriate "match" between public and private funding? A matching requirement creates incentives for participating firms to minimize costs and apply the results of such R&D. Setting a matching requirement at a very low share of total program costs may weaken such incentives and result in R&D that is of little relevance to an industry's competitive challenges. However, if the private matching requirement is set at a relatively high level (for example, above 75 percent of total program costs), firms may choose not to participate in collaborative R&D or will undertake projects that would have been launched in any event. The ideal matching requirement will balance these competing objectives, but there is little guidance from economic theory or prior experience to inform such a choice.

If R&D collaboration seeks to encourage research investments yielding high social returns, the case for tight controls on the dissemination of the results of such R&D is weak. The assignment to private firms of intellectual property rights to the results of such R&D that is allowed by the Bayh-Dole Act and other policies is intended to encourage the commercialization of these results by establishing a stronger reason for their owners to undertake such investments. But by limiting the access of other firms to these results, patents or restrictive licenses may slow the diffusion of R&D results, reducing the social returns from the publicly funded R&D. This dilemma is another one for which neither economic theory nor program experience provides much guidance. As a general rule, however, broad patents and restrictive licensing terms for patents resulting from publicly funded collaborative R&D should be discouraged. This policy recommendation suggests that the competitive effects of any greater tilt toward exclusivity in the licensing of these patents, such as that embodied in the Technology Transfer Improvements and Advancement Act, should be monitored carefully.

These dilemmas apply to public funding of R&D, especially civilian R&D performed within industry, regardless of whether R&D collaboration is involved. The mere presence of a collaborative relationship does not eliminate them, and in some cases may complicate their resolution.

The "taxonomy" of R&D collaborations discussed earlier is hardly exhaustive, but it suggests the need for a clearer assessment of the links between the goals of R&D collaborations and their design. For example, R&D collaborations established to support long-range R&D may be more effective if they link universities and industry, rather than being undertaken through industry-led consortia. At the same time, the effects of collaboration on the other missions of U.S. universities must be monitored carefully so as not to undercut performance in these areas. Small firms often face serious problems with R&D collaboration, because of the significant investments that participants must make in technology absorption and the inability of R&D collaboration to upgrade technological capabilities in firms lacking them. In addition, small firms often need much more than technological assistance alone in order to improve their competitive performance. R&D collaborations that seek to accelerate technology access and transfer must be designed to avoid administrative requirements that may instead slow these activities. In particular, negotiations over intellectual property rights must be handled flexibly and in a manner that is responsive to the needs of all the participants.

The variations among different types of R&D collaboration are substantial, and policymakers and managers alike should proceed with great caution in reaching sweeping conclusions or in developing detailed policies that seek to govern collaboration in all institutional venues, technologies, and industries. Broad guidelines are appropriate and consistent with Congress's role in ensuring that these undertakings serve the public interest. But the implementation of these guidelines and detailed policies governing R&D collaborations are best left to the agencies and institutions directly concerned with this activity. Greater flexibility for federal agencies in negotiating the terms of CRADAs within relatively broad guidelines, for example, would facilitate their more effective use and more careful consideration of alternatives to these instruments for collaboration.

The phenomenon of R&D collaboration has grown so rapidly that hard facts and robust generalizations about best practice and policy are exceedingly difficult to develop for all circumstances. A more comprehensive effort to collect data on R&D collaboration, perhaps spearheaded by the Commerce Department's Technology Administration, and greater efforts to capture and learn from the results of such ventures surely are one of the most urgent prerequisites to any effort to formulate a broader policy on R&D collaboration.

How to Find the Best University-Firm Match

University scientists and private firms are increasingly keen to engage in joint entrepreneurship, collaborating on research and development to advance knowledge and bring innovations to market. But only when the partners' strengths build up, rather than canceling each other out, will the alliance boost innovation.

Everyone has heard about Botox – derived from botulinum toxin – to smooth out wrinkles; but who knows that treatments for migraines, neck muscle spasms and speech impediments were developed from the same lethal neurotoxin? These treatments were the result of a fruitful collaboration between professors at a top US medical school and health care company Allergan – just one example of the many partnerships between academia and the private sector. As Denisa Mindruta points out, there is long-standing evidence that academic research has a significant impact on the productivity of private-sector research and development, as publications are influential channels of knowledge transfer. Unsurprisingly, firms with direct research ties to universities significantly increase their innovative performance. Conversely, scientists are always on the lookout for firms that will move published results towards commercialization. There is a long tradition of such collaboration in the US, Denisa Mindruta explains, citing the example of University of Illinois, where she studied for her Ph.D.: "Universities are more entrepreneurial, they encourage scientists to form start-ups, or 'spin-offs', to get venture capital and commercialize their inventions." But she also sees the trend coming to Europe, where scientists are more and more encouraged to transfer knowledge.

Finding the Best Partner

So how can universities and private companies form the most profitable alliances? The factors behind value creation remain underexplored, and Denisa Mindruta decided to study them from a "matching" approach. Economists have typically studied matching – the sorting process in a context of two-sided decision-making and competition for better partners – in marriage and labour markets. The researcher examined the matching of scientists and firms, based on the simple premise that scientists care about the quality of the firm and firms care about scientists' research excellence. The interaction of these preferences will lead to a sorting of partners, in other words "better" scientists will team up with "better" firms. But as Denisa Mindruta's research shows, the selection is not made along a linear pecking order, since the process is endogenous, i.e. the choice variables are partly function of other parameters: each party will try to choose a partner whose qualities reinforce their own. To study what drive alliances, the researcher examined collaborations between scientists at a top US medical school and their private-sector partners along three key dimensions, which she figured best reflected the typical strengths of potential partners: publishing capability, patenting capability and knowledge specialisation.

Publishing as an Innovation Signal

The first factor that Denisa Mindruta looked at was the quality of publications, weighing published articles by the number of citations they received. She used publishing as a proxy for dynamic, innovative research, and beyond a way of deploying knowledge, also a signal for a preference for "open science". Publishing, once the hallmark of academia, is also widespread in the corporate world. "Firms are now on a par with university departments in terms of publication," says the researcher. For both academic researchers and firms, there is an interest in publishing to advance novel ideas, but also to enhance standing in the scientific community and attract more talented people to work with. "What is important for scientists is also to get interesting projects to work on, or to place their Ph.D. students within firms," adds Denisa Mindruta. And indeed, her econometric model confirmed that firms' and university scientists' publication capabilities are complements in value creation, all other things being equal. In other words, the strengths of each partner build up and boost innovation. An example of such fruitful collaboration was a discovery made by academics, which could potentially reduce mortality in children with Pompe disease, a rare genetic disorder in which most children die before their first birthday. The discovery was based in part on an enzyme replacement therapy initially developed by biotechnology corporation Genzyme.

One Partner's Commercial Power is Enough

The second source of value creation examined was patenting capabilities. From the perspective of a university researcher, it makes sense to look for firms that will "take the next step to translate research into a concrete product", as Denisa Mindruta explains. Her hypothesis, corroborated by her model, shows that this feature is a substitute in value creation. In other terms, the strength of one partner substitutes for the shortcomings of the other. For example, a industry partner can advise a university laboratory on how to start producing drugs on a large scale. But if both partners have strong commercial abilities, they will not add up. In fact, the two are less likely to partner up. "Scientists who patent themselves, especially in the US, already have the opportunity to form their own companies" says the researcher. A final, surprising result of the interaction of capabilities was the negative relationship between a firm's patenting capabilities and university scientists' publishing capabilities: biotechnology firm' high-impact patents did not build up on important scientific papers, a possible sign that marketable inventions and valuable scientific knowledge follow different selection logics.

The Complement between Broad and Focused Expertise

Finally, Denisa Mindruta looked at the effect of each potential partner's type of knowledge: broad or specialised. There she found a complementary relationship between partners with different types of knowledge: one specialised partner will benefit from the "big picture" that only the other, more generalist partner will see; conversely, they will sometimes need an expert on another topic. In the example of botulinum toxin, a specialised firm (Allergan) reached out to scientists with broader expertise that could apply the firm's very specialised, proprietary knowledge to other domains.

Chapter 4

The Partners and their Roles

R&D Partnerships: Benefits and Considerations

The average business spends less than 5 percent of its revenue on research and development (R&D). As vital as researching the development of new products and services is to long-term success, the costs and risk involved in such initiatives often limit businesses from investing in their longevity.

Among other advantages, research and development partnerships offer businesses a way to maximize their return on R&D investments and gain quick or affordable access to technology that can galvanize new research techniques. So how are organisations around the world using R&D partnerships to their advantage?

What are R&D Partnerships?

R&D partnerships are strategic partnerships between businesses and organisations capable of developing a new product or service (or improving an old one) and others who have a financial interest in the development of such innovations. Investors are often entitled to a percentage of the product's profits, if any, along with other benefits.

By definition, a research and development partnership is a type of partnership devoted to the research and development of new products and services. This type of partnership is made up of limited partners who all contribute funds to pay for certain research and development opportunities. The partners providing the funding are entitled to a percentage of any income derived from the investment."

Due to the unpredictable nature of research, R&D partnerships are not without risk. In many cases, however, R&D partnerships bring about valuable innovations and often provide the only way organisations can stay ahead of their competition in the long run. R&D partnerships are especially popular among government entities, technology companies and medical and educational institutions.

Benefits of R&D Partnerships

R&D partnerships exist between parties from all sectors. In some cases industry members contract with a research group or groups to help them advance their business. In other cases government groups offer funding to research consortiums to spur innovation. Still other R&D partnerships, such as government-university-industry partnerships, incorporate members from a variety of sectors in order to reach a research goal. Below are some of the benefits these and other types of R&D partnerships can bring.

Competitive Edge

R&D partnerships aim to produce new or improved products or to innovate operations. When they succeed, R&D partnerships help organisations stay ahead of the competition and maintain customer satisfaction over time.

Profit Sharing

Depending on the nature of the partnership, investors will receive a percentage of the product's profits, if any, along with benefits like depreciation of equipment. Profit sharing is defined in the R&D partnership agreement.

Cost and Risk Sharing

Just as profits are shared among partners, so too are research and development costs and the risks associated with the investment of time, money and other resources. Sharing risk in this way can help members, especially those that are smaller or less established, take on more ambitious and potentially more valuable R&D projects.

Decreased Time-to-Market

By pooling resources like funding and special knowledge, members of R&D partnerships often produce results faster together than they could alone. This means that, through their collaboration, R&D partnerships can accelerate the creation phase and bring potential new products or systems to market faster.

Resource Sharing

Some R&D partnerships are designed to place more weight on resource sharing than on creating new products. In this case members have the opportunity to improve their own systems and offerings without investing in often costly assets like prototyping equipment, access to research documents, etc.

Access to New Markets

Often times partnering around R&D gives businesses the opportunity to test products in new markets. For example an organisation aiming to develop more hearty crops could enter into an R&D partnership to test new breeds on various continents.

Research and Development Tax Incentive

In some cases investing in R&D can reduce taxable income. If this is of importance, members should look into potential R&D tax credits before investing.

R&D Partnerships: Considerations

Though R&D partnerships can bring about a competitive edge, increased profits, and a faster time to market, certain considerations must be made before a project goes live. Financials, results monitoring and intellectual property should be special considerations during the partnership planning phase.

Financials

Whether a partnership is between research and development companies and industry members, government, university and industry entities or more, the most successful partnerships clearly define investments, profit sharing and the ability to buy back IP in their R&D partnership agreement.

Results Monitoring

It's not uncommon for R&D partnerships to involve multiple independent research teams. In these circumstances it's especially important that research quality and information sharing is monitored. According to Jean-Marcel Ribaut, director of the CGIAR Generation Challenge Programme for resource-poor farmers, this is one of the hardest things to get right:

"A key challenge in true partnership is to strike the right balance between management that serves the Programme as a whole and creating ownership so all partners can nurture a network spirit."

If R&D partners find a systematic way to share key information amongst themselves, track progress and spearhead separate areas of research, the partnership will be more likely to find success.

Intellectual Property

In the case of a cross-border R&D partnership, members should generally look to file patents and other intellectual property protection in both their home country and the country (or countries) the project is operating in. In some cases filing multiple international patents might be the best course of action. Checking with a patent law expert for best practices will help protect and retain your intellectual property.

R&D Partnerships in Action

R&D partnerships often allow industry leaders from different sectors to collaborate around common goals, pooling their knowledge and resources to advance technologies or systems. The Partnership for Research and Innovation in Sustainable Manufacturing, for example, is a collaboration between the University of Kentucky Institute for Sustainable Manufacturing and other industry members which aims to make U.S. manufacturing more competitive on a global scale. Specifically the Partnership aims to carry out a roadmapping effort for identifying and prioritizing significant challenges to achieving sustainable, closed-loop and advanced production processes across the U.S. manufacturing sector. The Partnership received $500,000 in support from the National Institute of Standards and Technology to pursue its goals.

Grow Your Business through an R&D Partnership

R&D partnerships have the potential to bring your business a competitive edge that will lead to long-term growth. When financials, results monitoring and IP concerns are handled well, R&D partnerships can be hugely beneficial.

Forming R&D Partnerships: 8 Keys to Success

1. There has to be mutual interest at the top and a willingness to explore being together. The management-level decision makers need to agree that they are interested in partnering. That buy-in at the top is essential.
2. Think about what *you* want first. In figuring out the focus of a potential partnership, each party should ask itself: “What are our strategic priorities and where are we willing to invest our resources?” Don’t worry yet about whether those priorities match up with the potential partner. If the partnership you create does not satisfy your own needs, then it is partnering for partnering’s sake and is doomed to fail and worse yet waste valuable resources (time and money) pursuing research that is not aligned with your organisations strategic direction.

3. Present your priorities and needs in terms the other will appreciate. Explain where the other party can contribute to your priorities (*why do you want to partner with them?*) as well as the strengths you can offer to address the other's priorities (*why should they want to partner with you?*). By identifying the larger needs where each believes the other can contribute, the potential partners can see where there is overlap.
4. If priorities overlap, then brace yourself to work hard to find the sweet-spot. Identifying a specific project to work together in a partnership for mutual benefit is challenging. Applying jointly for a funding opportunity makes it easier. It forces you to develop a statement of work (SOW) that specifies the goals and purpose of working together, what will be achieved, who is going to do which tasks, what the time frame is, and what the costs are of that work and what resources are needed. Then again, you can (and should!) develop a 1- or 2-page SOW even if there is no grant to go after.
5. Have the right people talk to each other at the right time. Early on, the management from the two parties need to talk to each other. But as things progress, bring together the potential partners' scientists, engineers, and innovators—those who are on the front lines of doing the actual work of the partnership. They are in the best position to hammer out the specifics of the SOW and will be more likely engaged and supportive of the project if they had a hand in working out the tasks and goals. In fact, if you don't get their buy-in, the project is almost certainly doomed. (So many ways to torpedo it without anyone being the wiser.)
6. It's okay to start small. The first time you work together as partners does not have to be an earth-shattering project. Most people don't get married on their first date. Think of it as taking the partnership on a test drive, doing a few small projects together to make sure you truly are a match. (This aligns well with the General Mills insights on open innovation.) Note that this concept can be difficult to sell internally. Some might fear that they are "settling" for a minor-impact project and losing the opportunity to play on a major-impact project. I believe the reverse is true. People like working with those that they have developed a trusting relationship. Starting small is an excellent way to build that trust. Once you've pulled off the smaller project, then you'll be ready when the bigger project arises.

7. Be willing to walk away. Patience and persistence are essential qualities for partnership development. But just as important is knowing when to give up and being able to walk away gracefully. Stopping partnership negotiations can be difficult, especially when you *really* want to partner with each other. So instead of thinking of it as an "I want to break up" situation, consider it a "The timing isn't right currently, so we can't be together now but maybe someday we can." It's okay to be just friends!
8. Consider using an intermediary. Okay, we may be a little biased on this point, but truly we have found that being an objective third-party (albeit representing our client's interests) has allowed Fuentek to effectively facilitate partnership negotiations. Part of this stems from our being able to understand the business aspects of partnership as well as the technical angles of collaborative R&D. Being in the middle helps us to see both parties' perspectives and identify innovative ways to overcome the barriers to partnering as well as to recognise when it just ain't gonna happen.

Public R&D – Private Industry Partnerships

Linkages between R&D agencies and industry in India effected through the facilitating institutionalised mechanisms of the government S&T departments and agencies as well as select academic institutions provide update on operational dimensions. Partnerships have assumed new importance in the context of globalisation. India has reached a stage when it should not be merely defencive to protect the domestic market, but should also aim at international markets with a medium and long-term strategy through partnership between R&D agencies and industry. New paradigms in the IPR generation and protection are posing novel challenges. Other factors such as transition to knowledge based economy, changing life cycles of products, expensive research emphasise the need of such partnerships

In India, like in most developing countries, the government budgetary allocation has been the main funding source for carrying out R&D in basic and applied sciences, which is evident from the statistics of the percentage share of various funding players on R&D in any given year. For example, in the year 1998-99 the percentage share in national expenditure on R&D of the Central Government was 62.5%; State Government 8.0%; public sector industries 5.0%; and private sector industries 21.6%. 83% of the R&D expenditure incurred by the Central Government sources came from 12 major scientific agencies, namely, the Department of Science and Technology (DST),

Council of Scientific & Industrial Research (CSIR), Department of Space (DOS), Department of Biotechnology (DBT), Defence Research & Development Organisation (DRDO), Department of Atomic Energy (DAE), Indian Council of Agricultural Research (ICAR), Indian Council of Medical Research (ICMR), Ministry of Information Technology (MIT), Ministry of New and renewable Energy (MNRE), Ministry of Environment and Forests (MoEF) and the rest from the other central ministries /departments /public sector industries. Amongst the major scientific agencies, DRDO accounted for 31.8% of the expenditure.

Opening up of economy and the global liberalisation policies of the Government causing severe competition in the global R&D base, particularly in strategic areas, awakened the industry to a great extent and it started looking outward. In view of the competitive environment in which the Indian industries had to compete even in the domestic market with imported products, it was expedient to focus the R&D efforts towards economic benefit of the country through better utilisation of research developments and capabilities available. The operation of market forces induced growth of forces supporting innovation. The Industry exhorted to graduate from the re-engineering culture to R&D culture to face the new challenges.

In order to obviate the highly independent identities of R&D agencies and industry and with a view to achieve techno-economic development India adopted a two pronged approach: one which relates to creating a climate for indigenous development of technology in the country and the other for the transfer and adaptation of technology imported from the advanced countries. The industrial development model pursued by India till the late eighties did not effectively encourage original R&D endeavour by industry. As a result, practically not a single globally competitive technology could emerge from India. The shift in the perception towards R&D began to change with the economic reforms of 1991 and a paradigm shift took place with India's accession to World Trade Organisation (WTO) in 1995. However, accessing globally competitive industrial technologies became more difficult due to the integration of the global trade/economy. Thus in order to survive, Indian industry had no option but to indigenously develop such technology.

The liberalised economy had given Indian industry valuable opportunity to develop new ideas and technologies, which could be sold globally. The process of globalisation compelled both the publicly funded R&D agencies and the industry to enter into a dialogue and work together to mutual advantage. However, despite the fact that in India the need for interaction between the industry and the R&D institutions was fairly well recognised, and that all the stakeholders in this interaction know that they are expected to benefit by collaborating with one another, the progress achieved so far has not been adequate.

The task of finding an appropriate scientific-engineering liaison is critical to the success of any new, university - R&D agency – industry interaction. Thus the Government of India (GOI) instituted several initiatives with focused endeavours to provide better opportunities for R&D agencies and the industries to work together and progress. The government support towards public sponsorship of R&D partnerships was the policy response to various market failures, which are not resolved by market mechanisms alone. It established partnership-facilitating agencies and launched programmes to specifically address the issues of generation and diffusion of new knowledge and technology through partnership at various stages of technology development cycle.

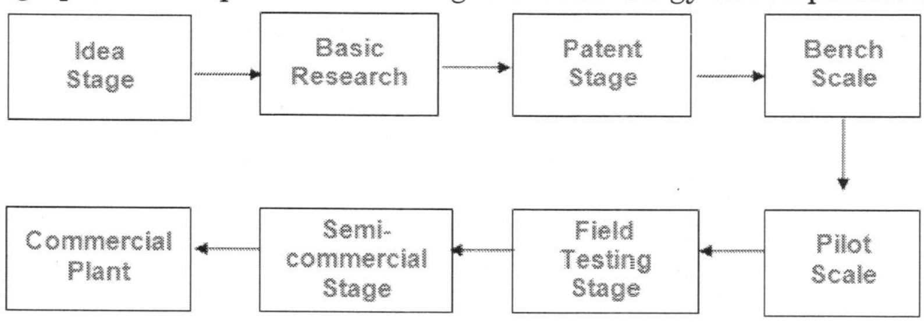

Figure: *Technology Development Cycle*

The government has traditionally been supporting the idea stage as part of its basic research efforts. Once the idea is generated it needs to be protected by securing the necessary patenting. For example, National Research Development Corporation (NRDC) provides funding support for this purpose. Schemes such as Technology Development and Demonstration Programme (TDDP, formerly Programme aimed at Technological Self Reliance (PATSER)) and Home Grown Technology (HGT) were instituted to support the R&D agencies/industries for prototype development, pilot plant establishment, test and evaluation of products, user trials etc. on indigenous technology with or without collaboration with each other. To enhance creativity & innovation, the GOI initiated a programme named, Technoprenaur Promotion Programme (TePP) for individual innovators, in formal & informal sector, and support for grassroot innovation to commercialization. This is the stage where intense interaction between the R&D and industry is required. Once a technology qualifies the techno-commercial requirements, it needs to be taken up for commercialisation. But the most important step at this stage is packaging the technology or a product into a saleable commodity, which requires specialised skills in design and engineering, not only for the product as such but the whole manufacturing system with economic viability. So there is a clear need of a special breed of technologists that could address this issue of realising the full potential of new scientific inventions through their engineering skills and market knowledge.

After establishing the concrete evidence of techno-economic feasibility of a technology or a product, there is still an element of uncertainty of the success of a technological venture. In order to take care of this risk, the Government established TDB in September 1996 and added a new element to the TDDP to extend support for incubation of proven R&D technologies for their commercialization.

Partnership Promoting Initiatives in All Sectors

Various mechanisms/programmes/fiscal incentives instituted by the GOI in the pre- and post-globalisation period are discussed below in chronological order.

The National Research Development Corporation: National Research Development Corporation (NRDC) was set up as early as in 1953 to address issues related to exploiting indigenous know-how, to act as a link between national research laboratories and entrepreneurs by transferring technologies developed by mostly public R&D agencies, and to financially support entrepreneurs for putting up pilot plant, prototype development and establishment of demonstration units and thus facilitating commercialisation of indigenous technologies. Current promotional activities of NRDC are being carried out under the Invention Promotion Programme (Proving Prize Award & Award of the World Intellectual Property Organisation (WIPO) to Meritorious Inventions; Protecting Inventions through IPR; IPR Consultancy; Incentive to Scientists and publications etc.) and the Technology Promotion Programme (Promotion of Rural and Household Technology; Export of Technology; Informatics for Technology Transfer and Technology Development Programme for Priority Projects). Its commercial activities include the licensing of technologies to industry; providing conditional grants for development of technologies to R&D laboratories and industries for setting up pilot plants to prove/scale up laboratory processes prior to commercialisation; providing IPR consultancy services to R&D institutes and industries; exporting Indigenous technologies and know-how; participating in equity to facilitate formation of new ventures using indigenous technologies; and executing turnkey projects abroad based on indigenous technologies. A large number of Indian technologies have been commercialised by industry under licence from NRDC in the areas of agro-food processing, biomedical devices, biotechnology, drugs and pharmaceuticals, chemical industries, eco-friendly chemicals, electronics, building materials, rural industries etc. NRDC has been exporting proven technologies and services to entrepreneurs/industries both in the developed as well as the developing countries that include USA, Germany, Malaysia, Burma, Nepal, Senegal, Indonesia, Madagascar, Philippine, Vietnam, Sri Lanka, Kenya, Brazil and Bangladesh.

In-house R&D Centres Recognition Scheme: The GOI launched an 'In-house R&D Centres Recognition Scheme' in 1973 for granting recognition to in-house R&D units in industry, which was initially being coordinated by DST, but was subsequently taken over by DSIR. At the time of launch one of the objectives of the scheme was to provide liberal import facilities to the recognised In-house R&D units under Open General License, which was later absorbed in the liberalised trade policies announced by the GOI in 1991. Recognising the need to establish their own R&D units and taking advantage of the incentives and support measures available, a number of industries set up their own in-house R&D units to meet the technical and technological needs of their production centres.

The number of in-house units recognised by DSIR has increased steadily from about 100 in 1973 to around 275 in 1975; around 700 by 1980; around 925 by 1985; around 1100 by 1990; around 1200 by 1995; and thereafter the number has been hovering between 1200 and 1250. On 31st December 2007, the number of recognised in-house R&D centres was 1253 which got raised to 1352 on 31st December 2008. Of these, nearly 1180 units are in the private sector and the remaining in public/joint sector. 157 of the total recognised R&D centres incurred in an annual expenditure of over Rs. 5.00 crores each and 307 centres' expenditure was in the range of Rs. 1.00 crore to Rs. 5.00 crore.

National Science and Technology Entrepreneurship Development Board : In 1982 the GOI set up a National Science & Technology Entrepreneurship Development Board (NSTEDB) under the aegis of DST with an aim to (a) promote knowledge based and innovation driven enterprises; (b) facilitate generation of entrepreneurship and self-employment opportunities for S&T persons; (c) facilitate information dissemination; (d) network various Central & State Government agencies for S&T based entrepreneurship development; and (e) act as a policy advisory body to the Government agencies for S&T based entrepreneurship development. The Board has representation from socio-economic and scientific Departments/Ministries, premier entrepreneurship development institutions and all India Financial Institutions.

The Board has since initiated a number of programmes, which have been successfully operating to meet the above objectives. Over 100 organisations, most of which are academic institutions and voluntary agencies, were drafted in the task of entrepreneurship development and employment generation. The Board has also initiated programmes jointly with International organisations such as the United Nations Development Programme (UNDP) on vocational training.

One of its major initiatives is Science and Technology Entrepreneurship Parks (STEPs). The concept of 'Technology Parks' existed since long in the developed world. However, the GOI launched the STEPs scheme in 1984-85 through NSTEDB in collaboration with the Indian financial institutions, namely, Industrial Development Bank of India (IDBI), Industrial Finance Corporation of India (IFCI) and Industrial Credit and Investment Corporation of India Ltd (ICICI) for promotion of innovation and entrepreneurship among scientific and technical persons. Under this scheme STEPs are established in and around academic and R&D institutions of excellence. The STEP has a focus to facilitate establishment of closer linkages on continuing basis between R&D agencies and industry and permit theory to influence practice for its continued up-gradation. So far 17 STEPs, have been established near the educational and research infrastructure spread over the country, which have by FY 2008-09 promoted nearly 788 units generating annual turnover of around Rs. 130 crores and employment for 5,000 persons. More than 100 new products and technologies have been developed by the STEP(s) promoted entrepreneurs. In addition, over 11,000 persons have been trained through various skill development programmes conducted by STEPs.

The Government increasingly realised that two distinct features, i.e. high growth and high risk, characterise the technology-based and knowledge-driven enterprises, coupled with time to market-necessitate development of special mechanisms to nurture innovation and entrepreneurship. NSTEDB made a beginning to establish Technology Business Incubator (TBI) by organising the first international workshop on TBIs in Bangalore jointly with the Asian and Pacific Centre for Transfer of Technology (APCTT) and the Directorate of Industries and

Commerce, Government of Karnataka during 29-31 January 2001. It concluded that TBIs are the tool for catalysing the development and growth of technology based small enterprises and the initiative. Thus, the initiative of the Government got formalised with a focus on integration of higher educational institutions, the seedbeds of new ideas and technologies, with business enterprises, which can yield good results. The setting up of TBIs was taken up as a major initiative in the 10th five-year plan. 16 TBIs were set up by the year 2005 in various higher learning institutions to leverage their strengths in a particular technological area.

For example, the Advanced Research Centre for Powder Metallurgy and New Materials (ARC-I) Hyderabad is involved not only in developing, upgrading and transferring the technologies for commercialisation, but also runs a TBI on Advanced Materials. Setting up of 40 TBIs was sanctioned by DST by 31st December 2008. Main factors for the growth of TBIs include access to skills and competencies, access to financing, access to marketing and environment for innovation. TBIs are a perfect example of the kind of Government – Private Sector – Local Institutions – University – R&D Institutions partnership that not only materialise new technologies and products but also meet the requirement of faculty and human resource development in the processes of technology development and commercialisation. Bigger companies also source new technologies or sponsor new technology development from these outfits. Other indirect advantages are the increase in entrepreneurship base and employment. The year-wise growth of STEPs and TBIs upto 2005 and the institutes housing them are shown in Figures respectively.

Entrepreneurship Development Cell (EDC) is the other major scheme of NSTEDB instituted with a mission to develop an institutional mechanism for providing various services including information to budding S&T entrepreneurs; creating entrepreneurial culture, fostering better linkages between the parent institution, industries and R&D agencies in the region and other related organisations engaged in promoting SMEs including Non-Government Organisations (NGOs); catalysing and promoting development of S&T based enterprises and promoting employment opportunities; and responding effectively to the emerging challenges and opportunities both at national and international level relating to SMEs and micro enterprises. The EDCs are established in academic institutions with requisite expertise and infrastructure. EDCs have been set up in 55 academic institutions of which 37 were already being supported by December 2008.

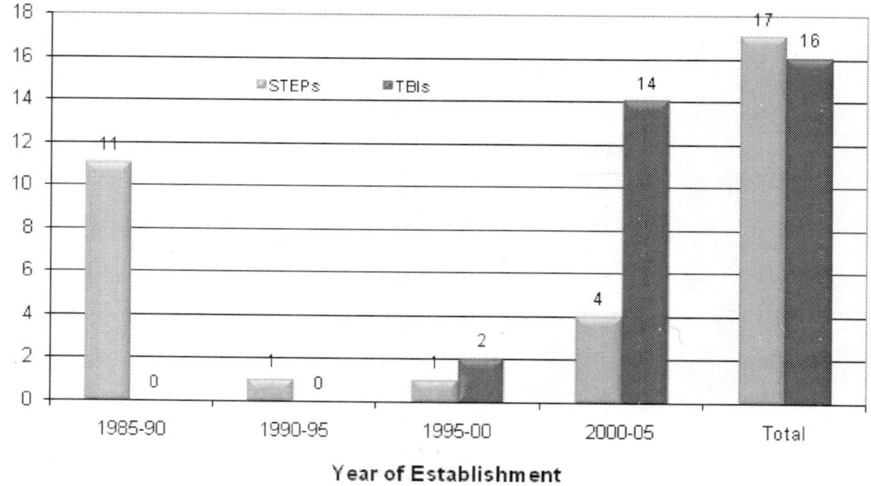

Figure: *Year-wise Establishment of STEPs and TBIs*

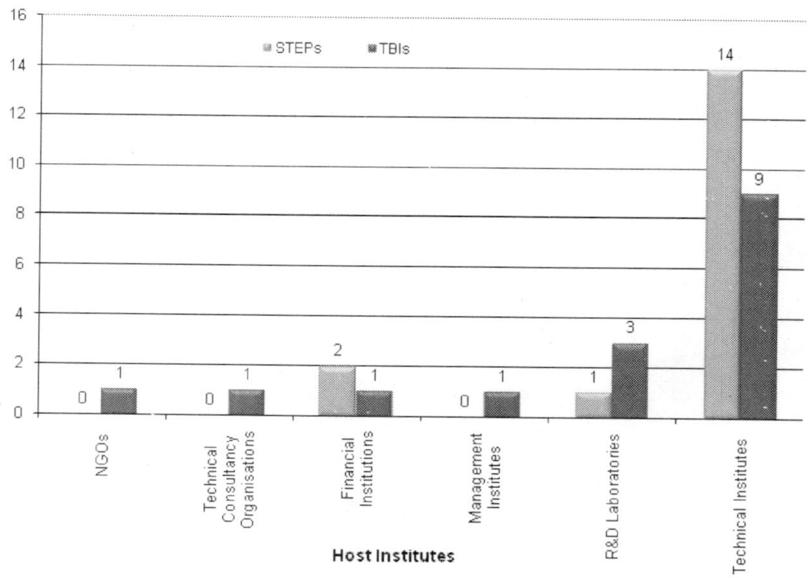

Figure: *Types of Institutes Hosting TBIs and STEPs*

NSTEDB in partnership with Federation for Indian Chambers of Commerce and Industry (FICCI) has launched a Technology Innovation Management and Entrepreneurship Service (TIME IS), which is a website providing all information required by the industry to promote technology development and commercialisation with/without partnership with R&D agencies i.e. information on industrial promotion policies; incentive schemes; industrial infrastructure facilities; new technologies; technology/equipment sources; funding options; open learning programmes on entrepreneurship; technology trends and ST Entrepreneur magazine.

Industrial R&D Promotion Programme: In order to promote the R&D activities in the industry and non-profit organisations several measures were evolved. A scheme was launched by DSIR to grant recognition to non-commercial voluntary Scientific & Industrial Organisations (SIROs) to enable them to be eligible for customs and excise duties on capital equipment, spares and consumables required for scientific research. 570 SIROs have been recognised by DSIR by the 2008-09 that are engaged in R&D in the areas of agriculture, medical, natural and applied sciences.

Home Grown Technology Programme and the *Programme Aimed at Technological Self-Reliance:* The GOI instituted the Home Grown Technology Programme (HGT) in 1993 and the Programme Aimed at Technological Self-Reliance (PATSER, now a component of TDDP) for supporting the knowledge and technology generation through partnerships from laboratory stage to pilot scale or prototype development stage. TIFAC and DSIR respectively coordinate these two programmes. In both the programmes the industry identifies a particular innovation, which would be useful for up-gradation of an existing technology or it explores the possibility of any new technology. Industry along with the technology provider, which could be an R&D agency, approaches the government and the support in the form of grants or loans is given to the industry for prototype development, pilot plant establishment, test and evaluation of products, user trials etc. This is the stage where intense interaction between the R&D organisation and industry is required.

The HGT programme promotes Indian capabilities for development of contemporary and novel products and processes. Operating in a project mode it catalyses R&D efforts and fosters closer linkages between the R&D agencies and the industry. Financial support under HGT is available on soft terms and the repayment is spread over a period of 5 years after successful completion of the project. The unique feature of HGT is the techno-managerial support mechanism of TIFAC for which purpose a separate group of experts is set up by TIFAC to guide each project. From the initiation of the scheme in 1992-93, till 2005-06, HGT has supported 77 projects, out of which 60 have been completed and the remaining are in different phases of completion.

TIFAC's contribution of Rs. 34.6 crores has catalyzed industry contribution of about Rs.70 crores. As regards the outcome of the 60 completed projects, 77% of these have resulted in commercially deployable technologies, out of which 46% have actually been commercialized. The important ones include pick and place robotic arm, HFC134-A standardised eco-friendly natural dyes, plasma incinerator for hospital wastes, eco-friendly kerosene substitute for printing industry, etc.

The PATSER aims to promote industry's efforts in development and demonstration of indigenous technologies, development of capital goods and absorption of imported technologies. The Government uses PATSER to catalyse the design, development, prototyping and commercialisation of innovations in and by the industry by means of financial support and institutional networking. NRDC manages the IP generated from the PATSER projects and also licenses the know-how so generated to other industries in India and abroad. The DSIR provides on a selective basis, partial financial support to research, development, design and engineering projects to be proposed by industry in the areas of the development and demonstration of new or improved product and process technologies, including those for specialised capital goods, for both domestic and export markets, as well as for absorption and up-gradation of imported technology.

Since its inception 193 R&D projects of industrial units of important industries such as metallurgy, electrical, electronics, instrumentation, mechanical engineering, earth moving and industrial machinery, chemicals and explosives, were supported under PATSER upto FY 2007-2008. Out of these 111 projects have been completed resulting in commercialisation of over 35 technologies/prototypes. Currently 31 companies are paying royalty/lump sum to DSIR as per the terms of the agreement. The programme has strengthened the linkages of industry with more than 30 research institutes/laboratories. TDDP has been expanded by adding two more components, namely "TDDP-Small Business" and "TDDP-Start Up".

Patent Facilitating Centre: Realising the important role of IP protection in gaining an advantageous position in the competitive technological game for achieving economic growth a Patent Facilitating Centre (PFC) was set up by DST under TIFAC in 1995. PFC was created as a single window facility to serve these institutions with a friendly approach and has been successfully reaching out to remote universities and R&D centres.

Technology Development Board: In September 1996, for the purpose of the development and application of indigenous technology in a dynamic economic environment, GOI enabled the placing of the proceeds of an existent cess @5% on all payments made by the industry towards the import of a technology into a fund called "Fund for Technology Development and Application" and to administer this fund the government constituted the Technology Development Board (TDB). Of the total of Rs. 1,279.16 crore from R&D cess collection during the year 1996-2007, the Government has made available to TDB a cumulative sum of Rs. 482.42 crore over the period of 11 years (1996-2007), which is 37.71% of the R&D cess collections made in 11 years. TDB is a unique organisation of its kind within the Government framework with the sole objective of translating the fruits of indigenous research into commercial products or services. It plays a pro-active role by encouraging commercial enterprises to take up technology-oriented projects of future importance in all sectors. The Board encourages industry to enter into hi-tech hi-risk areas and motivates industry to have firmer linkages with R&D. The board facilitates proactive dialogues between industry, scientists, technocrats and specialists and works in close association with industry bodies such as FlCCl and Confederation of Indian Industry (CII). It provides equity capital or soft loans at interest rate of 5% per annum to the industry and financial assistance to R&D agencies wanting to commercialise an indigenous development or imported technology for wider usage. The repayment of the loan together with interest thereon commences one year after the project is successfully completed or before the end of the fourth year from the date of disbursement of the loan, whichever is earlier. The loan amount along with the interest due thereon becomes recoverable in five annual instalments.

The TDB programme has made its mark in the technology development scene. During 1996-2007 the Board signed 173 agreements with the total project cost of Rs. 2,671.09 crore involving TDB's commitment of Rs. 780.95 crore against which TDB has disbursed Rs. 690.80 crore. The majority of the projects have been in the health, road transpiration, engineering, chemicals and IT sectors. Over 140 industries have so far been supported in the last few years and many products such as Hepatitis-B Vaccine, Lithium Ion Batteries, High Strength Alloys etc, have been successfully commercialised. The Board is supporting the ambitious project of commercialising indigenously designed multi-role aircraft.

In the recent past, with an aim to enhance its scope of commercialization of emerging technologies, TDB has partnered with the Unit Trust of

India (UTI) and APIDC Venture Capital Funds to widen its scope with a view to leverage investment in innovative projects and has also supported R&D initiatives by the incubators through Seed Support Fund.

Technopreneur Promotion Programme: In its endeavour to tap the vast innovative potential of the individual innovators having original ideas, the Government in August 1998 launched a novel programme known as Technopreneur Promotion Programme (TePP) institutionalised by DSIR with support from 20 outreach centres. The programme aims to promote and support untapped creativity of individual innovators; to assist the individual innovators to become technology based entrepreneurs and to assist the technopreneurs in networking and forge linkages with other constituents of the innovation chain for commercialisation of their developments. The selected & screened individual innovators having original ideas are provided financial support for converting them into working models, prototypes etc.

New Millennium Indian Technology Leadership Initiative: Another programme focusing on R&D agency – industry partnership, known as the New Millennium Indian Technology Leadership Initiative (NMITLI) was initiated by the Government in FY 2000-01 with the aim to help India attain global technology leadership position in select niche areas in a 'Team India' partnership mode, that fulfil national objectives. NMITLI therefore looks beyond present day technologies and seeks to build, capture and retain for India a leadership position based on technology by synergising the best competencies of publicly funded R&D institutions, academia and industry. The CSIR was given the responsibility to coordinate this massive programme.

NMITLI scheme provides funds in the form of grant-in-aid to R&D agencies, SIROs, Public Sector Units (PSUs) as well as NGOs and soft loan with 3% interest to industries for the joint project of 3-4 years duration. The quantum of funding depends on the nature of the projects, their attractiveness and feasibility criteria, risk factors and ability to capture the global leadership position. The funds are released to the individual partners only after the involved partners enter into a legal agreement with CSIR. The repayment of the loan component as well as interest by the industry partners is in 10 equal yearly instalments, which commences within six months of the completion of the project. With over 270 public R&D institutes/laboratories and 80 private industries networked together to implement 57 networked projects in diverse areas including Agriculture & Plant Biotechnology, General Biotechnology, Bioinformatics, Drugs & Pharmaceuticals, Chemicals, Materials, Information and Communication Technology and Energy with an initial outlay of Rs. 500 Cr., NMITLI is among the largest partnership facilitating programme in India today.

Relevance and Excellence in Achieving New Heights in Educational Institutions: On 24th July 2003, recognising the importance of supply of suitable human resource for accomplishing the technology development and commercialisation, for example, joint designing by academia-industry of the curricula in line with the business and market requirements, providing training and exposure, TIFAC launched a Technology Vision 2020 Mission Project called Relevance and Excellence in Achieving New Heights in Educational Institutions (REACH). The scheme aims to create a constellation of world class Centres of Relevance and Excellence (COREs) in diverse disciplines across the length and breadth of the country. Mission REACH intends to create 80-100 such COREs, which together will emerge as a network of mini IITs across the country, integrally connected physically and electronically through a mix of landline and V-SAT networking. By FY 2005-06, 26 TIFAC-COREs in various disciplines had been set up in smaller places which function in a tightly networked manner. For the first time these front-line entities are made to address vocational training requirements of the industries, a service that has not been forthcoming from them hitherto. The credibility of TIFAC-COREs and Mission REACH has increased over the years which is evident from the fact that financial stakes by industry and institute in the projects is increasing.

Sector Specific Partnership Enabling Programmes

The GOI has been promoting the R&D agency - industry partnership mechanisms in sectors specified below:

Automotive Sector: A Core Group on Automotive R&D was set up in 2003/2004 under DST involving the government, R&D agencies and industry. The Core Group aims at identifying frontier technologies. Based on the interactions and strengths available in the country, embedded control systems, telematics, hydrogen-powered vehicles, advanced materials and road safety are identified as focus areas. The uniqueness of this initiative is that the driver is the industry, which wants access to the latent technological capabilities in the public funded institutions.

Drugs & Pharmaceuticals: Another innovation enabling partnership has been in the upcoming field of biotechnology, particularly, drugs and pharmaceuticals. On the advice of the Planning Commission DST initiated the Drugs & Pharma Research Programme

(DPRD) in the FY 1994-95 with an aim to synergise strengths of publicly funded R&D agencies and Indian pharmaceutical Industry. Under DPRD, the DST provides grants to the R&D agencies, 100% for equipment and 70% of the total recurring expenditure, to prove the bench scale feasibility of the research. The remaining 30% recurring expenses are met by the participating industry. Since its inception till January 2009: 86 research projects have been supported resulting in filing of 6 product patents and 13 process patents, development of new chemical entities, vaccines, assay systems and drug delivery systems, and setting up national facilities. A peptide based anti-cancer drug for the treatment of colorectal cancer by Dabur Research Foundation is under Phase-II of clinical trial.

In FY 2004-05 DST had established a Pharmaceuticals Research and Development Support Fund (PRDSF) to support the Drugs & Pharma Research Programme in the country by extending soft loans @ 3% to the industry at the bench level feasibility stage of the research projects. A Drug Development Promotion Board (DDPB) under the administrative control of DST has been constituted to operationalise the PRDSF. The Drugs and Pharmaceuticals Research Programme (DPRD) has now been merged with PRDSF.

Biotechnology: The Department of Biotechnology (DBT) has established special mechanisms for enabling technology transfer to industry for commercialisation and large-scale use. These are, for example, the Micro-propagation Technology Parks (MTP) based on existing expertise and infrastructure of the two tissue culture pilot plant facilities at NCL, Pune and TERI, New Delhi. As the experience has been rewarding, DBT is promoting the concept of MTP to provide an interface between the R&D agencies and industry. It is important to cite the example of a technology for teak that has already been transferred to an international laboratory of UK.

For promotion, transfer and commercialisation of biotechnologies DBT established Biotech Consortium India Ltd. (BCIL) as a public limited company in 1990 under the Indian Companies Act 1956. BCIL is promoted by the financial institutions including IDBI, ICICI, UTI, IFCI and IFCI Venture Capital (VC) Funds Limited and the corporate sector including Ranbaxy Laboratories, Glaxo India, Cadila Laboratories, Lupin Laboratories, etc. which have since contributed Rs. 5.37 Cr. towards its core capital. It works in close association with them for syndication of funds for eligible biotech projects in addition to facilitating technology transfer. Over 9 technologies such as Biopesticides, ELISA, HIV-1/2, Hepititis A and reproductive hormones diagnostics etc. have been transferred to industry through BCIL from academic institutions like Jawaharlal Nehru University, New Delhi and various R&D agencies. So far more than 60 technologies and research leads from the Government funded R&D projects have been transferred by BCIL to Indian industries for scale up, validation and commercialization. Some of these products such as leprosy vaccine, HIV and hepatitis diagnostic kits, natural streptokinase, veterinary diagnostics, etc. are already in the market and some others are in pipeline.

With an aim to promote and compliment the R&D effort of the Indian biotech industry, DBT launched a scheme named "Small Business Innovation Research Initiative" (SBIRI) in 2005 to support early stage, pre-proof-of-concept research in biotechnology by industry; support late stage development and commercialisation of new indigenous technologies particularly those related to societal needs in the healthcare, food and nutrition, agriculture, environment and other sectors; nurture and mentor innovative and emerging technologies/ entrepreneurs; and to assist new enterprises to forge appropriate linkages with academia and government. The basic purpose of the scheme is to strengthen existing private industrial units whose product development is based on in-house innovative R&D, encourage other smaller businesses to increase their R&D capabilities and capacity and cultivate the entrepreneurial spirit by creating opportunities for starting new technology-based or knowledge-based businesses by science entrepreneurs.

DBT arranges national consultations after every three to six months to generate ideas in different sectors of biotechnology namely medical, agriculture, food, industry and environment.

Under this scheme DBT supports projects made solely by an in-house R&D unit(s) of the industrial firms; or by one or a group of industries/users in partnership with the national R&D organisations. SBIRI considers supporting only the capital investment on recurring costs. The scheme operates in two phases viz. for establishment of pre-proof-of-concepts of innovations and for product and process development. Its unique feature is that in both the phases, projects are implemented at the industry site. In Phase – I the following structure of funding is available to industry:

- 80% of the project cost as grant for projects costing upto Rs. 25 lakhs.
- 50% of the project cost as grant for projects costing between Rs. 25 lakhs and Rs. 100 lakhs, subject to a minimum of Rs. 20 lakhs and maximum of Rs. 50 lakhs.

- Govt. grant of Rs. 50 lakhs and interest free loan upto 50% of the project cost (subject to a limit of Rs. 50 lakhs) for projects costing beyond Rs. 100 lakhs

Soft loan upto Rs. 10 crores is considered for a project in Phase–II, which is available at simple interest rate of 1% for loan upto Rs. 100 lakhs and at 2% for loan amounting to more than Rs. 100 lakhs. The role of public R&D institutions at this stage too is critical, as many of the projects would continue to require technical support from the public funded R&D institutions. The partner in the public institution at this stage gets the R&D support as grant.

Uptill FY 2008-09, 37 projects had been sanctioned to 32 companies, which are worth Rs 155 crore. The private sector has committed an investment of around 48 percent of the total while the rest would be from SBIRI funds of the government. A sum of Rs 45 crore has been released to companies till date, out of which 16 projects are in the health sector, nine for industrial product and process development and eight in agriculture and allied areas. So far the biotech industry in the southern region has shown the maximum interest with Karnataka being the topmost state to submit proposals followed by Maharashtra, Andhra Pradesh, Tamil Nadu and Delhi.

Space: The Department of Space (DOS) has established a symbiotic partnership with Indian industries. DOS has established linkages with more than 500 industries (by the year 2005) in the small, medium and large-scale sectors, either through procurement contracts, know-how transfers or provision of technical consultancy. A Group on Technology Transfer and Industrial Consultancy was set up at the ISRO Headquarters to deal with all matters concerning transfer of technology developed by various laboratories of DOS. Till 2005, 285 technologies were transferred to industries for commercialisation and more than 270 technical consultancies were undertaken in various areas relevant to space technology in the broad areas of electro-mechanical, chemical and optics hardware to specialised software. DOS has formulated an Industry Participation Policy. The components of the policy include setting up of the modalities for identification of industries, commitment from DOS to these industries, utilisation of human resources and facilities available within the DOS, incentives for industries to promote space technology, etc. Sponsored Research Programme (RESPOND) of DOS has the main objective to strengthen the academic interaction through collaborative research, educational and scientific activities at the academic institutions. DOS operates a 'Technology Utilisation/ Vendor Development' programme to establish closer partnership with the Indian industries for maximal utilisation of the industrial capability. In 1992 DOS established a company named 'Antrix Corporation Limited' at Bangalore, which is the apex marketing agency with access to resources of DOS as well as Indian space industries. Antrix markets subsystems and components for satellites, undertakes order for satellites to user specifications, provides launch services and tracking facilities and also organises training of manpower and software development. ISRO's patent portfolio upto 2005 consisted of more than 205 patents, 10 trademarks and 22 copyrights.

Cooperative Research Associations: The Government has encouraged setting up of cooperative research associations in selected areas, viz., textile, building materials, rubber, tea, automobiles and electricals with active involvement of the industry. The government and the member industries jointly finance these cooperative associations. As per the experience of DSIR, the cooperative research concept has not grown adequately and that further encouragement is needed to enable this concept to flourish to the advantage of industry.

Partnership Enabling Initiatives of Some Select Scientific/Academic and industrial Institutions

Council of Scientific and Industrial Research: The Council of Scientific and Industrial Research (CSIR) was established in 1942 as a non-profit organisation with a variety of functions, ranging from promotion, guidance and coordination of scientific and industrial research, to founding of laboratories to further scientific and industrial research and exploitation of the research results for development of industry. CSIR today is a multidisciplinary, multi-location set-up comprising of thirty seven laboratories and thirty nine outreach centres. During Eleventh Five Year Plan, it is implementing six plan schemes viz. (i) National Laboratories', National S&T Human Resource Development', R&D management Support', 'Intellectual Property & Technology Management', 'New Millennium Indian Technology Leadership Initiative', and 'Institute of Translational Research'. Under National Laboratories scheme, CSIR as on January 2009 is implementing 96 projects covering all the areas of Science & Technology except Nuclear, Space and Atomic Energy. The projects comprise of 32 Supra-institutional projects, 46 Network projects, 7 Inter-agency projects and 11 Facility creation projects. The Planning Commission has approved these programmes. The flagship programmes viz, development and production of 14-seater small aircraft 'SARAS' involving National Aerospace Laboratories, Hindustan Aeronautics Limited; and Biotechnology programmes in the area of Drugs &

Pharmaceuticals involve partners from CSIR institutes, academia and industry. Some of the important initiatives are described below.

New Drug Development Programme: CSIR initiated a programme on New Drug Discovery in 1997 by pooling and networking existing resources of its institutes. Apart from 20 CSIR laboratories, the traditional knowledge based industry, and 13 universities are actively participating in this job. CSIR is working jointly with traditional medicine industry namely Arya Vaidya Sala (AVS), which is a non-profit making organisation, and Central Council of Research in Unani Medicine (CCRUM) of the Ministry of Health to screen selected medicinal plants and traditional preparations for deriving newer leads for drug development.

This coordinated programme has provided many leads on new chemical entities and new herbal formulations for cancer, tuberculosis, filarial, malaria, ulcer, and dementia. Interesting leads have been obtained on hepato-protective, immuno-modulation as well as dementia. Toxicity studies of antiulcer lead and antidementia leads have been completed. Few more leads for the identification of disease conditions are in hand for further study.

NMITLI: Based on the experience of CSIR in managing and implementing the networked programmes, CSIR was given the responsibility to coordinate NMITLI

The Centre for Genome Application: The Institute of Genomics & Integrative Biology (IGIB), a constituent institute under CSIR, and The Chatterjee Group based in Kolkata and USA through the Institute of Molecular Medicine have set up the Genomic Application Research Facility, namely The Centre for Genome Application (TCGA) at New Delhi in May 2004 with 50:50 financial participation of DST and The Chatterjee Group. This is for the first time, that any research institution in India has looked at opportunities in core-shared research facility by leveraging their domain specialisation and accessing competencies to provide high quality platform for scientific research. The main objectives of TCGA include Speeding up Research; Core Sharing facility for genomics and proteomic services; Nurturing Entrepreneurs; Incubator laboratories for start up entrepreneurs; Enabling Discovery and providing Laboratory facilities to scientists of national and international fame to implement their vision. The Centre has since grown as a world class facility.

Open Source Drug Discovery: an innovative Internet-based 'Open Source Drug Discovery' (OSDD) programme was launched by CSIR on 15th September 2008 to eliminate the scourge of infectious diseases that afflict the developing world. The Indian Government has committed Rs. 150 crores (US $38 million) towards this project of which 46 crores (US $12 million) has already been released. An equivalent amount of funding is proposed to be raised from international agencies and philanthropists.

OSDD, a Team India Consortium with Global Partnership, believes in knowledge sharing and constructive collaboration. It serves as a global platform where the best minds can collaborate & collectively endeavour to solve the complex problems associated with discovering novel therapies for neglected tropical diseases like Malaria, Tuberculosis, Leshmaniasis, etc. It is a concept to collaboratively aggregate the biological and genetic information available to scientists in order to use it to hasten the discovery of drugs. The initiative provides a unique opportunity for scientists, doctors, technocrats, students and others with diverse expertise to work for a common cause. Several scientists from research institutes and universities from India and abroad as well industrial partners are participating in this unique initiative.

Foundation for Innovation and Technology Transfer (IIT, Delhi): In 1992 the Indian Institute of Technology (IIT), Delhi set up a TTO named 'Foundation for Innovation and Technology Transfer (FITT)', as an autonomous registered society and interface organisation and has since been serving as a single window service to industry, drawing upon IIT Delhi as the primary resource. Keeping in view that graduating students of IIT Delhi complete more than 700 industry projects every year and of these at least 5-10 could be potentially commercialisable ideas, IIT Delhi initiated the 'Students-Faculty Led Incubation Program for Initiating Technology Start-Ups' through FITT. In the Incubation process FITT motivates students along with faculty supervisors to spend 6-24 months in IIT Delhi to upgrade/package technology ready for transfer to industry, that could be converted into "business", developing and marketing products and services or be acquired by an existing company. The graduate students, FITT, IIT and faculty members are the stakeholders in the incubation process. IIT Delhi has established its own TBI. The first company 'KRITIKAL Solutions Ltd.' physically moved into this TBI in Sept. 2002. By 2005, four companies were housed there. FITT also operates a scheme of 'Corporate Membership' It may be noted that joint centres have been set up by the industries like IBM and Monsanto in academic institutions like IIT Delhi as well as at IISc, Bangalore.

Society for Innovation and Development (IISc, Bangalore): The Society for Innovation and Development (SID) was founded in 1991 in close collaboration with IISc to enable India's innovations in S&T; by creating a purposeful and effective channel to help industries and business establishments to compete and prosper in the face of global competition, turbulent market conditions and fast moving technologies. Since its inception 389 research projects were initiated till July 2006 of which 100 were completed by 2005 and 142 by March 2006. By 2005 SID was already housing eight R&D Centres of Indian industries such as, Cadila Pharmaceutical Ltd., Cookson Electronics India Research Centre., Satyam Computer Services Limited, Cranes Software International Ltd., Himachal Futuristic Communication Limited, etc.

Confederation of Indian Industries: Confederation of Indian Industries (CII), an industry association, is operating an innovative scheme called 'CII TDB Technology Transfer Centres' Network (CII TDB T NET)' to bring industry closer to R&D agencies Presently 18 such Centres are operating at various technical universities across the country.

Innovation Centre of Entrepreneurship Development Institute: The Entrepreneurship Development Institute of India (EDI), an autonomous body, set up in 1983, sponsored by apex financial institutions, viz. IDBI, IFCI, ICICI and State Bank of India (SBI) and supported by Government of Gujarat is committed to entrepreneurship education, training and research. To achieve its objectives EDI with sponsorship of NSTEDB of DST has set up an Innovation Centre, which is a national facility for innovations and prepares and maintains 'Data Bank' on innovative projects and new and advanced technologies.

Initiatives of Financial Institutions for Promoting R&D Agency-Industry Partnerships

Venture Capital: The GOI guidelines for venture capital funds (VCF) were first issued in 1988; the guidelines for overseas investors were issued in 1995; and the Securities and Exchange Board of India (SEBI) VCF regulations were issued in 1996. In 1988 the Technical Development and Information Corporation of India (TDICI, now ICICI Ventures) was set up, soon followed by Gujarat Venture Finance Limited (GVFL) and Andhra Pradesh Industrial Development Corporation (APIDC) in early 90s, followed by entry of Foreign VC funds between 1995-1999 and emergence of successful India-centric VC firms from 2000 onwards. Thus the Indian VC industry is very young. The first origins of modern VC in India can be traced to the setting up of a Technology Development Fund (TDF) in the year 1987-88 by the Government through the levy of a cess on all technology import payments. Though young by international comparison, the

Indian VC industry has matured fast. Today there are about 150 VCFs (Government, Overseas, Corporate, and Domestic). The VC activity in India is mainly concentrated in a few places like Mumbai, Bangalore, Delhi and Chennai.

The VC firms as a rule do not participate at the initial stage and generally concentrate on projects that have prospects of fast growth. VC firms use high discount rates of around 40-50% in a period of 3-5 years while evaluating the projects. This restricts the VC firms to fund a number of R&D projects, that could be otherwise viable but do not meet their stringent criteria. Certain VCF are industry specific in that they fund enterprises only in certain industries such as pharmaceuticals, IT or food processing, whereas others may have a much wider spectrum. Again, certain funds may have a geographic focus like Uttar Pradesh, Maharashtra, Kerala, etc, whereas the others may fund across different territories.

Industrial Credit and Investment Corporation of India Bank Limited: The Technology Group of Industrial Credit and Investment Corporation of India (ICICI) funds new initiatives and for the World Bank the ICICI is implementing the Sponsored Research and Development Programme (SPREAD), design of which was finalised after extensive discussions with the industry, CSIR and other R&D agencies. The main objectives of the SPREAD programme is to encourage industry to substantially increase their R&D activities SPREAD programme supports projects at all stages of the R&D cycle starting from laboratory and pre-feasibility studies to prototyping and pilot plant operations. Projects are eligible only if the proposed development period is under 2 years. Assistance under SPREAD is limited to 50% of the cost of project or Rs. 1.5 Cr. The programme provided for a concessional interest @ 6.0% per annum for the development period (under 2 years) and then at near market rate of 15% per annum during the commercialisation phase. Under the SPREAD programme upto 2005, ICICI had assisted 101 projects with an aggregate assistance of about Rs. 70 Cr. Out of these, 48 have been commercialised indicating a high success rate for R&D funding. Three industrial sectors, namely pharma/biotechnology, electricals/electronics and chemicals/petrochemical constituted ~65 % of the portfolio and the projects in these sectors got success rates of over 50%. The number of projects supported under the scheme increased to 131 with the total sanction of Rs. 1,495 million by April 2009. It can be seen that CSIR laboratories and institutes of higher education (including IITs) played a major role in the success of the programme.

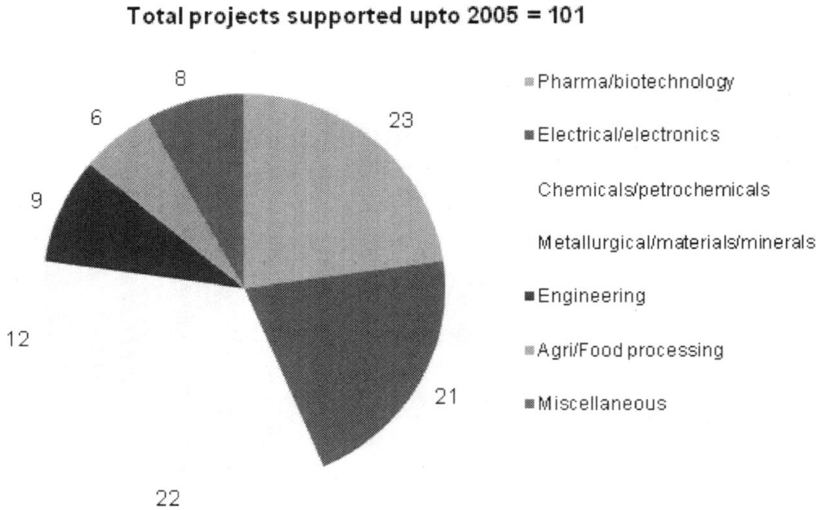

Figure: *Industrial Sectors of Projects supported by ICICI under SPREAD**

Source: *Technology Group of ICICI*

Table: *R&D Agencies that partnered more than one SPREAD Project*

Name of the Project Implementing Institute	***Number***
Bhabha Atomic Research Centre	2
Electronics Research and Development Corporation	3
Indian Institute of Chemical Technology, Hyderabad	7
Indian Institute of Petroleum	4
Indian Institute of Science	8
IIT, Mumbai	8
IIT, Chennai	5
IIT, Delhi	3
National Chemical Laboratory, Pune	11
Regional Research Centres	4
University Institute of Chemical Technology, Mumbai	7

Source: *Technology Group of ICICI*

Industrial Development Bank of India: Technology Financing Scheme of the Industrial Development Bank of India (IDBI) focuses on commercialisation of indigenous technology, adapting imported technology to wider domestic applications and projects envisaging higher than normal risk with potential for commensurate high returns. It prefers financing the technology development at the start-up level and provides the support in the form of equity, conditional and convertible loans (preference share). Its target return for 5-6 years has been 30% on equity investment.

Small Industry Development Bank of India: The Technology Development and Modernisation Fund Scheme of Small Industry Development Bank of India (SIDBI) was launched to provide support in purchase of capital equipment, need-based civil works and acquisition of additional land and need based additional margin money for working capital; acquisition of technical know-how, designs, and the like. The existing units in SSI sector which go in for modernisation / technology up-gradation and that have been in operation for at least three years, are eligible for support under this scheme. Units graduating out of SSI are also eligible, within the overall ceiling of Rs. 37.5 million for investment in plant & machinery. Assistance under this scheme is given by way of term loan in rupee currency or foreign currency. In select cases SIDBI may consider participating in equity also depending upon the exit route available to SIDBI for disinvestments in due course.

Cases of Technology Transfer

Various concepts employed in implementation of partnership programmes refer to: a) lap race concept wherein equipment or technology (low end) development and transfer involves R&D agency, industry and intermediary/promotional agency; b) mother licensee concept wherein the promoter setting up the first project based on the invention becomes the mother licensee; c) high technology, multi-ownership concept; d) concept based on societal needs; e) concept driven through Government legislation; f) disruptive technology concept – which has very long gestation period, requires larger funds through VC and a very large number of partnerships. The partnerships may be formalised through formal or informal arrangements such as collaborative projects, contracting or sponsoring research, consultancy, turn-key projects, or exchange of information / personnel or sharing of facilities.

In order to appreciate these modalities the summaries of fifteen cases of Technology transfer are discussed below. Twelve partnership projects were selected from CSIR institutions: Nine of these projects were implemented by one industry and one CSIR lab; one project involved partnership with a German R&D institute and industry besides partnering with Indian industry; one involved partners from more than one CSIR lab, universities and industry; and one involved participation from institutions other than CSIR. Three projects of non-CSIR institutions viz, ISRO, IPRI, CTCRI, CPRI were selected.

Out of the fifteen selected projects seven projects involved participation of intermediary agencies such as NRDC and TIFAC. The projects were so selected that they a) represented different S&T disciplines, b) involved the interface agencies to know the view of the partners on their schemes, c) involved a number of partners to understand various nuances of partnership implementation and d) had influence of the government policies. Salient features of the case studies are described in Table.

Table: *Summaries of Case Studies*

Case Study	Technology Developed	Main R&D Agency	Industry	Inter-mediary	Other Partners	Financing	Status of Commercialisation
1.	Palm Oil Technology	RRL – T, CMRI (CSIR) MERDO, CPCRI (ICAR)	AP Oil Federation	NRDC	DBT, Karnataka, AP & Maharashtra States	1.26 Cr by TDB, NCDC, Oil Mission	Commercialised
1.	Zeolite 'A' Intermediate for Detergent	CSMCRI (CSIR)	NALCO	NRDC	EIL	Equal share of Rs.30-40 Lakhs	Commercialised in India and abroad
1.	Rice Husk Particle Board	IPRI	PPBL	NRDC	-	50% NRDC Equity + 40 Lakh VCF-IDBI loan	Commercialised By MHEL Malaysia + Indonesian company
1.	Clot Busters TPA, UK, SK	IMT (CSIR)	Godrej	-	Cadila	-	Commercialised
1.	Specialty Monomers	NCL (CSIR)	Vinati Organics	-	-	Vinati Rs. 40 Lakh + TDB 40 Cr.	Commercialised
1.	Drug (Amlodipine) Molecule	NCL (CSIR)	Emcur Pimpri	-	-	Emcur Rs. 5 lakhs	Commercialised
1.	Leaf Cup Making Machine	CFTRI (CSIR)	10 Machine Fabricators	NRDC	SISI, NGO etc.	By R&D agency	Commercialised
1.	Biodegradable Plastics	CTCRI CPRI	Hindustan Lever	NRDC	SIRI	50% from HGT (DST)	Licensed and being considered for commercialisation
1.	Catalytic Process for Butadiene Conversion	NCL (CSIR)	Gharada Chemical			Gharada Rs. 20 lakhs	Licensed to industry, but could not get commercialised
1.	Sol-Gel Abrasives	RRL –T (CSIR)	Company 'X'	-	-	Rs. 35 lakhs from 'X'	Licensed, but could not get commercialised
1.	Flux Bonded Fly Ash Components	RRL –T (CSIR)	Company 'Y'	TIFAC	-	'Y' + Fly Ash Mission	Technology transfer in progress
1.	Cokeless Cupola for Foundries	NML (CSIR)	TKES	TIFAC	AIFA	Rs. 45 lakhs (TIFAC) + Rs. 20 lakhs (CSIR)	Technology transfer in progress, but not smooth
1.	Bioactive Molecules fm Plant Extracts	CSIR Labs	Arya Vaidya Sala	Dr. Valiathan	TSM Partners	Share as per Agreement	Technology development in progress
1.	FEM of Structures and Components	SERC (CSIR) ISR	-	-	NIIT INTES	'2+2' bilateral Project	Knowledge Generation
1.	Satellite Imagery Digitisation	ISRO	-	-	MPD, SOI (DST), IGNOU	-	Often free for societal needs

Assessing the Value of R&D Partnerships

Historically available tools for assessing the value generated by projects mainly address those with tangible deliverables (eg, the discovery of a new drug candidate). They also rely heavily on the quantitative, usually riskadjusted, values that can be assigned to these outputs. More recently, fuzzy approaches to real option valuation and decision trees using Boolean algebra have been developed, but these methods still rely on hard commercial valuations that are not realistic for early stage R&D projects. Partnerships with less tangible deliverables, such as fundamental science or technology development, are more difficult to value, particularly in a way that would enable comparisons across a diverse portfolio of projects. An additional complication is that some partnerships are comprised of multiple projects and can have an impact on different business areas, including those outside of R&D.

Without new assessment tools that enable comparison of such partnerships of disparate nature, R&D organisations will find it challenging to assess their relative value for investment decisions. It was therefore timely to develop a new assessment tool that would allow for differences in the various forms of partnerships and their outputs. In addition, such a tool could be valuable for setting expectations over the lifetime of a project and tracking progress.

Developing a New Assessment Tool

Our approach was constructed around three core principles that ensured the scoring methodology was both representative of the value added by an individual partnership and that each element of the assessment contributed to the overall score at an appropriate level:

1. Enable meaningful comparison of partnerships address a diverse range of scientific disciplines across all phases of R&D, from target identification to clinical studies, with diverse deliverables, such as basic scientific results, best practice recommendations or therapeutic agents. Estimating values based on cost of generating the deliverables relative to other means can be misleading, and ignore the fact that these savings alone are no indication of how important the deliverable is to the sponsoring organisation. Therefore, an assessment tool should not calculate the fiscal value generated from the partnership, but instead assess the impact that the output would have on the sponsoring organisation.
2. Apply weighting profiles to highlight important factors Not all elements of an assessment are necessarily of equal importance. For example, while the impact on non-R&D objectives may be

worth considering, the impact on an R&D objective may be of greater importance. Each element of the assessment therefore needs to be weighted according to its individual importance to the business.

The actual weightings applied to individual questions are highly dependent on the sponsoring organisation's strategy. Business requirements may change over time and the ability to change the associated weightings enables the assessment tool to be adapted for subsequent reviews should the strategy change. However, provided the weightings are agreed by a stakeholder group at the start of each process, and fixed throughout the assessment, the analysis should be consistent across projects.

3. Recognise that the value a partnership delivers often changes over time Recently started partnerships may not have had sufficient time, compared to older ones, to deliver the expected value, and this could restrict the utility of a scoring model based solely on tangible deliverables. A number of elements that address both the current value of the partnership and the perceived future value (the value considered realistically achievable within two years) were therefore included in the assessment tool. This understanding of the 'as is' and 'should be' scenarios enables a more realistic visualisation of the value a portfolio can deliver at a subsequent date, avoiding the danger of making decisions based on current value only. It also helps to identify the key areas where focus will be required to ensure that this future value is realised.

Using the Assessment Tool

Whilst this approach is applicable for general use across a range of partnerships, in the remainder of this article its use will be exemplified with a sub-set of Public-Private Partnerships (PPPs, also commonly referred to as research consortia) currently supported by GSK. In the context of this discussion, PPPs are defined as partnerships involving more than one pharmaceutical company and at least one public funding agency. The sub-set of PPPs selected, while diverse in nature, are generally focused on areas of pre-competitive science where the deliverables are less tangible than for therapeutic agent partnerships. Therefore, they are well-placed to demonstrate the value of this new assessment tool. A three-step approach was used:

Stage 1: Build the Assessment Tool

The assessment tool was based around a weighted scoring methodology, comprising a list of questions (or criteria) within four major categories. The criteria were carefully selected, worded and defined by the needs of the business, then organised into the categories summarised in Table. This enables the criteria to be closely aligned with specific R&D requirements and partnership strategy.

The shaded items in Figure represent timedependent criteria, where the present and future values could potentially be differentiated. The Impact on R&D Productivity and Access to Capability and Talent categories are completely populated with time-dependent criteria, while Strategic Interests and Delivery on Objectives are less so. This difference reflects the observation that alignment of partnership objectives to Strategic Interests, and the way they are managed to deliver on those objectives, should not change considerably over a two-year period. If this were not the case then the purpose of entering the partnership, or continuing it, should be questioned. Indeed, the only way to increase the value that these categories deliver would be to restructure the partnership. In the case of the Impact on R&D Productivity and Access to Capability and Talent categories, the value realised may change over time, particularly with recently-formed partnerships where the outputs have yet to be adopted or utilised extensively.

It is essential that assessment tools such as these are owned and promoted by senior executives and that the extended business units are fully engaged with both the need for assessment and the methodology employed. Working directly with members of the R&D executive, the criteria were tested and validated for reliability through an iterative series of workshops and feedback sessions where the criteria were challenged, reviewed, weighted and accepted by stakeholders.

Stage 2: Gather the Data

Many of the IT solutions used to gather information from key stakeholders do not address the level of complexity that often exists when balancing the needs of a company against the perceived benefits of an external venture. As a result, it is often easy to contradict preceding answers or simply assign a 'score' to a criterion without thinking through all the elements of potential value such as strategic alignment or organisational development.

For this reason, data were gathered through personal interviews with key stakeholders for each partnership using the criterion set as a basis for discussion. Each criterion was scored by the interviewee based on the discussion and their supporting comments were gathered.

To avoid middle-ground responses and force decisions, only four possible outcomes to each criterion were allowed, ranging in score from zero to three, which were assigned to a value relevant to that criterion. For example, in the Enhanced Disease and Patient Knowledge criterion, scores zero to three corresponded to 'Little or no Impact', 'Enhanced understanding of disease area', 'Significant impact on disease area or enhanced understanding of multiple disease areas', and 'Sets new direction in disease area or significant impact on several disease areas'. In each case, the selected score was supported by a full documentation of the collected comments of the interviewees.

Stage 3: Analyse and Interpret

The most useful portfolio analysis tools allow the user to explore and debate project data from a number of different angles. In the case of this assessment tool, there was a need to investigate various sub-sets of partnerships or different scoring categories from a number of perspectives. To facilitate data aggregation and analysis, a Microsoft Excel VBA tool was developed to import and analyse the criterion scores and comments that formed the output of key stakeholder interviews. This simple application also provided a convenient route to deliver a suite of graphical outputs that can easily be transferred to other Office applications for presentation and reporting.

Example: Evaluation of Public-Private Partnerships (PPPs)

Once the evaluation tool had been built using criteria appropriate for PPPs, and data gathered via interviews, the final step of analysis and interpretation could take place. Visualising the data in a number of formats, some of which are shown in the next few sections, enabled conclusions to be drawn, at differing levels of detail, either individually or as a portfolio.

An example analysis of individual partnerships is shown in Figure, focusing on three partnerships at different stages of their lifecycle, and with markedly different future prospects.

Partnership A

Partnership A is a PPP that was initiated recently. It is clear that the partnership is already rating well in the Strategic Interests and Delivery on Objectives categories. However, scores in the other two categories (Impact on R&D Productivity and Access to Capability and Talent) are less impressive.

It was previously suggested that the Strategic Interests and Delivery on Objectives categories often score higher earlier in the PPP lifecycle than the Impact on R&D Productivity and Access to Capability and Talent categories, and the results for Partnership A are in line with this. The future value plot suggests that all four categories will eventually score highly, and Partnership A exemplifies the need to consider the future value in addition to the present value of PPPs throughout the assessment.

It is important to note with Partnership A that it was recognised that full value would probably not be delivered within two years. However, it was felt that estimating the value beyond two years into the future would be so compromised by uncertainty as to be of little value.

Partnership B

The example in (Partnership B) is of a PPP started before Partnership A; it is delivering low or no value in all categories and experience thus far suggests it will not improve over time. Partnership B requires a more detailed analysis to determine why the prospect for delivery of value is so poor, both to see if it is salvageable and to understand what lessons could be learned for future partnerships.

Partnership C

Partnership C has been established for over a decade; it scores relatively well against all categories and very highly for Delivery on Objectives. Although delivery of value is not expected to increase over the next two years, the value it is already delivering means this is not a cause for concern. Analysis of the assessment data leads to key three observations:

1. New PPPs need time to mature in order to deliver their full potential. This is especially true for those with a primary focus on generating results through new experimental work, where the time taken to recruit staff and plan, perform and interpret experiments is considerable. Partnership A is an example of this. As a result, when accessing relatively new PPPs it is important to recognise the potential value they could deliver, rather than solely the present value. It was also apparent that the time it takes a partnership to deliver full value is commonly underestimated.
2. Established PPPs that are performing less well compared to others need further assessment. PPPs with a low current delivery value and a higher future value, should be monitored to ensure that the expected increase does occur, if necessary providing assistance to ensure this. Where both the present and future value is perceived to be low, such as Partnership B, more detailed analysis is required to understand why the PPP could not deliver better value and whether continued investment is appropriate.

3. The value delivered by a PPP does not have to increase continually over its lifetime provided it is delivering on the objectives. Established PPPs that deliver consistently high value (like Partnership C) are likely to be the ones that are the most stable and are ideally positioned to draw lessons from.

The Partnership Value Dashboard

In line with the previously-explained concerns about measuring the precise value of deliverables from each partnership, semi-quantitative estimates of value in terms of impact on the R&D pipeline were obtained from combining the scores in the four categories outlined in Figure. Presenting these as a dashboard produces a portfolio view and enables comparisons between partnerships.

The highest value is currently resulting from Partnership C, which is the second oldest PPP in the portfolio sub-set. It is clearly well established and, as highlighted previously, is delivering significant value across all four categories. Similarly, PPPs initiated more recently, in general, deliver lower current value. The tendency for more value to be delivered by older partnerships is not surprising, as all PPPs will take time to deliver maximum value. In addition, older partnerships that have not been delivering value will have been terminated or not renewed, meaning that an older partnership has to be good to have survived. Hence, in comparing the value of partnerships the likely improvement in delivery should also be considered. That is, focus is placed on the questions about the future value of each PPP.

A combined dashboard was developed that shows both the present and future value of the PPP portfolio. PPPs that were not scored as delivering an increase in overall value are marked with a white X; all the others are shown with the present and future values connected with an arrow in the direction of improvement. There were no examples of PPPs decreasing in expected future value.

This plot allows easy visualisation of the current and future value of the portfolio of partnerships and identifies those where more attention would be beneficial:

- The expected improvement in delivery value for Partnership A suggests that in two years' time it should be delivering the highest value.
- Lower value PPPs, with the exception of Partnership B, are expected to improve sufficiently over the next two years. These PPPs have all been initiated more recently, so the fact that they will improve is not necessarily surprising. However, it will

clearly be important to track their progress to ensure that the expected delivery occurs.

- Partnership C is unlikely to improve further but it is already performing very well.
- The current value delivered by Partnership D could be considered acceptable if it was early in its lifecycle, and value is expected to improve on a two year time scale. This is not the case, however, and it is appropriate to consider how the value delivered by this PPP could be improved or whether investment in this partnership should be terminated.

Partnership D is delivering almost to its full potential in the Delivery on Objectives category, but not in the others. This suggests it is delivering what it was established to do, but these deliverables are of limited value to the business. Partnership D has been running for more than 10 years, so it is not surprising that Strategic Interests will have changed over this timeframe, which, in turn, could limit the ability of the PPP to provide Access to Capability and Talent, and Impact on R&D Productivity. There are two approaches to consider in order to increase the value realised from Partnership D:

- Change externally: Adapt the objectives of the PPP to align better with current Strategic Interests, rather than those in place at the start of the PPP. This may also enable the partnership to deliver increased value in the Impact on R&D Productivity and Access to Capability and Talent categories.
- Change internally: Realign how the PPP output is utilised internally (eg, bringing the PPP to the attention of new internal groups) to increase the impact of the investment

Conclusions and Benefits of a Structured Assessment Tool for Partnerships

An assessment tool has been developed and used to evaluate major partnership commitments, identifying those that are:

- Delivering lower value than expected. In this case, programmes of work have been initiated to understand why value is being lost and changes to the partnerships have been implemented to ensure that the deliverables can be realised in the shortest amount of time. Of course, it may not be possible to recover fully some partnerships and, in these cases, sponsors can formalise an exit plan based on a well-constructed business case.
- Delivering high value. Such partnerships are important, not only because they deliver value directly to the R&D pipeline,

but also because they are essential tools to learn from to guide the evolution of partnerships and general partnering behaviours. Partnerships such as Partnership C, that deliver consistent value, and Partnership A, that is considered to improve dramatically over time, will be used as benchmarks in future assessments of the portfolio

Conclusion

With R&D organisations engaging in many partnerships, it is essential that value creation is identified early, so sponsors can learn from them and evolve their partnering strategy. It is also important that organisations can identify where value is not being realised such that they can take the appropriate action to either improve performance or redirect sponsorship to alternative partnerships of higher value. As such, the assessment process should be conducted regularly to ensure that the predicted increase in the value delivered from the portfolio of partnerships is realised and to build a long-term understanding of the partnering behaviours that drive successful collaborations.

This assessment tool is adaptable to the needs of differing portfolios through adjustment of the criteria and weighting profiles so that they are aligned with the strategic requirements of individual portfolios and organisations. It is also apparent that this assessment tool is applicable to other situations where diverse projects have multiple points of impact across R&D, in both academia and industry, and in sectors beyond Pharma. These share common themes with the partnerships described above:

- Benefits change over time.
- Value is difficult to estimate precisely.
- There is a need to maximise the value of the entire portfolio and make hard choices about future investment.

In Summary, This Assessment Tool Provides a Mechanism that can

- Flag easily issues in a portfolio of partnerships and aid the understanding of common factors contributing to success or failure throughout their lifecycle.
- Predict the likely value of partnerships both prior to engagement, and when the full return on investment has yet to be realised, and thereby avoid investment in low value ones.
- Identify areas for key focus in managing existing partnerships to deliver.

- Provide a framework to allow sponsors to consider the value of both intangible and tangible deliverables when a collaboration is under consideration.

Research and Development Business Models

A business model is usually defined as the method of doing business by which a company can sustain its existence and generate revenue. The role of a business model is to specify how a company positions itself within the value chain or, in other words, how the company translates its internal inputs, i.e. resources, capabilities and innovations into economic outputs.

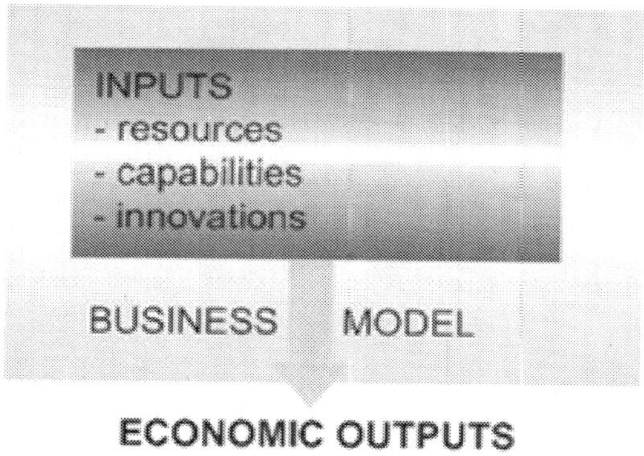

Figure: *Business model: connecting internal inputs to economic outputs*

This article is concerned with possible business models of independent R&D organisations, i.e. the organisations for which R&D activities remain both the core area of activity and the major source of income.

General Framework for Business Models

The framework describing the elements of a business model is illustrated in Figures and includes the following six basic components:

- value proposition – a description of the customer problem, the company's approach to solve the problem, and the value of this solution to the customer;
- market segment – a specific group to target having specific and known needs;
- value chain structure – the firm's position in the value chain and how the firm captures part of the value it creates;
- revenue generation and margins – how revenue is generated, the structure of costs, and profit margins aimed;

- position in the value network – competitors, complementors, and any value chain characteristics that can be utilised to offer higher value to the customer;
- competitive strategy – how the company develops a sustainable competitive advantage and uses it to improve its competitive position.

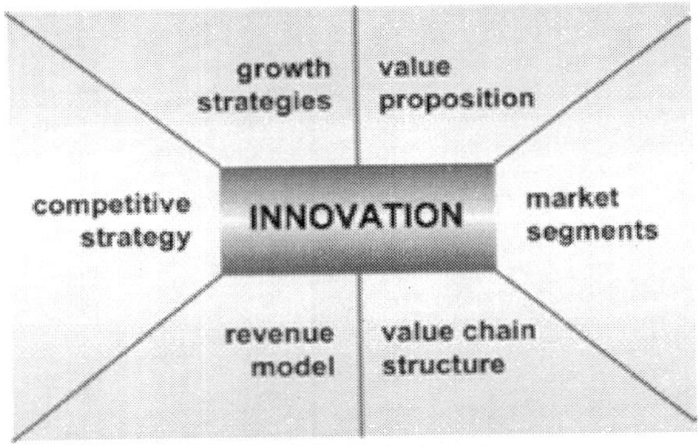

Figure: *Business model: converting innovation to economic value*

Malone and others define a business model based on two fundamental dimensions of what the business does:

- what types of rights are being sold,
- what type of assets is involved.

The heart of any business is what it sells, which concerns also a specific kind of legal right conferred to the buyer with the transaction. Malone and others recognise four basic asset rights being sold:

1. A Creator buys raw materials or components from suppliers and then creates a product sold to buyers. This is the typical business model in manufacturing.
2. A Distributor buys a product and then sells essentially the same product to someone else, usually providing additional value by transporting, repackaging, or by providing customer service. A key distinction between Creators and Distributors is that Creators design the products being sold.
3. A Landlord sells the right to use an asset for a specified period of time. The term Landlord describes here not only businesses providing temporary use of physical assets (like houses or airline seats), but also lenders of financial assets, and organisations providing temporary use of human assets.
4. A Broker facilitates sales by matching potential buyers and sellers. A Broker does not own the product being sold (unlike a

Distributor), receiving a fee (or commission) from the buyer, the seller, or both. This business model is common in real estate brokerage, stock brokerage and insurance brokerage.

The other dimension considered is the type of asset for which rights are being sold. Four types of assets are defined:

A. Physical assets include both: durable items (e.g. houses, computers, and machines) and nondurable items (e.g. food, clothing, paper).

B. Financial assets include cash and other assets, for instance stocks, bonds, and insurance policies that give their owners rights to potential future cash flows.

C. Intangible assets include legally protected intellectual property rights (patents, copyrights, trademarks, and trade secrets), and other intangible assets like knowledge, goodwill, and brand image.

D. Human assets include people's time and effort, which can be sold for a fee.

Based on the above definitions Malone [2] recognise business models that are briefly described below:

1A. An Entrepreneur – creates and sells financial assets, including firms. Examples are: serial entrepreneurs, "incubator" firms and other investors active in very early stage firms who finally sell the firms they create.

1B. A Manufacturer – Creates and Sells Physical Assets.

1C. An Inventor – creates and then sells intangible assets such as patents and copyrights. Firms using this business model exclusively are relatively rare, but some technology firms generate part of their revenues this way. Firms that license the use of their intangible assets while still retaining ownership are not classified as Inventors; they are Intellectual Landlords.

- 2A. A Financial Trader – buys and sells financial assets without significantly transforming (or designing) them. Banks, investment firms, and other financial institutions that invest for their own account are included in this business model.
- 2B. A Wholesaler/Retailer – buys and sells physical assets. This is the most common type of Distributor.
- 2C. An Intellectual Property (IP) Trader – buys and sells intangible assets. This business model includes firms that buy

and sell intellectual property such as copyrights, patents, domain names, etc.

- 3A. A Financial Landlord – lets others use cash (or other financial assets) under certain (often time-limited) conditions. There are two major subtypes of this business model: a Lender, who provides cash for a fee, and an Insurer, who provides financial reserves that the customers can use if they experience losses.
- 3B. A Physical Landlord – sells the right to use a physical asset. The asset may, for example, be a place or equipment. This business model is common in industries like real estate rental and leasing, accommodation, airlines and recreation.
- 3C. An Intellectual Landlord – licenses or otherwise gets paid for limited use of intangible assets. Three subtypes of Intellectual Landlord are recognised: a Publisher, who provides limited use of information assets such as software, newspapers, or databases in return for a purchase price or other fee, a Brand Manager, who gets paid for the use of a trademark, know-how, or brand, an Attractor, who attracts people's attention using television programs or web content and then "sells" that attention to advertisers.
- 3D. A Contractor – sells a service provided primarily by people, such as consulting, construction, education, personal care, package delivery, live entertainment or healthcare. Payment is a fee for service.
- 4A. A Financial Broker – matches buyers and sellers of financial assets.
- 4B. A Physical Broker – matches buyers and sellers of physical assets.
- 4C. An Intellectual Property (IP) broker – matches buyers and sellers of intangible assets.
- 4D. A Human Resources (HR) Broker – matches buyers and sellers of human services.

These business models can be presented in a more compact tabular form, as in Table. Four models are distinguished using blue colour. These models are used in the following discussion as reference models for independent R&D organisations.

Table: *Sixteen reference business models ('x' denotes illegal business models that are mentioned only for logical completeness)*

		Type of asset involved (A-D)			
		A. Financial	*B. Physical*	*C. Intangible*	*D. Human*
Rights being sold (1-4)	1. Creator	Entrepreneur	Manufacturer	Inventor	x
	2. Distributor	Financial Trader	Wholesaler, Retailer	IP Trader	x
	3. Landlord	Financial Landlord	Physical Landlord	Intellectual Landlord	Contractor
	4. Broker	Financial Broker	Physical Broker	IP Broker	HR Broker

Source: Based on: T.W. Malone, P. Weill, R.K. Lai, V.T. D'Urso, G. Herman, T.G. Apel, S. Woerner: Do some business models perform better than others? *MIT Sloan Research Paper*, No. 4615-06, May 2006, pp. 4-12

Business Models for Independent R&D Organisations

Constant discusses operational characteristics of an independent not-for-profit R&D organisation. Such organisation is similar to an independent for-profit organisation in the sense that it must operate effectively, and therefore has many similar operational characteristics. There are various potential income streams available to an independent not-for-profit R&D organisation:

- R&D projects,
- donations and subsidies,
- intellectual property rights,
- publishing and education,
- new product development.

Contract Research Projects

The principal income stream of the independent R&D organisation is that from contract research operations, which is project based. The income from a project depends on its size and on the type of the contract. Typical contract types for R&D projects are: cost-plus fixed fee, time and material, award fee, fixed price. The fixed fee contracts are the most sound from the financial point of view, however, at a higher risk than the other types. Since the R&D project is usually the financial lifeline of the R&D organisation, it takes a central role in the organisation and is served by all its elements. Using the reference model described above, this revenue path corresponds to the business model of the Inventor (1C).

Donations and Subsidies

Depending on the local regulations, donations [3] may be restricted to not-for-profit and non-profit organisations. Usually donations are not as viable source of income as R&D projects are. Moreover, it can take considerable time to meet the specified criteria or to undertake an effective campaign to raise money.

Intellectual Properties

Intellectual properties (IP) or intellectual assets (IA) are a very viable option for an R&D organisation. IP rights that are the property of the R&D organisation may come from contract research activities, from a self-funded research or from buying the rights from other parties. The IP rights could:

- generate new contract research work,
- constitute the basis for a new venture, e.g. a spin-off company,
- be sold to another party.

If the IP rights are to be commercialised through a new venture company, the R&D organisation becomes a parent organisation for the new company. The new company could have need for research work to be done by the parent organisation.

Publishing and Education

Another income stream available for some R&D organisations is the publication of technical information for sale in the form of articles, books, manuals, DVDs, CDs, or organising professional courses and trainings. This publishing activity may be related either to the established and widely known technical knowledge or to new information, not yet known in the marketplace. The latter case is related to selling IA, for instance know-how.

Using the reference model described above, the revenue paths based on trading IP rights or Publishing correspond to the business models of the IP Trader (2C) or the Intellectual Landlord (3C).

New Product Development

The R&D organisation can profit from new product development in various ways [3]. For some contract research projects customers (other organisations) want a new product to be developed. The customers introduce the newly developed product into manufacturing and markets, and derive profit from consequent sales. The R&D organisation makes a fee, which is a form of profit for the organisation.

Gaining profit from product development is dependent on the research contract terms. If staff members working on the project produce IP that are exclusively or partially owned by the R&D organisation, these IP rights can bring financial benefits.

Different marketing strategies can be followed by R&D organisations with respect to its principal revenue paths. Constant [3] recognises three major approaches, two reactive strategies involved with the contract research path for income and the third, a proactive strategy is used in the IP path. The term reactive strategy is used here to express the situation when the activity of the R&D organisation results from the communicated need of the customer – as a reaction to that need. The proactive strategy is followed when this is the organisation itself where the idea for new product or technology is born. And this new idea is consequently developed, managed and marketed to customers.

Reactive Strategies – Contract Research Project Path

The most common approach is, when the customer – government, industrial, trade or other organisation – develops a written request for proposal (RfP), request for quotation (RfQ) or invitation for bid (IfB) for a specific work to be done. After receiving the request the R&D organisation determines whether or not it wants to respond, taking into consideration different aspects, including:

- Is it within the current business area?
- Is any conflict of interest likely?
- Is it an opportunity to start a new business area?
- Are capabilities available to complete the job?
- Will capabilities be available or obtainable if some are missing?
- Who are the major competitors?
- Is it really a competitive bid or essentially sole-source proposition, i.e. the job designated for another organisation?
- What is the competition?
- What is the likelihood of success?
- What investments are necessary?
- What return on investment is expected?

If the initial decision is to respond, a Proposal (or Capture) Team is formed that is led by a Proposal Manager (or Capture Team Leader), who would eventually become the Project Manager in the case the contract is won. The Proposal Team might follow a formalised methodology (called a stage-gate review process [4]) of analysing the problem, developing the proposal and providing ground for organisation's executives to take decisions at predefined time moments (called gates) on whether to continue the effort (including the final decision to submit the proposal) or to abandon.

Another reactive strategy appears when the potential client approaches the R&D organisation and presents his need or problem. A meeting, a set of meetings or other type of information exchange between the appropriate staff members and the client is conveyed that is aimed at discussing the need and ensuring that the requirements are thoroughly understood. When the decision is made by the R&D organisation to propose, a Proposal Team is formed to prepare the proposal, as discussed above.

This latter type of reactive approach can be viewed as having certain advantages for the R&D organisation over the former one – based on an RfP:

- If the customer need was identified early it is likely that the customer would not approach competitors with the same need.
- Even if he approaches competitors in order to compare the offers, the first organisation discussing the need has the advantage of shaping the customer requirements in its favour and against the foreseen competitors, making it the essentially sole-source proposition.

Proactive Strategy – Intellectual Properties Path

The third strategy is based on a new idea the R&D organisation might have. The idea may be client related or not. It may concern a new product or the improvement of a product in terms of reliability, mean time between failures, maintainability, durability, ruggedness, sensitivity, accuracy, adaptability, user friendliness, life, cost, size, etc. The idea for new or improved product is first documented and a patent may be sought before the product is marketed to prospective customers.

One of these three generic strategies is responsible for the R&D organisation obtaining the contract that is sought. The contract gives all requirements to be met and defines how the IP rights shall be handled. The profit path for the R&D organisation is usually built into the contract, such as:

- the client owns all the IP rights conceived by project staff members,
- the R&D organisation shares in the right,
- the fee to be awarded for the contract work done.

In that case IP rights are not based on contract research project work, the benefit is solely that of the R&D organisation with a certain share of profits derived from the IP paid to the staff members who had the innovative idea.

Relations between R&D Organisation, Production Means and Sales of Products

When considering the ways the R&D organisation can make money on its innovations, the key issue is the relationship between the R&D institution, production capacity and sales. Typically, for an independent R&D organisation, the end product of a contract research project is a prototype of the product, often supplemented with the technical documentation needed to put the new product into production. Some R&D organisations have the capabilities to produce a limited number of units in-house. Alternatively, the organisation can subcontract production to a firm specialised in production in order to do the work.

Depending on the organisation status, the R&D organisation can or can not act as a manufacture of products because of its tax status. In the case of the independent not-for-profit organisations tax regulations can limit the amount of revenues generated from sales of products on the market, or even prevent the R&D organisation from production. In this case the not-for-profit organisation would have to have a separate for-profit division, which aims at commercialising innovations produced by the R&D organisation and to undertake the manufacturing and sales aspects. Alternatively, in order to profit from innovations the IP rights owned by the R&D organisation can be sold to other businesses, e.g. in the form of a license, or know-how.

Chapter 5

Decisive Role of Intellectual Property

Intellectual Property

Intellectual property (IP) rights are legally recognised exclusive rights to creations of the mind. Under intellectual property laws, owners are granted certain exclusive rights to a variety of intangible assets, such as musical, literary, and artistic works; discoveries and inventions; and words, phrases, symbols, and designs. Common types of intellectual property rights include copyright, trademarks, patents, industrial design rights, trade dress, and in some jurisdictions trade secrets.

Although many of the legal principles governing intellectual property rights have evolved over centuries, it was not until the 19th century that the term *intellectual property* began to be used, and not until the late 20th century that it became commonplace in the majority of the world. The British Statute of Anne (1710) and the Statute of Monopolies (1624) are now seen as the origins of copyright and patent law respectively.

History

Modern usage of the term *intellectual property* goes back at least as far as 1867 with the founding of the North German Confederation whose constitution granted legislative power over the protection of intellectual property (*Schutz des geistigen Eigentums*) to the confederation. When the administrative secretariats established by the Paris Convention (1883) and the Berne Convention (1886) merged in 1893, they located in Berne, and also adopted the term intellectual property in their new combined title, the United International Bureaux for the Protection of Intellectual Property.

The organisation subsequently relocated to Geneva in 1960, and was succeeded in 1967 with the establishment of the World Intellectual Property Organisation (WIPO) by treaty as an agency of the United Nations. According to Lemley, it was only at this point that the term really began to be used in the United States (which had not been a party to the Berne Convention), and it did not enter popular usage until passage of the Bayh-Dole Act in 1980.

"The history of patents does not begin with inventions, but rather with royal grants by Queen Elizabeth I (1558–1603) for monopoly privileges... Approximately 200 years after the end of Elizabeth's reign, however, a patent represents a legal [right] obtained by an inventor providing for exclusive control over the production and sale of his mechanical or scientific invention... [demonstrating] the evolution of patents from royal prerogative to common-law doctrine."

The term *intellectual property* can be found used in an October 1845 Massachusetts Circuit Court ruling in the patent case *Davoll et al. v. Brown.*, in which Justice Charles L. Woodbury wrote that "only in this way can we protect intellectual property, the labours of the mind, productions and interests are as much a man's own...as the wheat he cultivates, or the flocks he rears." The statement that "discoveries are...property" goes back earlier. Section 1 of the French law of 1791 stated, "All new discoveries are the property of the author; to assure the inventor the property and temporary enjoyment of his discovery, there shall be delivered to him a patent for five, ten or fifteen years." In Europe, French author A. Nion mentioned *propriété intellectuelle* in his *Droits civils des auteurs, artistes et inventeurs*, published in 1846.

Until recently, the purpose of intellectual property law was to give as little protection possible in order to encourage innovation. Historically, therefore, they were granted only when they were necessary to encourage invention, limited in time and scope.

The concept's origins can potentially be traced back further. Jewish law includes several considerations whose effects are similar to those of modern intellectual property laws, though the notion of intellectual creations as property does not seem to exist – notably the principle of Hasagat Ge'vul (unfair encroachment) was used to justify limited-term publisher (but not author) copyright in the 16th century. In 500 BCE, the government of the Greek state of Sybaris offered one year's patent "to all who should discover any new refinement in luxury".

Types

Common types of intellectual property rights include patents, copyright, industrial design rights, trademarks, trade dress, and in some jurisdictions trade secrets. There are also more specialised varieties of *sui generis* exclusive rights, such as circuit design rights (called mask work rights in U.S. law, protected under the Integrated Circuit Topography Act in Canadian law, and in European Union law by Directive 87/54/EEC of 16 December 1986 on the legal protection of topographies of semiconductor products), plant breeders' rights, plant variety rights, industrial design rights, supplementary protection certificates for pharmaceutical products and database rights (in European law).

Patent

A patent (/ÈpætYnt/ or /ÈpejtYnt/) is a set of exclusive rights granted by a sovereign state to an inventor or assignee for a limited period of time in exchange for detailed public disclosure of an invention. An invention is a solution to a specific technological problem and is a product or a process. Patents are a form of intellectual property.

The procedure for granting patents, requirements placed on the patentee, and the extent of the exclusive rights vary widely between countries according to national laws and international agreements. Typically, however, a granted patent application must include one or more claims that define the invention. A patent may include many claims, each of which defines a specific property right. These claims must meet relevant patentability requirements, such as novelty and non-obviousness. The exclusive right granted to a patentee in most countries is the right to prevent others, or at least to try to prevent others, from commercially making, using, selling, importing, or distributing a patented invention without permission.

Under the World Trade Organisation's (WTO) Agreement on Trade-Related Aspects of Intellectual Property Rights, patents should be available in WTO member states for any invention, in all fields of technology, and the term of protection available should be a minimum of twenty years. Nevertheless, there are variations on what is patentable subject matter from country to country.

Definition

The word *patent* originates from the Latin *patere*, which means "to lay open" (i.e., to make available for public inspection). More directly, it is a shortened version of the term *letters patent*, which was a royal decree granting exclusive rights to a person, predating the modern patent system. Similar grants included land patents, which were land grants by early state governments in the USA, and printing patents, a precursor of modern copyright.

In modern usage, the term *patent* usually refers to the right granted to anyone who invents any new, useful, and non-obvious process, machine, article of manufacture, or composition of matter. Some other types of intellectual property rights are also called *patents* in some jurisdictions: industrial design rights are called *design patents* in the US, plant breeders' rights are sometimes called *plant patents*, and utility models and *Gebrauchsmuster* are sometimes called *petty patents* or *innovation patents*.

The additional qualification *utility patent* is sometimes used (primarily in the US) to distinguish the primary meaning from these other types of patents. Particular species of patents for inventions include biological patents, business method patents, chemical patents and software patents.

History

Patents were systematically granted in Venice as of 1450, where they issued a decree by which new and inventive devices had to be communicated to the Republic in order to obtain legal protection against potential infringers. The period of protection was 10 years. These were mostly in the field of glass making. As Venetians emigrated, they sought similar patent protection in their new homes. This led to the diffusion of patent systems to other countries.

The English patent system evolved from its early medieval origins into the first modern patent system that recognised intellectual property in order to stimulate invention; this was the crucial legal foundation upon which the Industrial Revolution could emerge and flourish. By the 16th century, the English Crown would habitually abuse the granting of letters patent for monopolies. After public outcry, James I of England was forced to revoke all existing monopolies and declare that they were only to be used for "projects of new invention". This was incorporated into the Statute of Monopolies (1624) in which Parliament restricted the Crown's power explicitly so that the King could only issue letters patent to the inventors or introducers of original inventions for a fixed number of years. The Statute became the foundation for later developments in patent law in England and elsewhere.

Important developments in patent law emerged during the 18th century through a slow process of judicial interpretation of the law. During the reign of Queen Anne, patent applications were required to supply a complete specification of the principles of operation of the invention for public access. Legal battles around the 1796 patent taken out by James Watt for his steam engine, established the principles that patents could be issued for improvements of an already existing machine and that ideas or principles without specific practical application could also legally be patented. Influenced by the philosophy of John Locke, the granting of patents began to be viewed as a form of intellectual property right, rather than simply the obtaining of economic privilege.

The English legal system became the foundation for patent law in countries with a common law heritage, including the United States, New Zealand and Australia. In the Thirteen Colonies, inventors could obtain patents through petition to a given colony's legislature. In 1641, Samuel Winslow was granted the first patent in North America by the Massachusetts General Court for a new process for making salt.

The modern French patent system was created during the Revolution in 1791. Patents were granted without examination since inventor's right was considered as a natural one. Patent costs were very high (from 500 to 1500 francs). Importation patents protected new devices coming from foreign countries. The patent law was revised in 1844 - patent cost was lowered and importation patents were abolished.

The first Patent Act of the U.S. Congress was passed on April 10, 1790, titled "An Act to promote the progress of useful Arts". The first patent was granted on July 31, 1790 to Samuel Hopkins for a method of producing potash (potassium carbonate).

Law

Effects: A patent does not give a right to make or use or sell an invention. Rather, a patent provides, from a legal standpoint, the right to *exclude others* from making, using, selling, offering for sale, or importing the patented invention for the term of the patent, which is usually 20 years from the filing date subject to the payment of maintenance fees. From an economical and practical standpoint however, a patent is better and perhaps more precisely regarded as conferring upon its proprietor "a right to *try* to exclude by asserting the patent in court", for many granted patents turn out to be invalid once their proprietors attempt to assert them in court. A patent is a limited property right the government gives inventors in exchange for their agreement to share details of their inventions with the public. Like any other property right, it may be sold, licensed, mortgaged, assigned or transferred, given away, or simply abandoned.

A patent, being an exclusionary right, does not necessarily give the patent owner the right to exploit the invention subject to the patent. For example, many inventions are improvements of prior inventions that may still be covered by someone else's patent. If an inventor obtains a patent on improvements to an existing invention which is still under patent, they can only legally use the improved invention if the patent holder of the original invention gives permission, which they may refuse.

Some countries have "working provisions" that require the invention be exploited in the jurisdiction it covers. Consequences of not working an invention vary from one country to another, ranging from revocation of the patent rights to the awarding of a compulsory license awarded by the courts to a party wishing to exploit a patented invention. The patentee has the opportunity to challenge the revocation or license, but is usually required to provide evidence that the reasonable requirements of the public have been met by the working of invention.

Enforcement

Patents can generally only be enforced through civil lawsuits (for example, for a U.S. patent, by an action for patent infringement in a United States federal court), although some countries (such as France and Austria) have criminal penalties for wanton infringement. Typically, the patent owner seeks monetary compensation for past infringement, and seeks an injunction that prohibits the defendant from engaging in future acts of infringement. To prove infringement, the patent owner must establish that the accused infringer practises all the requirements of at least one of the claims of the patent. (In many jurisdictions the scope of the patent may not be limited to what is literally stated in the claims, for example due to the *doctrine of equivalents*).

An accused infringer has the right to challenge the validity of the patent allegedly being infringed in a countersuit. A patent can be found invalid on grounds described in the relevant patent laws, which vary between countries. Often, the grounds are a subset of requirements for patentability in the relevant country. Although an infringer is generally free to rely on any available ground of invalidity (such as a prior publication, for example), some countries have sanctions to prevent the same validity questions being relitigated. An example is the UK Certificate of contested validity.

Patent licensing agreements are contracts in which the patent owner (the licensor) agrees to grant the licensee the right to make, use, sell, and/or import the claimed invention, usually in return for a royalty or other compensation. It is common for companies engaged in complex technical fields to enter into multiple license agreements associated with the production of a single product. Moreover, it is equally common for competitors in such fields to license patents to each other under cross-licensing agreements in order to share the benefits of using each other's patented inventions.

Ownership

In most countries, both natural persons and corporate entities may apply for a patent. In the United States, however, only the inventor(s) may apply for a patent although it may be assigned to a corporate entity subsequently and inventors may be required to assign inventions to their employers under an employment contract. In most European countries, ownership of an invention may pass from the inventor to their employer by rule of law if the invention was made in the course of the inventor's normal or specifically assigned employment duties, where an invention might reasonably be expected to result from carrying out those duties, or if the inventor had a special obligation to further the interests of the employer's company.

The inventors, their successors or their assignees become the proprietors of the patent when and if it is granted. If a patent is granted to more than one proprietor, the laws of the country in question and any agreement between the proprietors may affect the extent to which each proprietor can exploit the patent. For example, in some countries, each proprietor may freely license or assign their rights in the patent to another person while the law in other countries prohibits such actions without the permission of the other proprietor(s).

The ability to assign ownership rights increases the liquidity of a patent as property. Inventors can obtain patents and then sell them to third parties. The third parties then own the patents and have the same rights to prevent others from exploiting the claimed inventions, as if they had originally made the inventions themselves.

Governing Laws

The grant an enforcement of patents are governed by national laws, and also by international treaties, where those treaties have been given effect in national laws. Patents are granted by national or regional patent offices. A given patent is therefore only useful for protecting an invention in the country in which that patent is granted. In other words, patent law is territorial in nature. When a patent application is published, the invention disclosed in the application becomes prior art and enters the public domain (if not protected by other patents) in countries where a patent applicant does not seek protection, the application thus generally becoming prior art against anyone (including the applicant) who might seek patent protection for the invention in those countries.

Commonly, a nation forms a patent office with responsibility for operating that nation's patent system, within the relevant patent laws. The patent office generally has responsibility for the grant of patents, with infringement being the remit of national courts.

The authority for patent statutes in different countries varies. In the UK, substantive patent law is contained in the Patents Act 1977 as amended. In the United States, the Constitution empowers Congress to make laws to "promote the Progress of Science and useful Arts..." The laws Congress passed are codified in Title 35 of the United States Code and created the United States Patent and Trademark Office.

There is a trend towards global harmonization of patent laws, with the World Trade Organisation (WTO) being particularly active in this area. The TRIPs Agreement has been largely successful in providing a forum for nations to agree on an aligned set of patent laws. Conformity with the TRIPs agreement is a requirement of admission to the WTO and so compliance is seen by many nations as important. This has also led to many developing nations, which may historically have developed different laws to aid their development, enforcing patents laws in line with global practice.

In addition, there are international treaty procedures, such as the procedures under the European Patent Convention (EPC) [constituting the European Patent Organisation (EPOrg)], that centralize some portion of the filing and examination procedure. Similar arrangements exist among the member states of ARIPO and OAPI, the analogous treaties among African countries, and the nine CIS member states that have formed the Eurasian Patent Organisation. A key international convention relating to patents is the Paris Convention for the Protection of Industrial Property, initially signed in 1883. The Paris Convention sets out a range of basic rules relating to patents, and although the convention does not have direct legal effect in all national jurisdictions, the principles of the convention are incorporated into all notable current patent systems. The most significant aspect of the convention is the provision of the right to claim priority: filing an application in any one member state of the Paris Convention preserves the right for one year to file in any other member state, and receive the benefit of the original filing date. Another key treaty is the Patent Cooperation Treaty (PCT), administered by WIPO and covering more than 140 countries.

Application and Prosecution

A patent is requested by filing a written application at the relevant patent office. The person or company filing the application is referred to as "the applicant". The applicant may be the inventor or its assignee. The application contains a description of how to make and use the invention that must provide sufficient detail for a person skilled in the art (i.e., the relevant area of technology) to make and use the invention. In some countries there are requirements for providing specific information such as the usefulness of the invention, the best mode of performing the invention known to the inventor, or the technical problem or problems solved by the invention. Drawings illustrating the invention may also be provided.

The application also includes one or more claims that define what a patent covers or the "scope of protection".

After filing, an application is often referred to as "patent pending". While this term does not confer legal protection, and a patent cannot be enforced until granted, it serves to provide warning to potential infringers that if the patent is issued, they may be liable for damages.

Once filed, a patent application is "prosecuted". A patent examiner reviews the patent application to determine if it meets the patentability requirements of that country. If the application does not comply, objections are communicated to the applicant or their patent agent or attorney through an Office action, to which the applicant may respond. The number of Office actions and responses that may occur vary from country to country, but eventually a final rejection is sent by the patent office, or the patent application is granted, which after the payment of additional fees, leads to an issued, enforceable patent. In some jurisdictions, there are opportunities for third parties to bring an opposition proceeding between grant and issuance, or post-issuance.

Once granted the patent is subject in most countries to renewal fees to keep the patent in force. These fees are generally payable on a yearly basis. Some countries or regional patent offices (e.g. the European Patent Office) also require annual renewal fees to be paid for a patent application before it is granted.

Costs

The costs of preparing and filing a patent application, prosecuting it until grant and maintaining the patent vary from one jurisdiction to another, and may also be dependent upon the type and complexity of the invention, and on the type of patent.

The European Patent Office estimated in 2005 that the average cost of obtaining a European patent (via a Euro-direct application, i.e. not based on a PCT application) and maintaining the patent for a 10-year term was around €32,000. Since the London Agreement entered into force on May 1, 2008, this estimation is however no longer up-to-date, since fewer translations are required.

In the United States, in 2000 the cost of obtaining a patent (patent prosecution) was estimated to be from $10,000 to $30,000 per patent. When patent litigation is involved (which in year 1999 happened in about 1,600 cases compared to 153,000 patents issued in the same year), costs increase significantly: while 95% of patent litigation cases are settled out of court, but when the case reaches the court, direct legal costs of patent litigation are on average in the order of a million dollars per case, not including associated business costs.

Alternatives to Applying for a Patent

A defencive publication is the act of publishing a detailed description of a new invention without patenting it, so as to establish prior art and public identification as the creator/originator of an invention, although a defencive publication can also be anonymous. A defencive publication prevents others from later being able to patent the invention.

A trade secret is information that is intentionally kept confidential and that provides a competitive advantage to its possessor. Trade secrets are protected by nondisclosure agreements and employment law, each of which prevents information leaks such as breaches of confidentiality and corporate espionage. Compared to patents, the advantages of trade secrets are that the value of a trade secret continues until it is made public, whereas a patent is only in force for a specified time, after which others may freely copy the invention; does not require payment of fees to governmental agencies or filing paperwork; has an immediate effect; and does not require any disclosure of information to the public. The key disadvantage of a trade secret is its vulnerability to reverse engineering.

Economics

Rationale: Primary incentives embodied in the patent system include incentives to invent in the first place; to disclose the invention once made; to invest the sums necessary to experiment, produce and market the invention; and to design around and improve upon earlier patents.

1. Patents provide incentives for economically efficient research and development (R&D). A study conducted annually by the IPTS shows that the 2,000 largest global companies invested more than 430 billion euros in 2008 in their R&D departments. If the investments can be considered as inputs of R&D, real

products and patents are the outputs. Based on these groups, a project named Corporate Invention Board, had measured and analyzed the patent portfolios to produce an original picture of their technological profiles. Supporters of patents argue that without patent protection, R&D spending would be significantly less or eliminated altogether, limiting the possibility of technological advances or breakthroughs. Corporations would be much more conservative about the R&D investments they made, as third parties would be free to exploit any developments. This second justification is closely related to the basic ideas underlying traditional property rights.

2. In accordance with the original definition of the term “patent”, patents are intended to facilitate and encourage disclosure of innovations into the public domain for the common good. If inventors did not have the legal protection of patents, in many cases, they might prefer or tend to keep their inventions secret. Awarding patents generally makes the details of new technology publicly available, for exploitation by anyone after the patent expires, or for further improvement by other inventors. Furthermore, when a patent’s term has expired, the public record ensures that the patentee’s invention is not lost to humanity.
3. In many industries (especially those with high fixed costs and either low marginal costs or low reverse engineering costs — computer processors, and pharmaceuticals for example), once an invention exists, the cost of commercialization (testing, tooling up a factory, developing a market, etc.) is far more than the initial conception cost. (For example, the internal rule of thumb at several computer companies in the 1980s was that post-R&D costs were 7-to-1.) Unless there is some way to prevent copies from competing at the marginal cost of production, companies don’t invest in making the invention a product.

One effect of modern patent usage is that a small-time inventor can use the exclusive right status to become a licensor. This allows the inventor to accumulate capital from licensing the invention and may allow innovation to occur because he or she may choose not to manage a manufacturing buildup for the invention. Thus the inventor’s time and energy can be spent on pure innovation, allowing others to concentrate on manufacturability.

Another effect of modern patent usage is to both enable and incentivize competitors to design around (or to “invent around” according to R S Praveen Raj) the patented invention. This may promote healthy competition among manufacturers, resulting in gradual improvements of the technology base. This may help augment national economies and confer better living standards to the citizens. The 1970 Indian Patent Act allowed the Indian pharmaceutical industry to develop local technological capabilities in this industry. This act transformed India from a bulk importer of pharmaceutical drugs to a leading exporter. The rapid evolution of Indian pharmaceutical industry since the mid-1970s highlights the fact that the design of the patent act was instrumental in building local capabilities even in a developing country like India.

Criticism

Legal scholars, economists, scientists, engineers, activists, policymakers, industries, and trade organisations have held differing views on patents and engaged in contentious debates on the subject. Recent criticisms primarily from the scientific community focus on the core tenant of the intended utility of patents, as now some argue they are retarding innovation. Critical perspectives emerged in the nineteenth century, and recent debates have discussed the merits and faults of software patents, nanotechnology patents and biological patents.

These debates are part of a larger discourse on intellectual property protection which also reflects differing perspectives on copyright.

Copyright

Copyright is a legal right created by the law of a country, that grants the creator of an original work exclusive rights to its use and distribution, usually for a limited time, with the intention of enabling the creator (e.g. the photographer of a photograph or the author of a book) to receive compensation for their intellectual effort.

Copyright is a form of intellectual property, applicable to any expressed representation of a creative work. It is often shared, then percentage holders are commonly called rightsholders: legally, contractually and in associated "*rights*" business functions. Generally rightsholders have "the right to copy", but also the right to be credited for the work, to determine who may adapt the work to other forms, who may perform the work, who may financially benefit from it, and other related rights.

As far back as 1787, the United States Constitution provided for the protection of copyrights "to promote the Progress of Science and useful Arts." The contemporary intent of copyright is to promote the creation of new works by giving authors control of and profit from them. Copyrights are said to be territorial, which means that they do not extend beyond the territory of a specific state unless that state is a party to an international agreement. Today, however, this is less relevant since most countries are parties to at least one such agreement. While many aspects of national copyright laws have been standardized through international copyright agreements, copyright laws of most countries have some unique features. Typically, the duration of copyright is the whole life of the creator plus fifty to a hundred years from the creator's death, or a finite period for anonymous or corporate creations. Some jurisdictions have required formalities to establishing copyright, but most recognise copyright in any completed work, without formal registration. Generally, copyright is enforced as a civil matter, though some jurisdictions do apply criminal sanctions.

Most jurisdictions recognise copyright limitations, allowing "fair" exceptions to the creator's exclusivity of copyright, and giving users certain rights. The development of digital media and computer network technologies have prompted reinterpretation of these exceptions, introduced new difficulties in enforcing copyright, and inspired additional challenges to copyright law's philosophic basis. Simultaneously, businesses with great economic dependence upon copyright, such as those in the music business, have advocated the extension and expansion of their intellectual property rights, and sought additional legal and technological enforcement.

Justification

The usual justification of copyright is to enable creators of intellectual wealth to financially support themselves and give them a motive to continue publishing their creations. Without copyright, artists, authors, journalists, photographers, or anyone else who creates non-material economic wealth would have to find another way to support themselves. For example, they could publish a small subset of their creations and then request payment before they published more. In a capitalist economic system, food and housing cost money; so authors, directors, painters, photographers, poets and other creators must find other jobs to support themselves if they can't get compensated for their creative work. With copyright in place, the author of a book or the photographer of a photograph can charge users who want to get a copy of their creations and thus support themselves. Before copyright, authors generally requested a large-sum one-off payment from the printer of their book before publishing it. With copyright in place, and assuming efficient enforcement, authors, photographers and other intellectual workers can publish their creations immediately and wait for licensing requests from people who want to use or re-publish their works. Examples of this model for funding photography are Alamy, Corbis, Getty Images, and other stock photography image banks).

Anti-copyright critics claim copyright law protects corporate interests while criminalizing legitimate uses, while proponents argue the law is fair and just, protecting the interest of the creator.

History

Copyright came about with the invention of the printing press and with wider public literacy. As a legal concept, its origins in Britain were from a reaction to printers' monopolies at the beginning of the 18th century. Charles II of England was concerned by the unregulated copying of books and passed the Licensing of the Press Act 1662 by Act of Parliament, which established a register of licensed books and required a copy to be deposited with the Stationers' Company, essentially continuing the licensing of material that had long been in effect.

The British Statute of Anne (1710) further alluded to individual rights of the artist. It began, "Whereas Printers, Booksellers, and other Persons, have of late frequently taken the Liberty of Printing... Books, and other Writings, without the Consent of the Authors... to their very great Detriment, and too often to the Ruin of them and their Families:". A right to benefit financially from the work is articulated, and court rulings and legislation have recognised a right to control the work, such as ensuring that the integrity of it is preserved. An irrevocable right to be recognised as the work's creator appears in some countries' copyright laws.

Copyright laws allow products of creative human activities, such as literary and artistic production, to be preferentially exploited and thus incentivized. Different cultural attitudes, social organisations, economic models and legal frameworks are seen to account for why copyright emerged in Europe and not, for example, in Asia. In the Middle Ages in Europe, there was generally a lack of any concept of literary property due to the general relations of production, the specific organisation of literary production and the role of culture in society. The latter refers to the tendency of oral societies, such as that of Europe in the medieval period, to view knowledge as the product and expression of the collective, rather than to see it as individual property. However, with copyright laws, intellectual production comes to be seen as a product of an individual, with attendant rights. The most significant point is that patent and copyright laws support the expansion of the range of creative human activities that can be commodified. This parallels the ways in which capitalism led to the commodification of many aspects of social life that earlier had no monetary or economic value.

The Statute of Anne was the first real copyright act, and gave the publishers rights for a fixed period, after which the copyright expired. Copyright has grown from a legal concept regulating copying rights in the publishing of books and maps to one with a significant effect on nearly every modern industry, covering such items as sound recordings, films, photographs, software, and architectural works.

Prior to the passage of the United States Constitution, several states passed their own copyright laws between 1783 and 1787, the first being Connecticut. Contemporary scholars and patriots such as Noah Webster, John Trumbull (poet), and Joel Barlow were instrumental in securing the passage of these statutes.

The Copyright Clause of the United States Constitution (1787) authorized copyright legislation: "To promote the Progress of Science and useful Arts, by securing for limited Times to Authors and Inventors the exclusive Right to their respective Writings and Discoveries." That is, by guaranteeing them a period of time in which they alone could *profit* from their works, they would be enabled and encouraged to invest the time required to create them, and this would be good for society as a whole. A right to profit from the work has been the philosophical underpinning for much legislation extending the duration of copyright, to the life of the creator and beyond, to their heirs.

The original length of copyright in the United States was 14 years, and it had to be explicitly applied for. If the author wished, they could apply for a second 14 year monopoly grant, but after that the work entered the public domain, so it could be used and built upon by others.

Thomas Jefferson, who strongly advocated the ability of the public to share and build upon the works of others, proposed as part of the Bill of Rights that a short timespan be protected:

Art. 9. Monopolies may be allowed to persons for their own productions in literature and their own inventions in the arts for a term not exceeding – years but for no longer term and no other purpose.

The 1886 Berne Convention first established recognition of copyrights among sovereign nations, rather than merely bilaterally. Under the Berne Convention, copyrights for creative works do not have to be asserted or declared, as they are automatically in force at creation: an author need not "register" or "apply for" a copyright in countries adhering to the Berne Convention. As soon as a work is "fixed", that is, written or recorded on some physical medium, its author is automatically entitled to all copyrights in the work, and to any derivative works unless and until the author explicitly disclaims them, or until the copyright expires. The Berne Convention also resulted in foreign authors being treated equivalently to domestic authors, in any country signed onto the Convention. The UK signed the Berne Convention in 1887 but did not implement large parts of it until 100 years later with the passage of the *Copyright, Designs and Patents Act of 1988*. The United States did not sign the Berne Convention until 1989.

The United States and most Latin American countries instead entered into the Buenos Aires Convention in 1910, which required a copyright notice on the work (such as *all rights reserved*), and permitted signatory nations to limit the duration of copyrights to shorter and renewable terms. The Universal Copyright Convention was drafted in 1952 as another less demanding alternative to the Berne Convention, and ratified by nations such as the Soviet Union and developing nations.

The regulations of the Berne Convention are incorporated into the World Trade Organisation's TRIPS agreement (1995), thus giving the Berne Convention effectively near-global application. The 2002 WIPO Copyright Treaty enacted greater restrictions on the use of technology to copy works in the nations that ratified it.

Scope

Copyright may apply to a wide range of creative, intellectual, or artistic forms, or "works". Specifics vary by jurisdiction, but these can include poems, theses, plays and other literary works, motion pictures, choreography, musical compositions, sound recordings, paintings, drawings, sculptures, photographs, computer software, radio and television broadcasts, and industrial designs. Graphic designs and industrial designs may have separate or overlapping laws applied to them in some jurisdictions.

Copyright does not cover ideas and information themselves, only the form or manner in which they are expressed. For example, the copyright to a Mickey Mouse cartoon restricts others from making copies of the cartoon or creating derivative works based on Disney's particular anthropomorphic mouse, but does not prohibit the creation of other works about anthropomorphic mice in general, so long as they are different enough to not be judged copies of Disney's. Note additionally that Mickey Mouse is not copyrighted because characters cannot be copyrighted; rather, Steamboat Willie is copyrighted and Mickey Mouse, as a character in that copyrighted work, is afforded protection.

In many jurisdictions, copyright law makes exceptions to these restrictions when the work is copied for the purpose of commentary or other related uses. It should be noted that US copyright does NOT cover names, title, short phrases or Listings (such as ingredients, recipes, labels, or formulas). However there are protections available for those areas copyright does not cover – such as trademarks and patents.

Copyright laws are standardized somewhat through international conventions such as the Berne Convention and Universal Copyright Convention. These multilateral treaties have been ratified by nearly all countries, and international organisations such as the European Union or World Trade Organisation require their member states to comply with them.

Obtaining and Enforcing Copyright

Typically, a work must meet minimal standards of originality in order to qualify for copyright, and the copyright expires after a set period of time (some jurisdictions may allow this to be extended). Different countries impose different tests, although generally the requirements are low; in the United Kingdom there has to be some 'skill, labour, and judgment' that has gone into it. In Australia and the United Kingdom it has been held that a single word is insufficient to comprise a copyright work. However, single words or a short string of words can sometimes be registered as a trademark instead.

Copyright law recognises the right of an author based on whether the work actually is an original creation, rather than based on whether it is unique; two authors may own copyright on two substantially identical works, if it is determined that the duplication was coincidental, and neither was copied from the other.

In all countries where the Berne Convention standards apply, copyright is automatic, and need not be obtained through official registration with any government office. Once an idea has been reduced to tangible form, for example by securing it in a fixed medium (such as a drawing, sheet music, photograph, a videotape, or a computer file), the copyright holder is entitled to enforce his or her exclusive rights. However, while registration isn't needed to exercise copyright, in jurisdictions where the laws provide for registration, it serves as *prima facie* evidence of a valid copyright and enables the copyright holder to seek statutory damages and attorney's fees. (In the USA, registering *after* an infringement only enables one to receive actual damages and lost profits.)

The original holder of the copyright may be the *employer* of the author rather than the author himself, if the work is a "work for hire". For example, in English law the *Copyright, Designs and Patents Act* 1988 provides that if a copyrighted work is made by an employee in the course of that employment, the copyright is automatically owned by the employer which would be a "Work for Hire."

Copyrights are generally enforced by the holder in a civil law court, but there are also criminal infringement statutes in some jurisdictions. While central registries are kept in some countries which aid in proving claims of ownership, registering does not necessarily prove ownership, nor does the fact of copying (even without permission) necessarily prove that copyright was infringed. Criminal sanctions are generally aimed at serious counterfeiting activity, but are now becoming more commonplace as copyright collectives such as the RIAA are increasingly targeting the file sharing home Internet user. Thus far, however, most such cases against file sharers have been settled out of court. (See: Legal aspects of file sharing)

Cost of Enforcing Copyright

In most jurisdictions the copyright holder must bear the cost of enforcing copyright. This will usually involve engaging legal representation, administrative and or court costs. These costs, including time, should be taken into consideration when evaluating the benefits of enforcing copyright. In light of this, many copyright disputes are settled by a direct approach to the infringing party in order to settle the dispute out of court.

Copyright Notices in the United States

Before 1989, the use of a copyright notice – consisting of the copyright symbol (©, the letter C inside a circle), the abbreviation "Copr.", or the word "Copyright", followed by the year of the first publication of the work and the name of the copyright holder – was part of U. S. statutory requirements. Several years may be noted if the work has gone through substantial revisions. The proper copyright notice for sound recordings of musical or other audio works is a sound recording copyright symbol (!, the letter P inside a circle), which indicates a sound recording copyright, with the letter P indicating a "phonorecord". Similarly, the phrase *All rights reserved* was once required to assert copyright.

In 1989 the United States enacted the Berne Convention Implementation Act, amending the 1976 Copyright Act to conform to most of the provisions of the Berne Convention. As a result, the use of copyright notices has become optional to claim copyright, because the Berne Convention makes copyright automatic. However, the lack of notice of copyright using these marks may have consequences in terms of reduced damages in an infringement lawsuit – using notices of this form may reduce the likelihood of a defence of "innocent infringement" being successful.

"Poor Man's Copyright"

A widely circulated strategy to avoid the cost of copyright registration is referred to as the "poor man's copyright". It proposes that the creator send the work to himself in a sealed envelope by registered mail, using the postmark to establish the date. This technique has not been recognised in any published opinions of the United States courts. The United States Copyright Office makes it clear that the technique is no substitute for actual registration. The United Kingdom Intellectual Property Office discusses the technique and notes that the technique (as well as commercial registries) does not constitute dispositive proof that the work is original nor who the creator of the work is.

Exclusive Rights

Several exclusive rights typically attach to the holder of a copyright:

- to produce copies or reproductions of the work and to sell those copies (including, typically, electronic copies)
- to import or export the work
- to create derivative works (works that adapt the original work)
- to perform or display the work publicly
- to sell or cede these rights to others
- to transmit or display by radio or video.

The phrase "exclusive right" means that only the copyright holder is free to exercise those rights, and others are prohibited from using the work without the holder's permission. Copyright is sometimes called a "negative right", as it serves to *prohibit* certain people (e.g., readers, viewers, or listeners, and primarily publishers and would be publishers) from doing something they would otherwise be able to do, rather than *permitting* people (e.g., authors) to do something they would otherwise be unable to do. In this way it is similar to the unregistered design right in English law and European law. The rights of the copyright holder also permit him/her to *not* use or exploit their copyright, for some or all of the term. There is, however, a critique which rejects this assertion as being based on a philosophical interpretation of copyright law that is not universally shared. There is also debate on whether copyright should be considered a property right or a moral right.

Useful Articles

If a pictorial, graphic or sculptural work is a useful article, it is copyrighted only if its aesthetic features are separable from its utilitarian features. A useful article is an article having an intrinsic utilitarian function that is not merely to portray the appearance of the article or to convey information. They must be separable from the functional aspect to be copyrighted.

Limitations and Exceptions to Copyright

Idea–Expression Dichotomy and the Merger Doctrine: The idea–expression divide differentiates between ideas and expression, and states that copyright protects only the original expression of ideas, and not the ideas themselves. This principle, first clarified in the 1879 case of Baker v. Selden, has since been codified by the Copyright Act of 1976 at 17 U.S.C. § 102(b).

The First-Sale Doctrine and Exhaustion of Rights

Copyright law does *not* restrict the owner of a copy from reselling legitimately obtained copies of copyrighted works, provided that those copies were originally produced by or with the permission of the copyright holder. It is therefore legal, for example, to resell a copyrighted book or CD. In the United States this is known as the first-sale doctrine, and was established by the courts to clarify the legality of reselling books in second-hand bookstores. Some countries may have parallel importation restrictions that allow the copyright holder to control the aftermarket. This may mean for example that a copy of a book that does not infringe copyright in the country where it was printed does infringe copyright in a country into which it is imported for retailing. The first-sale doctrine is known as exhaustion of rights in other countries and is a principle which also applies, though somewhat differently, to patent and trademark rights. It is important to note that the first-sale doctrine permits the transfer of the particular legitimate copy involved. It does not permit making or distributing additional copies.

In addition, copyright, in most cases, does not prohibit one from acts such as modifying, defacing, or destroying his or her own legitimately obtained copy of a copyrighted work, so long as duplication is not involved. However, in countries that implement moral rights, a copyright holder can in some cases successfully prevent the mutilation or destruction of a work that is publicly visible.

Fair Use and Fair Dealing

Copyright does not prohibit all copying or replication. In the United States, the fair use doctrine, codified by the Copyright Act of 1976 as 17 U.S.C. Section 107, permits some copying and distribution without permission of the copyright holder or payment to same. The statute does not clearly define fair use, but instead gives four non-exclusive factors to consider in a fair use analysis. Those factors are:

1. the purpose and character of one's use
2. the nature of the copyrighted work
3. what amount and proportion of the whole work was taken, and
4. the effect of the use upon the potential market for or value of the copyrighted work.

In the United Kingdom and many other Commonwealth countries, a similar notion of fair dealing was established by the courts or through legislation. The concept is sometimes not well defined; however in Canada, private copying for personal use has been expressly permitted by statute since 1999. In *Alberta (Education) v. Canadian Copyright Licensing Agency (Access Copyright)*, 2012 SCC 37, the Supreme Court of Canada concluded that limited copying for educational purposes could also be justified under the fair dealing exemption. In Australia, the fair dealing exceptions under the *Copyright Act 1968* (Cth) are a limited set of circumstances under which copyrighted material can be legally copied or adapted without the copyright holder's consent. Fair dealing uses are research and study; review and critique; news reportage and the giving of professional advice (i.e. legal advice). Under current Australian law it is still a breach of copyright to copy, reproduce or adapt copyright material for personal or private use without permission from the copyright owner. Other technical exemptions from infringement may also apply, such as the temporary reproduction of a work in machine readable form for a computer.

In the United States the AHRA (Audio Home Recording Act Codified in Section 10, 1992) prohibits action against consumers making noncommercial recordings of music, in return for royalties on both media and devices plus mandatory copy-control mechanisms on recorders.

Section 1008. Prohibition on Certain Infringement Actions

No action may be brought under this title alleging infringement of copyright based on the manufacture, importation, or distribution of a digital audio recording device, a digital audio recording medium, an analog recording device, or an analog recording medium, or based on the noncommercial use by a consumer of such a device or medium for making digital musical recordings or analog musical recordings.

Later acts amended US Copyright law so that for certain purposes making 10 copies or more is construed to be commercial, but there is no general rule permitting such copying. Indeed making one complete copy of a work, or in many cases using a portion of it, for commercial purposes will not be considered fair use. The Digital Millennium Copyright Act prohibits the manufacture, importation, or distribution of devices whose intended use, or only significant commercial use, is to bypass an access or copy control put in place by a copyright owner. An appellate court has held that fair use is not a defence to engaging in such distribution.

Accessible Copies

It is legal in several countries including the United Kingdom and the United States to produce alternative versions (for example, in large print or braille) of a copyrighted work to provide improved access to a work for blind and visually impaired persons without permission from the copyright holder.

Transfer and Licensing, and Assignment

A copyright, or aspects of it, may be assigned or transferred from one party to another. For example, a musician who records an album will often sign an agreement with a record company in which the musician agrees to transfer all copyright in the recordings in exchange for royalties and other considerations. The creator (and original copyright holder) benefits, or expects to, from production and marketing capabilities far beyond those of the author. In the digital age of music, music may be copied and distributed at minimal cost through the Internet, however the record industry attempts to provide promotion and marketing for the artist and his or her work so it can reach a much larger audience. A copyright holder need not transfer all rights completely, though many publishers will insist. Some of the rights may be transferred, or else the copyright holder may grant another party a non-exclusive license to copy and/or distribute the work in a particular region or for a specified period of time.

A transfer or licence may have to meet particular formal requirements in order to be effective, for example under the Australian Copyright Act 1968 the copyright itself must be expressly transferred in writing. Under the U.S. Copyright Act, a transfer of ownership in copyright must be memorialized in a writing signed by the transferor. For that purpose, ownership in copyright includes exclusive licenses of rights. Thus exclusive licenses, to be effective, must be granted in a written instrument signed by the grantor. No special form of transfer or grant is required. A simple document that identifies the work involved and the rights being granted is sufficient. Non-exclusive grants (often called non-exclusive licenses) need not be in writing under U.S. law. They can be oral or even implied by the behaviour of the parties. Transfers of copyright ownership, including exclusive licenses, may and should be recorded in the U.S. Copyright Office. (Information on recording transfers is available on the Office's web site.) While recording is not required to make the grant effective, it offers important benefits, much like those obtained by recording a deed in a real estate transaction.

Copyright may also be licensed. Some jurisdictions may provide that certain classes of copyrighted works be made available under a prescribed statutory license (e.g. musical works in the United States used for radio broadcast or performance). This is also called a compulsory license, because under this scheme, anyone who wishes to copy a covered work does not need the permission of the copyright holder, but instead merely files the proper notice and pays a set fee established by statute (or by an agency decision under statutory guidance) for every copy made. Failure to follow the proper procedures would place the copier at risk of an infringement suit. Because of the difficulty of following every individual work, copyright collectives or collecting societies and performing rights organisations (such as ASCAP, BMI, and SESAC) have been formed to collect royalties for hundreds (thousands and more) works at once. Though this market solution bypasses the statutory license, the availability of the statutory fee still helps dictate the price per work collective rights organisations charge, driving it down to what avoidance of procedural hassle would justify.

Free Licences

There are a large number of free licenses, where users are granted several rights, for example those mention in the Free Software Definition, Open Source Definition, Debian Free Software Guidelines or Definition of Free Cultural Works. Examples of free licences are the GNU General Public License, BSD license and some Creative Commons licenses.

Founded in 2001, by James Boyle, Lawrence Lessig, and Hal Abelson the Creative Commons (CC) is a non-profit organisation which aims to facilitate the legal sharing of creative works. To this end, the organisation provides a number of copyright license options to the public, free of charge. These licenses allow copyright holders to define conditions under which others may use a work and to specify what types of use are acceptable.

Terms of use have traditionally been negotiated on an individual basis between copyright holder and potential licensee. Therefore, a general CC license outlining which rights the copyright holder is willing to waive enables the general public to use such works more freely. Six general types of CC licenses are available. These are based upon copyright holder stipulations such as whether he or she is willing to allow modifications to the work, whether he or she permits the creation of derivative works and whether he or she is willing to permit commercial use of the work. As of 2009 approximately 130 million individuals had received such licenses.

Duration

Copyright Term

Copyright subsists for a variety of lengths in different jurisdictions. The length of the term can depend on several factors, including the type of work (e.g. musical composition, novel), whether the work has been published, and whether the work was created by an individual or a corporation. In most of the world, the default length of copyright is the life of the author plus either 50 or 70 years. In the United States, the term for most existing works is a fixed number of years after the date of creation or publication. Under most countries' laws (for example, the United States and the United Kingdom), copyrights expire at the end of the calendar year in question.

The length and requirements for copyright duration are subject to change by legislation, and since the early 20th century there have been a number of adjustments made in various countries, which can make determining the duration of a given copyright somewhat difficult. For example, the United States used to require copyrights to be renewed after 28 years to stay in force, and formerly required a copyright notice upon first publication to gain coverage. In Italy and France, there were post-wartime extensions that could increase the term by approximately 6 years in Italy and up to about 14 in France. Many countries have extended the length of their copyright terms (sometimes retroactively). International treaties establish minimum terms for copyrights, but individual countries may enforce longer terms than those.

In the United States, all books and other works published before 1923 have expired copyrights and are in the public domain. In addition, works published before 1964 that did not have their copyrights renewed

28 years after first publication year also are in the public domain. Hirtle points out that the great majority of these works (including 93% of the books) were not renewed after 28 years and are in the public domain. Books originally published outside the US by non-Americans are exempt from this renewal requirement, if they are still under copyright in their home country.

But if the intended exploitation of the work includes publication (or distribution of derivative work, such as a film based on a book protected by copyright) outside the U.S., the terms of copyright around the world must be considered. If the author has been dead more than 70 years, the work is in the public domain in most, but not all, countries.

In 1998 the length of a copyright in the United States was increased by 20 years under the Copyright Term Extension Act. This legislation was strongly promoted by corporations which had valuable copyrights which otherwise would have expired, and has been the subject of substantial criticism on this point.

As a curiosity, the famous work *Peter Pan, or The Boy Who Wouldn't Grow Up* has a complex – and disputed – story of copyright expiry.

Public Domain

Copyright, like other intellectual property rights, is subject to a statutorily determined term. Once the term of a copyright has expired, the formerly copyrighted work enters the public domain and may be freely used or exploited by anyone. Courts in common law countries, such as the United States and the United Kingdom, have rejected the doctrine of a common law copyright. Public domain works should not be confused with works that are publicly available. Works posted in the internet, for example, are publicly available, but are not generally in the public domain. Copying such works may therefore violate the author's copyright.

Copyright Infringement

For a work to be considered to infringe upon copyright, its use must have occurred in a nation that has domestic copyright laws and/or adheres to a bilateral treaty or established international convention such as the Berne Convention or WIPO Copyright Treaty. Improper use of materials outside of legislation is deemed "unauthorized edition", not copyright infringement.

Copyright infringement most often occurs to software, film and music. However, infringement upon books and other text works remains common, especially for educational reasons. Statistics regarding the effects of copyright infringement are difficult to determine. Studies have attempted to determine whether there is a monetary loss for industries affected by copyright infringement by predicting what portion of pirated works would have been formally purchased if they had not been freely available. Other reports indicate that copyright infringement does not have an adverse effect on the entertainment industry, and can have a positive effect.

Industrial Design Right

An industrial design right is an intellectual property right that protects the visual design of objects that are not purely utilitarian. An industrial design consists of the creation of a shape, configuration or composition of pattern or colour, or combination of pattern and colour in three-dimensional form containing aesthetic value. An industrial design can be a two- or three-dimensional pattern used to produce a product, industrial commodity or handicraft.

Under the Hague Agreement Concerning the International Deposit of Industrial Designs, a WIPO-administered treaty, a procedure for an international registration exists. An applicant can file for a single international deposit with WIPO or with the national office in a country party to the treaty. The design will then be protected in as many member countries of the treaty as desired. Design rights started in the United Kingdom in 1787 with the Designing and Printing of Linen Act and have expanded from there.

An industrial design right can be viewed as a sui generis intellectual property right similar to copyright.

Legislation

Kenya: According to industrial property Act 2001, an industrial design is defined as "any composition of lines or colours or any three-dimensional form whether or not associated with lines or colours, provided that such composition or form gives a special appearance to a product of industry or handicraft and can serve as pattern for a product of industry or handicraft" .

An industrial design is registrable if it is new. An industrial design is deemed to be new if it has not been disclosed to the public, anywhere in the world, by publication in tangible form or, in Kenya by use or in any other way, prior to the filing date or, where applicable, the priority date of the application for registration. However a disclosure of the industrial design is not taken into consideration if it occurred not earlier than twelve months before the filing date or, where applicable, the priority date of the application and if it was by reason or in consequence of acts committed by the applicant or his predecessor in title; or an evident abuse committed by a third party in relation to the applicant or his predecessor in title.

India

India's Design Act, 2000 was enacted to consolidate and amend the law relating to protection of design and to comply with the articles 25 and 26 of TRIPS agreement. The new act, (earlier Patent and Design Act, 1911 was repealed by this act) now defines "design" to mean only the features of shape, configuration, pattern, ornament, or composition of lines or colours applied to any article, whether in two- or three-dimensional, or in both forms, by any industrial process or means, whether manual or mechanical or chemical, separate or combined, which in the finished article appeal to and are judged solely by the eye; but does not include any mode or principle of construction.

Indonesia

In Indonesia the protection of the Right to Industrial Design shall be granted for 10 (ten) years commencing from the filing date and there is not any renewal or annuity after the given period.

- Industrial Designs that are Granted Protection
  1. The Right to Industrial Design shall be granted for an Industrial Design that is novel/new
  2. An Industrial Design shall be deemed new if on the filing date, such Industrial Design is not the same as any previous disclosure.
  3. The previous disclosure as referred to in point 2 shall be one which before :
     a. The filing date or
     b. The Priority Date, if the applicant is filed with priority right.
     c. Has been announced or used in Indonesia or out side Indonesia.

An industrial design shall not be deemed to have been announced if within the period of 6 (six) months at the latest before the filing date, such industrial design

a. Has been displayed in a national or international exhibition in Indonesia or overseas that is official or deemed to be official; or,

b. Has been used in Indonesia by the designer in an experiment for the purposes of education, research or development.

Canada

Canadian law affords ten years of protection to industrial designs that are registered; there is no protection for unregistered designs. The *Industrial Design Act* defines "design" or "industrial design" to mean "features of shape, configuration, pattern or ornament and any combination of those features that, in a finished article, appeal to and are judged solely by the eye." The design must also be original: in 2012, the Patent Appeal Board rejected a design for a trash can, and gave guidance as to what the Act requires:

- The degree of originality required to register an original design is greater than that laid down by Canadian copyright legislation, but less than that required to register a patent.
- The articles being compared should not be examined side by side, but separate so that imperfect recollection comes into play.
- One is to look at the design as a whole.
- Any change must be substantial. It must not be trivial or infinitesimal.

During the existence of an exclusive right, no person can "make, import for the purpose of trade or business, or sell, rent, or offer or expose for sale or rent, any article in respect of which the design is registered." The rule also applies to kits and substantial differences are in reference to previously published designs.

Registering an industrial design in Canada may be appropriate for a variety of articles such as consumer products, vehicles, sports equipment, packaging, etc., having an original aesthetic appearance, and may even be used to protect new technologies such as electronic icons. Industrial designs can also serve to complement other forms of intellectual property rights such as patents and trade-marks.

The Canadian courts see infrequent litigation concerning industrial designs — the first case in almost two decades took place in 2012 between Bodum and Trudeau Corporation concerning visual features of double wall drinking glasses.

It is possible for a registered design to also receive protection under Canadian copyright or trademark law:

- a "useful article" (ie, one with a utilitarian function) will receive copyright protection where it is reproduced in a quantity of fifty or less, but that limitation does not apply with respect to:
  - o a graphic or photographic representation that is applied to the face of an article

  - o a trademark or a representation thereof or a label
  - o material that has a woven or knitted pattern or that is suitable for piece goods or surface coverings or for making wearing apparel
  - o a representation of a real or fictitious being, event or place that is applied to an article as a feature of shape, configuration, pattern or ornament
- where a registered design has become publicly identifiable with the product, it may be eligible for registration as a "distinguishing guise" under trademark law, but such registration cannot be used to limit the development of any art or industry.

Europe

Registered and unregistered Community designs are available which provide a unitary right covering the European Community. Protection for a registered Community design is for up to 25 years, subject to the payment of renewal fees every five years. The unregistered Community design lasts for three years after a design is made available to the public and infringement only occurs if the protected design has been copied.

United Kingdom

In addition to the design protection available under Community designs, UK law provides its own national registered design right and an unregistered design right. The unregistered right, which exists automatically if the requirements are met, can last for up to 15 years. The registered design right can last up to 25 years subject to the payment of maintenance fees. The topography of semi-conductor circuits are also covered by Integrated circuit layout design protection, a form of protection which lasts 10 years.

Japan

Article 1 of the Japanese Design Law states: "This law was designed to protect and utilise designs and to encourage creation of designs in order to contribute to industrial development". The protection period in Japan is 20 years from the day of registration.

United States

U.S. design patents last fourteen years from the date of grant and cover the ornamental aspects of utilitarian objects. Objects that lack a use beyond that conferred by their appearance or the information they convey, may be covered by copyright—a form of intellectual property of much longer duration that exists as soon as a qualifying work is created. In some circumstances, rights may also be acquired in trade dress, but trade dress protection is akin to trademark rights and requires that the design have source significance or "secondary meaning." It is useful only to prevent source misrepresentations; trade dress protection.

Australia

In Australia, design patent registration lasts for 5 years, with an option to be extended once for an additional 5 years. For the patent to be granted, a formalities exam is needed. If infringement action is to be taken, the design needs to become certified which involves a substantive examination.

Trademark

A trademark, trade mark, or trade-mark is a recognisable sign, design or expression which identifies products or services of a particular source from those of others. The trademark owner can be an individual, business organisation, or any legal entity. A trademark may be located on a package, a label, a voucher or on the product itself. For the sake of corporate identity trademarks are also being displayed on company buildings.

Usage

Trademarks are used to claim exclusive properties of products or services.

The usage of trademarks by its owner can cause legal issues if this usage makes them guilty of false advertising or if the trademark is offencive.

Trademarks can be owned, but also licensed. Many toy suppliers are licensees. For example:

- Bullyland obtained a license to produce Smurf figurines.
- The Lego Group purchased a license from Lucasfilm in order to be allowed to launch Lego Star Wars.
- TT Toys is a manufacturer of licensed ride-on replica cars for children.

The unauthorized usage of trademarks by producing and trading counterfeit consumer goods is known as brand piracy.

The owner of a trademark may pursue legal action against trademark infringement. Most countries require formal registration of a trademark as a precondition for pursuing this type of action. The United States, Canada and other countries also recognise common law trademark rights, which means action can be taken to protect an unregistered trademark if it is in use. Still common law trademarks offer the holder in general less legal protection than registered trademarks.

A Trademark may be Designated by the Following Symbols

- ™ (the "trademark symbol", which is the letters "TM", for an unregistered trademark, a mark used to promote or brand goods)
- ! (which is the letters "SM" in superscript, for an unregistered service mark, a mark used to promote or brand services)
- ® (the letter "R" surrounded by a circle, for a registered trademark)

A trademark is typically a name, word, phrase, logo, symbol, design, image, or a combination of these elements. There is also a range of non-conventional trademarks comprising marks which do not fall into these standard categories, such as those based on colour, smell, or sound (like jingles). The term *trademark* is also used informally to refer to any distinguishing attribute by which an individual is readily identified, such as the well-known characteristics of celebrities. When a trademark is used in relation to services rather than products, it may sometimes be called a service mark, particularly in the United States.

Fundamental Concepts

The essential function of a trademark is to exclusively identify the commercial source or origin of products or services, so a trademark, properly called, *indicates source* or serves as a *badge of origin*. In other words, trademarks serve to identify a particular business as the source of goods or services. The use of a trademark in this way is known as *trademark use*. Certain exclusive rights attach to a registered mark.

It should be noted that trademark rights generally arise out of the use of, or to maintain exclusive rights over, that sign in relation to certain products or services, assuming there are no other trademark objections.

Different goods and services have been classified by the International (Nice) Classification of Goods and Services into 45 Trademark Classes (1 to 34 cover goods, and 35 to 45 services). The idea behind this system is to specify and limit the extension of the intellectual property right by determining which goods or services are covered by the mark, and to unify classification systems around the world.

History

In trademark treatises it is usually reported that blacksmiths who made swords in the Roman Empire are thought of as being the first users of trademarks. Other notable trademarks that have been used for a long time include Löwenbräu, which claims use of its lion mark since 1383. The first trademark legislation was passed by the Parliament of England under the reign of King Henry III in 1266, which required all bakers to use a distinctive mark for the bread they sold.

The first modern trademark laws emerged in the late 19th century. In France the first comprehensive trademark system in the world was passed into law in 1857 with the "Manufacture and Goods Mark Act". In Britain, the 1862 Merchandise Marks Act made it a criminal offence to imitate another's trade mark 'with intent to defraud or to enable another to defraud'. In 1875 the Trade Marks Registration Act was passed which allowed formal registration of trade marks at the UK Patent Office for the first time. Registration was considered to comprise prima facie evidence of ownership of a trade mark and registration of marks began on 1 January 1876. The 1875 Act defined a registrable trade mark as 'a device, or mark, or name of an individual or firm printed in some particular and distinctive manner; or a written signature or copy of a written signature of an individual or firm; or a distinctive label or ticket'.

In the United States, Congress first attempted to establish a federal trademark regime in 1870. This statute purported to be an exercise of Congress' Copyright Clause powers. However, the Supreme Court struck down the 1870 statute in the *Trade-Mark Cases* later on in the decade. In 1881, Congress passed a new trademark act, this time pursuant to its Commerce Clause powers. Congress revised the Trademark Act in 1905. The Lanham Act of 1946 updated the law and has served, with several amendments, as the primary federal law on trademarks.

The Trademarks Act of 1938 in the United Kingdom set up the first registration system based on the "intent-to-use" principle. The Act also established an application publishing procedure and expanded the rights of the trademark holder to include the barring of trademark use even in cases where confusion remained unlikely. This Act served as a model for similar legislation elsewhere.

Oldest Registered Trademarks

The oldest registered trademark has various different claimants, enumerated below:

- United Kingdom: 1876 – The Bass Brewery's Red Triangle for ale was the first trademark to be registered under the Trade Mark Registration Act 1875.
- United States: A design mark with an eagle and a ribbon and the words "Economical, Brilliant" was the first registered trademark, filed by the Averill Chemical Paint Company on August 30, 1870 under the Trademark Act of 1870. However, in the *Trade-Mark Cases*, 100 U.S. 82 (1879), the U.S. Supreme Court held the 1870 Act to be unconstitutional. The oldest U.S. registered trademark still in use is trademark reg. no 11210, a depiction of the Biblical figure Samson wrestling a lion, registered in the United States on May 27, 1884 by the J.P. Tolman Company (now Samson Rope Technologies, Inc.), a rope-making company.
- United States: In 1923, the businessman and author Edgar Rice Burroughs registered his fictitious character Tarzan as a trademark; even after the copyright to the Tarzan story expired, his company used ownership of the trademarks relating to the character (which unlike copyrights, do not have a limited length) to control the production of media using its imagery and license the character for use in other works (such as adaptations). This practice is a precursor to the modern concept of a media franchise.

Symbols

The two symbols associated with U.S. trademarks ™ (the trademark symbol) and ® (the registered trademark symbol) represent the status of a mark and accordingly its level of protection. While ™ can be used with any common law usage of a mark, ® may only be used by the owner of a mark following registration with the relevant national authority, such as the U.S. Patent and Trademark Office (USPTO or PTO). The proper manner to display either symbol is immediately following the mark in superscript style.

Terminology

Terms such as "mark", "brand" and "logo" are sometimes used interchangeably with "trademark". "Trademark", however, also includes any device, brand, label, name, signature, word, letter, numerical, shape of goods, packaging, colour or combination of colours, smell, sound, movement or any combination thereof which is capable of distinguishing goods and services of one business from those of others. It must be capable of graphical representation and must be applied to goods or services for which it is registered. Specialised types of trademark include certification marks, collective trademarks and defencive trademarks. A trademark which is popularly used to describe a product or service (rather than to distinguish the product or services from those of third parties) is sometimes known as a genericized trademark. If such a mark becomes synonymous with that product or service to the extent that the trademark owner can no longer enforce its proprietary rights, the mark becomes generic.

A "trademark look" is an informal term for a characteristic look for a performer or character of some sort. It is usually not legally trademark protected and the term is not used in the trademark law.

Registration

The law considers a trademark to be a form of property. Proprietary rights in relation to a trademark may be established through actual use in the marketplace, or through registration of the mark with the trademarks office (or "trademarks registry") of a particular jurisdiction. In some jurisdictions, trademark rights can be established through either or both means. Certain jurisdictions generally do not recognise trademarks rights arising through use. If trademark owners do not hold registrations for their marks in such jurisdictions, the extent to which they will be able to enforce their rights through trademark infringement proceedings will therefore be limited. In cases of dispute, this disparity of rights is often referred to as "first to file" as opposed to "first to use." Other countries such as Germany offer a limited amount of common law rights for unregistered marks where to gain protection, the goods or services must occupy a highly significant position in the marketplace — where this could be 40% or more market share for sales in the particular class of goods or services.

In the United States, the registration process includes several steps. First, the trademark owner files an application to register the trademark. About three months after it is filed, the application is reviewed by an examining attorney at the U.S. Patent and Trademark Office. The examining attorney checks for compliance with the rules of the Trademark Manual of Examination Procedure. This review includes procedural matters such as making sure the applicant's goods or services are identified properly. It also includes more substantive matters such as making sure the applicant's mark is not merely descriptive or likely to cause confusion with a pre-existing applied-for or registered mark. If the application runs afoul of any requirement, the examining attorney will issue an office action requiring the applicant to address certain issues or refusals prior to registration of the mark. If the examining attorney approves the application, it will be "published for opposition." During this 30-day period third parties who may be affected by the registration of the trademark may step forward to file an Opposition Proceeding to stop the registration of the mark. If an Opposition proceeding is filed it institutes a case before the Trademark Trial and Appeal Board to determine both the validity of the grounds for the opposition as well as the ability of the applicant to register the mark at issue. Finally, provided that no third-party opposes the registration of the mark during the opposition period or the opposition is ultimately decided in the applicant's favour the mark will be registered in due course.

Outside of the United States the registration process is substantially similar to that found in the U.S. save for one notable exception in many countries: registration occurs prior to the opposition proceeding. In short, once an application is reviewed by an examiner and found to be entitled to registration a registration certificate is issued subject to the mark being open to opposition for a period of typically 6 months from the date of registration.

A registered trademark confers a bundle of exclusive rights upon the registered owner, including the right to exclusive use of the mark in relation to the products or services for which it is registered. The law in most jurisdictions also allows the owner of a registered trademark to prevent unauthorized use of the mark in relation to products or services which are identical or "colourfully" similar to the "registered" products or services, and in certain cases, prevent use in relation to entirely dissimilar products or services. The test is always whether a consumer of the goods or services will be confused as to the identity of the source or origin. An example may be a very large multinational brand such as "Sony" where a non-electronic product such as a pair of sunglasses might be assumed to have come from Sony Corporation of Japan despite not being a class of goods that Sony has rights in.

Once trademark rights are established in a particular jurisdiction, these rights are generally only enforceable in that jurisdiction, a quality which is sometimes known as territoriality. However, there is a range of international trademark laws and systems which facilitate the protection of trademarks in more than one jurisdiction.

Search

In the United States the USPTO maintains a database of registered trademarks. The database is open to the public. A licensed attorney may be required to interpret the search results. As trademarks are governed by federal law, state law, and common law, a thorough search as to the availability of a mark is very important. In the United States obtaining a trademark search and relying upon the results of an opinion issued by an attorney may insulate a trademark user from being required to pay treble damages and attorney's fees in a trademark infringement case as it demonstrates that the trademark user performed due diligence and was using the mark in good faith. The USPTO internally captures more information about trademarks than what they publicly disclose on their official search website, such as the complete contents of every logo trademark filing.

Trademarks may also be searched on third-party databases such as LexisNexis, Dialog, and Compu-Mark.

In Europe and if a community trademark has to be filed, searches have to be conducted with the OHIM (Community Trademark Office) and with the various national offices. An alternative solution is to conduct a trademark search within private databases.

Classification systems exist to help in searching for marks. One example is the "International Classification of the Figurative Elements of Marks", better known as the Vienna Classification.

Ability to Register

In most systems, a trademark can be registered if it is able to distinguish the goods or services of a party, will not confuse consumers about the relationship between one party and another, and will not otherwise deceive consumers with respect to the qualities.

Distinctive Character

Maintaining Rights: Trademarks rights must be maintained through actual lawful use of the trademark. These rights will cease if a mark is not actively used for a period of time, normally 5 years in most jurisdictions. In the case of a trademark registration, failure to actively use the mark in the lawful course of trade, or to enforce the registration in the event of infringement, may also expose the registration itself to become liable for an application for the removal from the register after a certain period of time on the grounds of "non-use". It is not necessary for a trademark owner to take enforcement action against all infringement if it can be shown that the owner perceived the infringement to be minor and inconsequential. This is designed to prevent owners from continually being tied up in litigation for fear of cancellation. An owner can at any time commence action for infringement against a third party as long as it had not previously notified the third party of its discontent following third party use and then failed to take action within a reasonable period of time (called acquiescence). The owner can always reserve the right to take legal action until a court decides that the third party had gained notoriety which the owner 'must' have been aware of. It will be for the third party to prove their use of the mark is substantial as it is the onus of a company using a mark to check they are not infringing previously registered rights. In the US, owing to the overwhelming number of unregistered rights, trademark applicants are advised to perform searches not just of the trademark register but of local business directories and relevant trade press. Specialised search companies perform such tasks prior to application.

All jurisdictions with a mature trademark registration system provide a mechanism for removal in the event of such *non use*, which is usually a period of either three or five years. The intention to use a trademark can be proven by a wide range of acts as shown in the "Wooly Bull" and *Aston v Harlee* cases.

In the U.S., failure to use a trademark for this period of time will result in *abandonment* of the mark, whereby any party may use the mark. An abandoned mark is not irrevocably in the public domain, but may instead be re-registered by any party which has re-established exclusive and active use, and must be associated or linked with the original mark owner. A mark is registered in conjunction with a description of a specific type of goods, and if the party uses the mark but in conjunction with a different type of goods, the mark may still be considered abandoned, as was the case in Lens.com, Inc. v. 1-800 Contacts, Inc.. If a court rules that a trademark has become "generic" through common use (such that the mark no longer performs the essential trademark function and the average consumer no longer considers that exclusive rights attach to it), the corresponding registration may also be ruled invalid.

Unlike other forms of intellectual property (e.g., patents and copyrights) a registered trademark can, theoretically, last forever. So long as a trademark's use is continuous a trademark holder may keep the mark registered with the U.S. Patent and Trademark Office by filing Section 8 Affidavit(s) of Continuous Use as well as Section 9 Applications for renewal, as required.

Specifically, once registered with the U.S. Patent and Trademark Office the owner of a trademark is required to file a Section 8 Affidavit of Continuous Use to maintain the registration between the 5th and 6th year anniversaries of the registration of the mark or during the 6-month grace period following the 6th-year anniversary of the registration. During this period, a trademark owner may concurrently opt to file a Section 15, Declaration of Incontestability. A mark declared incontestable is immune from future challenge, except in instances where the mark becomes generic, the mark is abandoned, or if the registration was acquired fraudulently. Note, if the Section 8 Affidavit is filed during the 6-month grace period additional fees to file the Affidavit with the U.S. Patent and Trademark Office will apply.

In addition to requirement above, U.S. trademark registrations are also required to be renewed on or about every 10-year anniversary of the registration of the trademark. The procedure for 10-year renewals is somewhat different from that for the 5th-6th year renewal. In brief, registrants are required to file both a Section 8 Affidavit of Continuous Use as well as a Section 9 Application for Renewal every ten years to maintain their registration.

Enforcing Rights

The extent to which a trademark owner may prevent unauthorized use of trademarks which are the same as or similar to its trademark depends on various factors such as whether its trademark is registered, the similarity of the trademarks involved, the similarity of the products or services involved, and whether the owner's trademark is *well known* or, under U.S. law relating to trademark dilution, *famous*.

If a trademark has not been registered, some jurisdictions (especially Common Law countries) offer protection for the business reputation or goodwill which attaches to unregistered trademarks through the tort of passing off. Passing off may provide a remedy in a scenario where a business has been trading under an unregistered trademark for many years, and a rival business starts using the same or a similar mark.

If a trademark has been registered, then it is much easier for the trademark owner to demonstrate its trademark rights and to enforce these rights through an infringement action. Unauthorized use of a registered trademark need not be intentional in order for infringement to occur, although damages in an infringement lawsuit will generally be greater if there was an intention to deceive.

For trademarks which are considered to be well known, infringing use may occur where the use occurs in relation to products or services which are not the same as or similar to the products or services in relation to which the owner's mark is registered. A growing area of law relating to the enforcement of trademark rights is secondary liability, which allows for the imputation of liability to one who has not acted directly to infringe a trademark but whose legal responsibility may arise under the doctrines of either contributory or vicarious liability.

Limits and Defences to Claims of Infringement

Trademark is subject to various defences, such as abandonment, limitations on geographic scope, and fair use. In the United States, the fair use defence protects many of the interests in free expression related to those protected by the First Amendment. Fair use may be asserted on two grounds, either that the alleged infringer is using the mark to describe accurately an aspect of its products, or that the alleged infringer is using the mark to identify the mark owner. One of the most visible proofs that trademarks provide a limited right in the U.S. comes from the comparative advertising that is seen throughout U.S. media. An example of the first type is that although Maytag owns the trademark "Whisper Quiet", makers of other products may describe their goods as being "whisper quiet" so long as these products do not fall under the same category of goods the trademark is protected under.

An example of the second type is that Audi can run advertisements saying that a trade publication has rated an Audi model higher than a BMW model, since they are only using "BMW" to identify the competitor. In a related sense, an auto mechanic can truthfully advertise that he services Volkswagens, and a former *Playboy* Playmate of the Year can identify herself as such on her website.

Wrongful or Groundless Threats of Infringement

Various jurisdictions have laws which are designed to prevent trademark owners from making wrongful threats of trademark infringement action against other parties. These laws are intended to prevent large or powerful companies from intimidating or harassing smaller companies.

Where one party makes a threat to sue another for trademark infringement, but does not have a genuine basis or intention to carry out that threat, or does not carry out the threat at all within a certain period, the threat may itself become a basis for legal action. In this situation, the party receiving such a threat may seek from the Court a declaratory judgment; also known as a declaratory ruling.

Other Aspects

Public Policy: Trademark law is designed to fulfill the public policy objective of consumer protection, by preventing the public from being misled as to the origin or quality of a product or service. By identifying the commercial source of products and services, trademarks facilitate identification of products and services which meet the expectations of consumers as to quality and other characteristics.

Trademarks may also serve as an incentive for manufacturers, providers or suppliers to consistently provide quality products or services to maintain their business reputation. Furthermore, if a trademark owner does not maintain quality control and adequate supervision in relation to the manufacture and provision of products or services supplied by a licensee, such "naked licensing" will eventually adversely affect the owner's rights in the trademark. For US law *see, ex.* Eva's Bridal Ltd. v. Halanick Enterprises, Inc. 639 F.3d 788 (7th Cir. 2011). This proposition has, however, been watered down by the judgment of the House of Lords in the case of Scandecor Development AB v. Scandecor Marketing AB et al. [2001] UKHL 21; wherein it has been held that the mere fact that a bare license (equivalent of the United States concept of a naked license) has been granted did not automatically mean that a trademark was liable to mislead.

By the same token, trademark holders must be cautious in the sale of their mark for similar reasons as apply to licensing. When assigning an interest in a trademark, if the associated product or service is not transferred with it, then this may be an "assignment-in-gross" and could lead to a loss of rights in the trademark. It is still possible to make significant changes to the underlying goods or services during a sale without jeopardizing the trademark, but companies will often contract with the sellers to help transition the mark and goods or services to the new owners to ensure continuity of the trademark.

Comparison with Patents, Designs and Copyright

While trademark law seeks to protect indications of the commercial source of products or services, patent law generally seeks to protect new and useful inventions, and registered designs law generally seeks to protect the look or appearance of a manufactured article. Trademarks, patents and designs collectively form a subset of intellectual property known as industrial property because they are often created and used in an industrial or commercial context.

By comparison, copyright law generally seeks to protect original literary, artistic and other creative works. Continued active use and re-registration can make a trademark perpetual, whereas copyright usually lasts for the duration of the author's lifespan plus 60 years for works by individuals, and some limited time after creation for works by bodies corporate. This can lead to confusion in cases where a work passes into the public domain but the character in question remains a registered trademark.

Although intellectual property laws such as these are theoretically distinct, more than one type may afford protection to the same article. For example, the particular design of a bottle may qualify for copyright protection as a non-utilitarian [sculpture], or for trademark protection based on its shape, or the 'trade dress' appearance of the bottle as a whole may be protectable. Titles and character names from books or movies may also be protectable as trademarks while the works from which they are drawn may qualify for copyright protection as a whole. Trademark protection does not apply to utilitarian features of a product such as the plastic interlocking studs on lego bricks.

Drawing these distinctions is necessary, but often challenging for the courts and lawyers, especially in jurisdictions where patents and copyrights pass into the public domain, depending on the jurisdiction. Unlike patents and copyrights, which in theory are granted for one-off fixed terms, trademarks remain valid as long as the owner actively uses and defends them and maintains their registrations with the competent authorities. This often involves payment of a periodic renewal fee. As a trademark must be used to maintain rights in relation to that mark, a trademark can be 'abandoned' or its registration can be cancelled or revoked if the mark is not continuously used. By comparison, patents and copyrights cannot be 'abandoned' and a patent holder or copyright owner can generally enforce their rights without taking any particular action to maintain the patent or copyright. Additionally, patent holders and copyright owners may not necessarily need to actively police their rights. However, a failure to bring a timely infringement suit or action against a known infringer may give the defendant a defence of implied consent or estoppel when suit is finally brought.

Like patents and copyrights, trademarks can be bought, sold, and transferred from one company or another. Unlike patents and copyrights, trademarks may not remain in tact through this process. Where trademarks have been acquired for the purpose of marketing generic (non-distinctive) products, courts have refused to enforce them.

Dilution

A trademark is *diluted* when the use of similar or identical trademarks in other non-competing markets means that the trademark in and of itself will lose its capacity to signify a single source. In other words, unlike ordinary trademark law, dilution protection extends to trademark uses that do not confuse consumers regarding who has made a product. Instead, dilution protection law aims to protect sufficiently strong trademarks from losing their singular association in the public mind with a particular product, perhaps imagined if the trademark were to be encountered independently of any product (e.g., just the word Pepsi spoken, or on a billboard). Under trademark law, dilution occurs either when unauthorized use of a mark "blurs" the "distinctive nature of the mark" or "tarnishes it."

Sale, Transfer and Licensing

In various jurisdictions a trademark may be sold with or without the underlying goodwill which subsists in the business associated with the mark. However, this is not the case in the United States, where the courts have held that this would "be a fraud upon the public". In the U.S., trademark registration can therefore only be sold and assigned if accompanied by the sale of an underlying asset. Examples of assets whose sale would ordinarily support the assignment of a mark include the sale of the machinery used to produce the goods that bear the mark, or the sale of the corporation (or subsidiary) that produces the trademarked goods.

Licensing

Licensing means the trademark owner (the licensor) grants a permit to a third party (the licensee) in order to commercially use the trademark legally. It is a contract between the two, containing the scope of content and policy. The essential provisions to a trademark license identify the trademark owner and the licensee, in addition to the policy and the goods or services agreed to be licensed.

Most jurisdictions provide for the use of trademarks to be licensed to third parties. The licensor must monitor the quality of the goods being produced by the licensee to avoid the risk of trademark being deemed abandoned by the courts. A trademark license should therefore include appropriate provisions dealing with quality control, whereby the licensee provides warranties as to quality and the licensor has rights to inspection and monitoring.

Domain Names

The advent of the domain name system has led to attempts by trademark holders to enforce their rights over domain names that are similar or identical to their existing trademarks, particularly by seeking control over the domain names at issue. As with dilution protection, enforcing trademark rights over domain name owners involves protecting a trademark outside the obvious context of its consumer market, because domain names are global and not limited by goods or service.

This conflict is easily resolved when the domain name owner actually uses the domain to compete with the trademark owner. Cybersquatting, however, does not involve competition. Instead, an unlicensed user registers a domain name identical to a trademark, and offers to sell the domain to the trademark owner. Typosquatters—those registering common misspellings of trademarks as domain names—have also been targeted successfully in trademark infringement suits. "Gripe sites", on the other hand, tend to be protected as free speech, and are therefore more difficult to attach as trademark infringement.

This clash of the new technology with preexisting trademark rights resulted in several high profile decisions as the courts of many countries tried to coherently address the issue (and not always successfully) within the framework of existing trademark law. As the website itself was not the product being purchased, there was no actual consumer confusion, and so initial interest confusion was a concept applied instead. Initial interest confusion refers to customer confusion that creates an initial interest in a competitor's "product" (in the online context, another party's website). Even though initial interest confusion is dispelled by the time any actual sales occur, it allows a trademark infringer to capitalize on the goodwill associated with the original mark.

Several cases have wrestled with the concept of initial interest confusion. In Brookfield Commc'ns v. West Coast Ent'mt the court found initial interest confusion could occur when a competitor's trademarked terms were used in the HTML metatags of a website, resulting in that site appearing in the search results when a user searches on the trademarked term. In *Playboy v. Netscape*, the court found initial interest confusion when users typed in Playboy's trademarks into a search engine, resulting in the display of search results alongside unlabelled banner ads, triggered by keywords that included Playboy's marks, that would take users to Playboy's competitors. Though users might ultimately realise upon clicking on the banner ads that they were not Playboy-affiliated, the court found that the competitor advertisers could have gained customers by appropriating Playboy's goodwill since users may be perfectly happy to browse the competitor's site instead of returning the search results to find the Playboy sites.

In Lamparello v. Falwell, however, the court clarified that a finding of initial interest confusion is contingent on financial profit from said confusion, such that, if a domain name confusing similar to a registered trademark is used for a non-trademark related website, the site owner will not be found to have infringed where they do not seek to capitalize on the mark's goodwill for their own commercial enterprises.

In addition, courts have upheld the rights of trademark owners with regard to commercial use of domain names, even in cases where goods sold there legitimately bear the mark. In the landmark decision Creative Gifts, Inc. v. UFO, 235 F.3d 540 (10th Cir. 2000) (New Mexico), defendants had registered the domain name "Levitron.com" to sell goods bearing the trademark "Levitron" under an at-will license from the trademark owner. The 10th Circuit affirmed the rights of the trademark owner with regard to said domain name, despite arguments of promissory estoppel. Most courts particularly frowned on cybersquatting, and found that it was itself a sufficiently commercial use (i.e., "trafficking" in trademarks) to reach into the area of trademark infringement. Most jurisdictions have since amended their trademark laws to address domain names specifically, and to provide explicit remedies against cybersquatters.

In the US, the legal situation was clarified by the Anticybersquatting Consumer Protection Act, an amendment to the Lanham Act, which explicitly prohibited cybersquatting. It defines cybersquatting as "(occurring) when a person other than the trademark holder registers the domain name of a well-known trademark and then attempts to profit from this by either ransoming the domain name back to the trademark holder or using the domain name to divert business from the trademark holder to the domain name holder". The provision states that "[a] person shall be liable in a civil action by the owner of the mark ... if, without regard to the goods or services of the person, that person (i) had a bad faith intent to profit from the mark ...; and registers, traffics in, or uses domain name [that is confusingly similar to another's mark or dilutes another's mark]".

This international legal change has also led to the creation of ICANN Uniform Domain-Name Dispute-Resolution Policy (UDRP) and other dispute policies for specific countries (such as Nominet UK's DRS) which attempt to streamline the process of resolving who should own a domain name (without dealing with other infringement issues such as damages). This is particularly desirable to trademark owners when the domain name registrant may be in another country or even anonymous.

Registrants of domain names also sometimes wish to register the domain names themselves (e.g., "XYZ.COM") as trademarks for perceived advantages, such as an extra bulwark against their domain being hijacked, and to avail themselves of such remedies as *confusion* or passing off against other domain holders with confusingly similar or intentionally misspelled domain names.

As with other trademarks, the domain name will not be subject to registration unless the proposed mark is actually used to identify the registrant's goods or services to the public, rather than simply being the location on the Internet where the applicant's web site appears. Amazon.com is a prime example of a protected trademark for a domain name central to the public's identification of the company and its products.

Terms which are not protectable by themselves, such as a generic term or a merely descriptive term that has not acquired secondary meaning, may become registrable when a Top-Level Domain Name (e.g. dot-COM) is appended to it. An example of such a domain name ineligible for trademark or service mark protection as a generic term, but which currently has a registered U.S. service mark, is "HEARSAY.COM".

Among trademark practitioners there remains a great deal of debate around trademark protection under ICANN's proposed generic top-level domain name space expansion. World Trademark Review has been reporting on the at times fiery discussion between trademark owners and domainers.

International Law

Although there are systems which facilitate the filing, registration or enforcement of trademark rights in more than one jurisdiction on a regional or global basis it is currently not possible to file and obtain a single trademark registration which will automatically apply around the world. Like any national law, trademark laws apply only in their applicable country or jurisdiction, a quality which is sometimes known as "territoriality".

Territorial Application

The inherent limitations of the territorial application of trademark laws have been mitigated by various intellectual property treaties, foremost amongst which is the WTO Agreement on Trade-Related Aspects of Intellectual Property Rights. TRIPS establishes legal compatibility between member jurisdictions by requiring the harmonization of applicable laws. For example, Article 15(1) of TRIPS provides a definition for "sign" which is used as or forms part of the definition of "trademark" in the trademark legislation of many jurisdictions around the world.

Madrid System

The major international system for facilitating the registration of trademarks in multiple jurisdictions is commonly known as the "Madrid system". Madrid provides a centrally administered system for securing trademark registrations in member jurisdictions by extending the protection of an "international registration" obtained through the World Intellectual Property Organisation. This international registration is in turn based upon an application or registration obtained by a trade mark applicant in its home jurisdiction.

The primary advantage of the Madrid system is that it allows a trademark owner to obtain trademark protection in many jurisdictions by filing one application in one jurisdiction with one set of fees, and make any changes (e.g. changes of name or address) and renew registration across all applicable jurisdictions through a single administrative process. Furthermore, the "coverage" of the international registration may be extended to additional member jurisdictions at any time.

INTA's Position

INTA strongly supports and encourages governments of WIPO member countries to take all action necessary to adhere to the Madrid Protocol. The Association encourages countries to optimize their trademark office operations under the harmonized registration procedures in order to reduce costs and other burdens for local and international trademark owners.

Through its advocacy strategy launched in 2006, INTA, in partnership with the USPTO, WIPO and other IP associations, has played a leading role in promoting the Madrid Protocol in Latin American countries, including Argentina, Brazil, Colombia, Nicaragua and Peru. INTA policy seminars conducted throughout the region have championed the advantages of joining the Madrid System, but also have helped identify some of the challenges that must be addressed by local authorities and IP stakeholders.

Trademark Law Treaty

The Trademark Law Treaty establishes a system pursuant to which member jurisdictions agree to standardize procedural aspects of the trademark registration process. It is not necessarily respective of rules within individual countries.

Community Trade Mark System

The Community Trade Mark (CTM) system is the trademark system which applies in the European Union, whereby registration of a trademark with the Office for Harmonization in the Internal Market (Trade Marks and Designs) (i.e. OHIM, the trademarks office of the European Union), leads to a registration which is effective throughout the EU as a whole. The CTM system is therefore said to be unitary in character, in that a CTM registration applies indivisibly across all

European Union member states. However, the CTM system did not replace the national trademark registration systems; the CTM system and the national systems continue to operate in parallel to each other.

If one resides outside the EU, they must have professional representative to the procedures before the OHIM. If they are a European resident, they don't have to have professional representation to file an opposition, however, it is strongly recommended by the OHIM.

One of the tasks of a CTM owner is the monitoring of the later applications whether any of those is similar to his/her earlier trademark. Monitoring is not easy and usually requires professional expertise. To conduct a monitoring there is the so-called Trademark Watching service where it can be checked if someone tries to get registered marks that are similar to the existing marks.

Oppositions should be filed on the standard opposition form in any official language of the European Union, however, the substantive part of the opposition (e.g. the argumentations) can be submitted only in the language of the opposed application, that is one of the working languages of the OHIM, e.g. English, Spanish, German. Worth noting that in most of the cases the opponents file their oppositions in English.

Well-Known Status

Well-known trade mark status is commonly granted to famous international trade marks in less-developed legal jurisdictions.

Pursuant to Article 6 *bis* of the Paris Convention, countries are empowered to grant this status to marks that the relevant authority considers are 'well known'. In addition to the standard grounds for trade mark infringement (same/similar mark applied same/similar goods or services, and a likelihood of confusion), if the mark is deemed well known it is an infringement to apply the same or a similar mark to dissimilar goods/services where there is confusion, including where it takes unfair advantage of the well-known mark or causing detriment to it. A well-known trademark does not have to be registered in the jurisdiction to bring a trade mark infringement action (equivalent to bringing a passing off claim without having to show goodwill and having a lesser burden of proof).

Protection of Well-Known Marks

Many countries protect unregistered well-known marks in accordance with their international obligations under the Paris Convention for the Protection of Industrial Property and the Agreement on Trade-Related Aspects of Intellectual Property Rights (the TRIPS Agreement). Consequently, not only big companies but also SMEs may have a good chance of establishing enough goodwill with customers so that their marks may be recognised as well-known marks and acquire protection without registration. It is, nevertheless, advisable to seek registration, taking into account that many countries provide for an extended protection of registered well-known marks against dilution (Art. 16.3 TRIPS), i.e., the reputation of the mark being weakened by the unauthorized use of that mark by others.

A number of trademark laws merely implement obligations under Article 16.3 of the TRIPS Agreement and protect well-known registered trademarks only under the following conditions: 1- that the goods and services for which the other mark is used or is seeking protection are not identical with or similar to the goods for which the well-known mark acquired its reputation 2- that the use of the other mark would indicate a connection between these goods and the owner of the well-known mark, and 3 - that their interests are likely to be damaged by such use.

Trade Dress

Trade dress is a legal term of art that generally refers to characteristics of the visual appearance of a product or its packaging (or even the design of a building) that signify the source of the product to consumers. Trade dress is a form of intellectual property.

United States

In the U.S., like trademarks, a product's trade dress is legally protected by the Lanham Act, the federal statute which regulates trademarks and trade dress. Trade dress protection is intended to protect consumers from packaging or appearance of products that are designed to imitate other products; to prevent a consumer from buying one product under the belief that it is another. For example, the shape, colour, and arrangement of the materials of a children's line of clothing can be protectable trade dress (though, the design of the garments themselves is not protected), as can the design of a magazine cover, the appearance and décor of a chain of Mexican-style restaurants, and a method of displaying wine bottles in a wine shop.

Statutory Source

Under section 43(a) of the Lanham Act, a product's trade dress can be protected without formal registration with the PTO. In relevant part, section 43(a) states the following:

"Any person who, on or in connection with any goods or services, or any container for goods, uses in commerce any word, term, name, symbol, or device, or any combination thereof, or any false designation of origin, false or misleading description of fact, or false or misleading representation of fact, which

(A) is likely to cause confusion, or to cause mistake, or to deceive [...] as to the origin, sponsorship, or approval of his or her goods, services, or commercial activities by another person, or

(B) in commercial advertising or promotion, misrepresents the nature, characteristics, qualities, or geographic origin of his or her or another person's goods, services, or commercial activities, shall be liable in a civil action by any person who believes that he or she is likely to be damaged by such an act."

This statute allows the owner of a particular trade dress ("container for goods") to sue an infringer (a person or entity who illegally copies that trade dress) for violating section 43(a) without registering that trade dress with any formal agency or system (unlike the registration and application requirements for enforcing other forms of intellectual property, such as patents). It is commonly seen as providing "federal common law" protection for trade dress (and trademarks).

Formal Registration

Trade dress may be registered with the United States Patent and Trademark Office (PTO) in either the Principal Register or the Supplemental Register. Although registration is not required for legal protection, registration offers several advantages. In the Principal Register, a registrant gains nationwide constructive use and constructive notice, which prevent others from using or registering that registrant's trade dress (without contesting the registration). Further, a registrant in the Principal Register gains incontestable status after five years, which eliminates many of the ways for another party to challenge the registration. Registration under the Supplemental Register allows the registrant to protect its trade dress in foreign countries, although the protections are much more limited than protections under the Principal Register in the U.S.

Legal Requirements

It can be difficult to obtain protection for trade dress, as applicants must prove that the design has secondary meaning to consumers and is then further limited by the functionality doctrine.

Functionality

To gain registration in the Principal Register or common law protection under the Lanham Act, a trade dress must not be "functional." That is, the configuration of shapes, designs, colours, or materials that make up the trade dress in question must not serve a utility or function outside of creating recognition in the consumer's mind. For example, even though consumers associated a distinct spring design for wind resistant road signs with a particular company, the spring design was not protectable for trade dress purposes because the springs served the function of withstanding heavy wind conditions.

What is considered "functional" depends upon the specific product or thing sought to be protected. For example, the colour red in a line of clothing may not be functional (and thus part of protectable trade dress) whereas the same colour on a stop sign would be functional because the colour red serves the function of putting drivers on alert (and thus would not be part of a protectable trade dress).

Distinctiveness

To gain registration in the Principal Register or common law protection under the Lanham Act, a trade dress must be "distinctive." This means that consumers perceive a particular trade dress as identifying a source of a product.

Claimed trade dress in the product design — as opposed to product packaging — context can no longer be "inherently distinctive"; it must acquire distinctiveness through "secondary meaning." Distinctiveness through secondary meaning means that although a trade dress is not distinctive on its face, the use of the trade dress in the market (the "good will" of the trade dress) has created an association between that trade dress and a source in the mind of the consumer.

Although the law is evolving, as it stands now, product packaging (including packaging in very general terms, such as a building's décor) may be inherently distinctive. However, product design, that is the design or shape of the product itself, may not be inherently distinctive, and must acquire secondary meaning to be protected.

Protection for Electronic Interfaces and Websites

Although the exact boundaries of protection are still uncertain, courts are beginning to allow trade dress protection for the overall "look and feel" of a website. In *Blue Nile, Inc. v. Ice.com, Inc.*, the plaintiff sued the defendant for copying the overall "look and feel" of plaintiff's retail jewellery websites, including the design of plaintiff's search pages. Although the court ordered more factual development before it could rule definitively on the issue, the court did hold that it was possible for the look and feel of the websites to have trade dress protection if the plaintiff's copyright claims did not already cover those parts. In *SG*

Services, Inc. v. God's Girls, Inc., the court denied trade dress protection for the plaintiff's website because the plaintiff did not demonstrate that the website was non-functional or distinctive. This case shows the court's willingness to consider trade dress protection for a website, even though the court did not find protection in this case. It is notable, however, that the *SG Services* court did not look at the overall "look and feel" of the website, but rather, at specific characteristics (such as colour) of the website that the plaintiff claimed were infringed.

Although the future of trade dress protection for websites is still very unclear, much thought has been given to this area and it will likely continue to be actively developing area for courts and litigants.

India

In view of the recent developments in trading and commercial practices and to give effect to important judicial pronouncements, a need for simplification and harmonization of trademark management systems was felt. The new *Trade Marks Act*, 1999, which came into force in September 2003 is the result of this realisation.

The new legal definition of a trade mark under the Act consists of the shape of goods, packaging or combination of colours or any combination thereof. A package is now protected under the Act, which includes any case, box container, receptacle, vessel, casket, bottle, wrapper, label, band, ticket, reel, frame, capsule, cap, lid, stopper, and cork. Thus, the new definition of trademark in India broadly encompasses almost all the elements of trade dress under the US law. Under the Indian trademark law, any distinctive and identifying mark, which is capable of distinguishing the goods and services of one owner from that of another, may be utilised as Trademark and such marks are afforded protection under the law. The Trade Marks Act, 1999 is a reproduction of the UK's Trade Marks Act 1994 as India follow the English Trade Mark laws from the beginning. Unlike the United States *Lanham Act*, 1946 the English *Trade Marks Act*, 1994 and the Indian Act, 1999 do not have provisions like section 43(a) (of *Lanham Act*) to protect unregistered trade dress or allow registration of trade dress which qualifies the tests of distinctiveness and source identifier.

United Kingdom

Trade dress can be protected as getup under the law of passing off in the UK. Passing off is a common law remedy for protecting an unregistered trademark. Getup, packaging, business strategy, marketing techniques, advertisement themes etc. can also be protected under passing off.

Trade Secret

A trade secret is a formula, practice, process, design, instrument, pattern, commercial method, or compilation of information which is not generally known or reasonably ascertainable by others, and by which a business can obtain an economic advantage over competitors or customers. In some international jurisdictions, such secrets are referred to as "confidential information", but are generally not referred to as "classified information" in the United States, since that refers to government secrets protected by a different set of laws and practices.

Definition

The precise language by which a trade secret is defined varies by jurisdiction (as do the particular types of information that are subject to trade secret protection). However, there are three factors that, although subject to differing interpretations, are common to all such definitions: a trade secret is information that:

- Is not generally known to the public;
- Confers some sort of economic benefit on its holder (where this benefit must derive *specifically* from its not being publicly known, not just from the value of the information itself);
- Is the subject of reasonable efforts to maintain its secrecy.

These three aspects are also incorporated in the TRIPS Agreement in Article 39.

By comparison, under U.S. law, "A trade secret, as defined under 18 U.S.C. § 1839(3) (A), (B) (1996), has three parts: (1) information; (2) reasonable measures taken to protect the information; and (3) which derives independent economic value from not being publicly known".

Protection

Trade secrets are by definition *not* disclosed to the world at large. Instead, owners of trade secrets seek to protect trade secret information from competitors by instituting special procedures for handling it, as well as technological and legal security measures. Legal protections include non-disclosure agreements (NDA) and non-compete clauses. In exchange for an opportunity to be employed by the holder of secrets, an employee may sign an agreement not to reveal his or her prospective employer's proprietary information. An employee may also surrender or assign to his employer the right to his own intellectual work produced during the course (or as a condition) of employment. Violation of the agreement generally carries the possibility of heavy financial penalties. These penalties operate as a disincentive to reveal trade secrets.

However, proving a breach of an NDA against a former employee who is legally working for a competitor can be very difficult. A holder of a trade secret may also require similar agreements from other parties he deals with, such as vendors or licensees.

A company can protect its confidential information through non-compete and non-disclosure contracts with its employees (within the constraints of employment law, including only restraint that is reasonable in geographic- and time-scope). The law of protection of confidential information effectively allows a perpetual monopoly in secret information – it does not expire as would a patent. The lack of formal protection, however, means that a third party is not prevented from independently duplicating and using the secret information once it is discovered.

Secret formulae are often protected by restricting the key information to a few trusted individuals. Famous examples of products protected by trade secrets are Chartreuse liqueur and Coca-Cola.

Protection of trade secret can, in principle, extend indefinitely and therefore may provide an advantage over patent protection, which lasts only for a specific period of time. Coca-Cola, for example, has no patent for its formula and has been very effective in protecting it for many more years than the twenty years of protection that a patent would have provided. In fact, Coca-Cola refused to reveal its trade secret under at least two judges' orders. The disadvantage is that there is no protection once information protected as trade secret is uncovered by others through reverse engineering, for example, whereas patent has a guaranteed time of protection in exchange for disclosing the information to the public.

Misappropriation

Companies often try to discover one another's trade secrets through lawful methods of reverse engineering or employee poaching on one hand, and potentially unlawful methods including industrial espionage on the other. Acts of industrial espionage are generally illegal in their own right under the relevant governing laws. The importance of that illegality to trade secret law is as follows: If a trade secret is acquired by improper means (a somewhat wider concept than "illegal means" but inclusive of such means), the secret is generally deemed to have been *misappropriated*. Thus if a trade secret has been acquired via industrial espionage, its acquirer will probably be subject to legal liability for acquiring it improperly. (The holder of the trade secret is nevertheless obliged to protect against such espionage to some degree in order to safeguard the secret. As noted above, under most trade secret regimes, a trade secret is not deemed to exist unless its purported holder takes reasonable steps to maintain its secrecy.)

History

Roman Law: Commentators starting with A. Arthur Schiller assert that trades secrets were protected under Roman law by a claim known as, "*actio servi corrupti*", interpreted as an "action for making a slave worse" (or an action for corrupting a servant). The Roman law is described as follows:

The Roman owner of a mark or firm name was legally protected against unfair usage by a competitor through the *actio servi corrupti* ... which the Roman jurists used to grant commercial relief under the guise of private law actions. "If, as the writer believes [writes Schiller], various private cases of action were available in satisfying commercial needs, the state was acting in exactly the same fashion as it does at the present day."

The suggestion that trade secret law has its roots in Roman law was introduced in 1929 in a *Columbia Law Review* article called "Trade Secrets and the Roman Law: The *Actio Servi Corrupti*", which has been reproduced in Schiller's, *An American Experience in Roman Law* 1 (1971). However, the University of Georgia Law School professor Alan Watson argued in *Trade Secrets and Roman Law: The Myth Exploded* that the *actio servi corrupti* was not used to protect trade secrets p. 19. Rather, he explained:

Schiller is sadly mistaken as to what was going on. ... The *actio servi corrupti* presumably or possibly could be used to protect trade secrets and other similar commercial interests. That was not its purpose and was, at most, an incidental spin-off. But there is not the slightest evidence that the action was ever so used. In this regard the *actio servi corrupti* is not unique. Exactly the same can be said of many private law actions including those for theft, damage to property, deposit, and production of property. All of these could, I suppose, be used to protect trade secrets, etc., but there is no evidence they were. It is bizarre to see any degree the Roman actio servi corrupti as the counterpart of modern law for the protection of trade secrets and other such commercial interests.

19th Century

Trade secret law as we know it today made its first appearance in England in 1817 in *Newbery v James*, and in the United States in 1837 in *Vickery v. Welch.* While those cases involved the first known common law causes of action based on a modern concept of trade secret laws, neither involved injunctive relief; rather, they involved damages only. In England, the first case involving injunctive relief came in 1820 in *Yovatt v Winyard*, while in the United States, it took until the 1866 case *Taylor v. Blanchard*.

Trade secrets law continued to evolve throughout the United States as a hodgepodge of state laws. In 1939, the American Law Institute issued the Restatement of Torts, containing a summary of trade secret laws across states, which served as the primary resource until the latter part of the century. As of 2013, however, only four states—Massachusetts, New Jersey, New York, and Texas—still rely on the Restatement as their primary source of guidance (other than their body of state case law). It has also been recently theorized that the doctrine of trade secrets should protect competitively valuable, personal information of company executives, in a concept known as "executive trade secrets".

Current Regulation

United States: Although trade secrets law evolved under state common law, prior to 1974, the question of whether patent law preempted state trade secrets law had been unanswered. In 1974, the United States Supreme Court issued the landmark decision, *Kewanee Oil Co. v. Bicron Corp.,* which resolved the question in favour of allowing the states to freely develop their own trade secret laws.

In 1979 several U.S. states adopted the Uniform Trade Secrets Act (UTSA), which was further amended in 1985, with approximately 47 states having adopted it as the basis for trade secret law. Another significant development is the Economic Espionage Act of 1996 (18 U.S.C. §§ 1831–1839), which makes the theft or misappropriation of a trade secret a federal crime. This law contains two provisions criminalizing two sorts of activity. The first, 18 U.S.C. § 1831(a), criminalizes the theft of trade secrets to benefit foreign powers. The second, 18 U.S.C. § 1832, criminalizes their theft for commercial or economic purposes. (The statutory penalties are different for the two offences.)

Commonwealth Jurisdictions

In Commonwealth common law jurisdictions, confidentiality and trade secrets are regarded as an equitable right rather than a property right (with the exception of Hong Kong where a judgment of the High Court indicates that confidential information may be a property right). The Court of Appeal of England and Wales in the case of *Saltman Engineering Co Ltd v. Campbell Engineering Ltd* held that the action for breach of confidence is based on a principle of preserving "good faith". The test for a cause of action for breach of confidence in the common law world is set out in the case of *Coco v. A.N. Clark (Engineers) Ltd*:

- The information itself must have the necessary quality of confidence about it;
- That information must have been imparted in circumstances imparting an obligation of confidence;
- There must be an unauthorized use of that information to the detriment of the party communicating it.

The "quality of confidence" highlights that trade secrets are a legal concept. With sufficient effort or through illegal acts (such as break and enter), competitors can usually obtain trade secrets. However, so long as the owner of the trade secret can prove that reasonable efforts have been made to keep the information confidential, the information remains a trade secret and generally remains legally protected. Conversely, trade secret owners who cannot evidence reasonable efforts at protecting confidential information, risk losing the trade secret, even if the information is obtained by competitors illegally. It is for this reason that trade secret owners shred documents and do not simply recycle them.

A successful plaintiff is entitled to various forms of judicial relief, including:

- An injunction
- An account of profits or an award of damages
- A declaration

Comparison to Other Types of Intellectual Property Law

In the United States, trade secrets are not protected by law in the same manner as trademarks or patents. Specifically, both trademarks and patents are protected under federal statutes, the Lanham Act and Patent Act, respectively. Instead, trade secrets are protected under state laws, and most states have enacted the Uniform Trade Secrets Act (UTSA), except for Massachusetts, New York, and North Carolina. One of the differences between patents and trademarks, on the one hand, and trade secrets, on the other, is that trade secret is protected only when the secret is *not* disclosed.

Comparison with Trademarks

To acquire rights in a trademark under U.S. law, one must simply use the mark "in commerce". It is possible to register a trademark in the United States, both at the federal and state levels. (Registration of trademarks confers some advantages, including stronger protection in certain respects, but it is not required in order to get protection.) Registration may be required in order to file a lawsuit for trademark infringement. Other nations have different trademark policies and this information may not apply to them. Assuming the mark in question meets certain other standards of protectibility, it is protected from infringement on the grounds that other uses might confuse consumers as to the origin or nature of the goods once the mark has been associated with a particular supplier. (Similar considerations apply to service marks and trade dress.) By definition, a trademark enjoys no protection (*qua* trademark) until and unless it is "disclosed" to consumers, for only then are consumers able to associate it with a supplier or source in the requisite manner. (That a company plans to *use* a certain trademark might itself be protectible as a trade secret, however, until the mark is actually made public.)

Comparison with Patents

To acquire a patent, full information about the method or product has to be supplied to the patent office and upon publication or issuance, will then be available to all. After expiration of the patent, competitors can copy the method or product legally. The temporary monopoly on the subject matter of the patent is regarded as a tradeoff for thus disclosing the information to the public.

One popular misconception held by many is that trade secret protection is incompatible with patent protection. It is typically said that if you apply for a patent you can no longer maintain a trade secret on the invention, but this is an oversimplification. It is true that in order to obtain a patent you must disclose your invention so that others will be able to both make and use the invention, and, to obtain a patent in the United States, if you have any preferences you must likewise disclose your preferences. What is typically not appreciated though is that the critical time for satisfying this disclosure requirement is at the time the application is filed. In many if not most situations, improvements will be made to an invention even after filing of the patent application, and additional information will be learned. None of this additional information must be disclosed and can instead be kept as a secret. Virtually all patent licenses include clauses that require the inventor to disclose any trade secrets they have. Frequently it is this information not disclosed in the patent that is the most commercially viable. Thus, if you are attempting to sell or license your patent rights you want to make sure that you take steps to continue to maintain your trade secrets as secrets, otherwise they will be lost.

Accordingly, before disclosing any secrets not already protected by an issued patent you should use a non-disclosure agreement.

Compared to patents, the advantages of trade secrets are that a trade secret is not limited in time (it "continues indefinitely as long as the secret is not revealed to the public", whereas a patent is only in force for a specified time, after which others may freely copy the invention), a trade secret does not imply any registration costs, has an immediate effect, does not require compliance with any formalities, and does not imply any disclosure of the invention to the public. The disadvantages of trade secrets include that "others may be able to legally discover the secret and be thereafter entitled to use it", "others may obtain patent protection for legally discovered secrets", and a trade secret is more difficult to enforce than a patent.

Objectives

The stated objective of most intellectual property law (with the exception of trademarks) is to "Promote progress." By exchanging limited exclusive rights for disclosure of inventions and creative works, society and the patentee/copyright owner mutually benefit, and an incentive is created for inventors and authors to create and disclose their work. Some commentators have noted that the objective of intellectual property legislators and those who support its implementation appears to be "absolute protection". "If some intellectual property is desirable because it encourages innovation, they reason, more is better. The thinking is that creators will not have sufficient incentive to invent unless they are legally entitled to capture the full social value of their inventions". This absolute protection or full value view treats intellectual property as another type of "real" property, typically adopting its law and rhetoric. Other recent developments in intellectual property law, such as the America Invents Act, stress international harmonization.

Financial Incentive

These exclusive rights allow owners of intellectual property to benefit from the property they have created, providing a financial incentive for the creation of an investment in intellectual property, and, in case of patents, pay associated research and development costs. Some commentators, such as David Levine and Michele Boldrin, dispute this justification.

In 2013 the United States Patent & Trademark Office approximated that the worth of intellectual property to the U.S. economy is more than US$5 trillion and creates employment for an estimated 18 million American people. The value of intellectual property is considered similarly high in other developed nations, such as those in the European Union. In the UK, IP has become a recognised asset class for use in pension-led funding and other types of business finance. However, in 2013, the UK Intellectual Property Office stated: "There are millions of intangible business assets whose value is either not being leveraged at all, or only being leveraged inadvertently".

Economic Growth

The WIPO treaty and several related international agreements are premised on the notion that the protection of intellectual property rights is essential to maintaining economic growth. The *WIPO Intellectual Property Handbook* gives two reasons for intellectual property laws:

One is to give statutory expression to the moral and economic rights of creators in their creations and the rights of the public in access to those creations. The second is to promote, as a deliberate act of Government policy, creativity and the dissemination and application of its results and to encourage fair trading which would contribute to economic and social development.

The Anti-Counterfeiting Trade Agreement (ACTA) states that "effective enforcement of intellectual property rights is critical to sustaining economic growth across all industries and globally".

Economists estimate that two-thirds of the value of large businesses in the United States can be traced to intangible assets. "IP-intensive industries" are estimated to generate 72 percent more value added (price minus material cost) per employee than "non-IP-intensive industries".

A joint research project of the WIPO and the United Nations University measuring the impact of IP systems on six Asian countries found "a positive correlation between the strengthening of the IP system and subsequent economic growth."

Economists have also shown that IP can be a disincentive to innovation when that innovation is drastic. IP makes excludable non-rival intellectual products that were previously non-excludable. This creates economic inefficiency as long as the monopoly is held. A disincentive to direct resources toward innovation can occur when monopoly profits are less than the overall welfare improvement to society. This situation can be seen as a market failure, and an issue of appropriability.

Morality

According to Article 27 of the Universal Declaration of Human Rights, "everyone has the right to the protection of the moral and material interests resulting from any scientific, literary or artistic production of which he is the author". Although the relationship between intellectual property and human rights is a complex one, there are moral arguments for intellectual property.

The arguments that justify intellectual property fall into three major categories. Personality theorists believe intellectual property is an extension of an individual. Utilitarians believe that intellectual property stimulates social progress and pushes people to further innovation. Lockeans argue that intellectual property is justified based on deservedness and hard work.

Various moral justifications for private property can be used to argue in favour of the morality of intellectual property, such as:

1. *Natural Rights/Justice Argument*: this argument is based on Locke's idea that a person has a natural right over the labour and/or products which is produced by his/her body. Appropriating these products is viewed as unjust. Although Locke had never explicitly stated that natural right applied to products of the mind, it is possible to apply his argument to intellectual property rights, in which it would be unjust for people to misuse another's ideas. Locke's argument for intellectual property is based upon the idea that labourers have the right to control that which they create. They argue that we own our bodies which are the labourers, this right of ownership extends to what we create. Thus, intellectual property ensures this right when it comes to production.
2. *Utilitarian-Pragmatic Argument*: according to this rationale, a society that protects private property is more effective and prosperous than societies that do not. Innovation and invention in 19th century America has been said to be attributed to the development of the patent system. By providing innovators with "durable and tangible return on their investment of time, labour, and other resources", intellectual property rights seek to maximize social utility. The presumption is that they promote public welfare by encouraging the "creation, production, and distribution of intellectual works". Utilitarians argue that without intellectual property there would be a lack of incentive to produce new ideas. Systems of protection such as Intellectual property optimize social utility.

3. *"Personality" Argument*: this argument is based on a quote from Hegel: "Every man has the right to turn his will upon a thing or make the thing an object of his will, that is to say, to set aside the mere thing and recreate it as his own". European intellectual property law is shaped by this notion that ideas are an "extension of oneself and of one's personality". Personality theorists argue that by being a creator of something one is inherently at risk and vulnerable for having their ideas and designs stolen and/or altered. Intellectual property protects these moral claims that have to do with personality.

Lysander Spooner (1855) argues "that a man has a natural and absolute right—and if a natural and absolute, then necessarily a perpetual, right—of property, in the ideas, of which he is the discoverer or creator; that his right of property, in ideas, is intrinsically the same as, and stands on identically the same grounds with, his right of property in material things; that no distinction, of principle, exists between the two cases".

Writer Ayn Rand argued in her book *Capitalism: The Unknown Ideal* that the protection of intellectual property is essentially a moral issue. The belief is that the human mind itself is the source of wealth and survival and that all property at its base is intellectual property. To violate intellectual property is therefore no different morally than violating other property rights which compromises the very processes of survival and therefore constitutes an immoral act.

Infringement, Misappropriation, and Enforcement

Unauthorized use of intellectual property rights, called "infringement" with respect to patents, copyright, and trademarks, and "misappropriation" with respect to trade secrets, may be a breach of civil law or criminal law, depending on the type of intellectual property, jurisdiction, and the nature of the action.

Patent infringement typically is caused by using or selling a patented invention without permission from the patent holder. The scope of the patented invention or the extent of protection is defined in the claims of the granted patent. There is safe harbor in many jurisdictions to use a patented invention for research. This safe harbor does not exist in the US unless the research is done for purely philosophical purposes, or in order to gather data in order to prepare an application for regulatory approval of a drug. In general, patent infringement cases are handled under civil law (e.g., in the United States) but several jurisdictions incorporate infringement in criminal law also (for example, Argentina, China, France, Japan, Russia, South Korea).

Copyright infringement is reproducing, distributing, displaying or performing a work, or to make derivative works, without permission from the copyright holder, which is typically a publisher or other business representing or assigned by the work's creator. It is often called "piracy". While copyright is created the instance a work is fixed, generally the copyright holder can only get money damages if the owner registers the copyright. Enforcement of copyright is generally the responsibility of the copyright holder. The ACTA trade agreement, signed in May 2011 by the United States, Japan, Switzerland, and the EU, requires that its parties add criminal penalties, including incarceration and fines, for copyright and trademark infringement, and obligated the parties to active police for infringement. There is a safe harbor to use copyrighted works under the fair use doctrine.

Trademark infringement occurs when one party uses a trademark that is identical or confusingly similar to a trademark owned by another party, in relation to products or services which are identical or similar to the products or services of the other party. As with copyright, there are common law rights protecting a trademark, but registering a trademark provides legal advantages for enforcement. Infringement can be addressed by civil litigation and, in several jurisdictions, under criminal law. In the United States, the Trademark Counterfeiting Act of 1984 criminalized the intentional trade in counterfeit goods and services and ACTA amplified the penalties.

Trade secret misappropriation is different from violations of other intellectual property laws, since by definition trade secrets are secret, while patents and registered copyrights and trademarks are publicly available. In the United States, trade secrets are protected under state law, and states have nearly universally adopted the Uniform Trade Secrets Act. The United States also has federal law in the form of the Economic Espionage Act of 1996 (18 U.S.C. §§ 1831–1839), which makes the theft or misappropriation of a trade secret a federal crime. This law contains two provisions criminalizing two sorts of activity. The first, 18 U.S.C. § 1831(a), criminalizes the theft of trade secrets to benefit foreign powers. The second, 18 U.S.C. § 1832, criminalizes their theft for commercial or economic purposes. (The statutory penalties are different for the two offences.) In Commonwealth common law jurisdictions, confidentiality and trade secrets are regarded as an equitable right rather than a property right but penalties for theft are roughly the same as the United States.

As of 2011 trade in counterfeit copyrighted and trademarked works was a $600 billion industry worldwide and accounted for 5–7% of global trade.

Criticisms

The Term Itself: Criticism of the term *intellectual property* ranges from discussing its vagueness and abstract overreach to direct contention to the semantic validity of using words like *property* in fashions that contradict practice and law. Many detractors think this term specially serves the doctrinal agenda of parties opposing reform or otherwise abusing related legislations; for instance, by associating one view with certain attitude, or disallowing intelligent discussion about specific and often unrelated aspects of copyright, patents, trademarks, etc.

Free Software Foundation founder Richard Stallman argues that, although the term *intellectual property* is in wide use, it should be rejected altogether, because it "systematically distorts and confuses these issues, and its use was and is promoted by those who gain from this confusion". He claims that the term "operates as a catch-all to lump together disparate laws [which] originated separately, evolved differently, cover different activities, have different rules, and raise different public policy issues" and that it creates a "bias" by confusing these monopolies with ownership of limited physical things, likening them to "property rights". Stallman advocates referring to copyrights, patents and trademarks in the singular and warns against abstracting disparate laws into a collective term.

Similarly, economists Boldrin and Levine prefer to use the term "intellectual monopoly" as a more appropriate and clear definition of the concept, which they argue, is very dissimilar from property rights.

Law professor, writer and political activist Lawrence Lessig, along with many other copyleft and free software activists, has criticized the implied analogy with physical property (like land or an automobile). They argue such an analogy fails because physical property is generally rivalrous while intellectual works are non-rivalrous (that is, if one makes a copy of a work, the enjoyment of the copy does not prevent enjoyment of the original). Other arguments along these lines claim that unlike the situation with tangible property, there is no natural scarcity of a particular idea or information: once it exists at all, it can be re-used and duplicated indefinitely without such re-use diminishing the original. Stephan Kinsella has objected to *intellectual property* on the grounds that the word "property" implies scarcity, which may not be applicable to ideas.

Entrepreneur and politician Rickard Falkvinge and hacker Alexandre Oliva have independently compared George Orwell's fictional dialect Newspeak to the terminology used by intellectual property supporters as a linguistic weapon to shape public opinion regarding copyright debate and DRM.

Alternative Terms

In civil law jurisdictions, intellectual property has often been referred to as intellectual rights, traditionally a somewhat broader concept that has included moral rights and other personal protections that cannot be bought or sold. Use of the term *intellectual rights* has declined since the early 1980s, as use of the term *intellectual property* has increased. Alternative terms *monopolies on information* and *intellectual monopoly* have emerged among those who argue against the "property" or "intellect" or "rights" assumptions, notably Richard Stallman. The backronyms *intellectual protectionism* and *intellectual poverty*, whose initials are also *IP*, have found supporters as well, especially among those who have used the backronym *digital restrictions management*. The argument that an intellectual property right should (in the interests of better balancing of relevant private and public interests) be termed an *intellectual monopoly privilege* (IMP) has been advanced by several academics including Birgitte Andersen and Thomas Alured Faunce.

Objections to Overbroad Intellectual Property Laws

Some critics of intellectual property, such as those in the free culture movement, point at intellectual monopolies as harming health (in the case of pharmaceutical patents), preventing progress, and benefiting concentrated interests to the detriment of the masses, and argue that the public interest is harmed by ever-expansive monopolies in the form of copyright extensions, software patents, and business method patents. More recently scientists and engineers are expressing concern that patent thickets are undermining technological development even in high-tech fields like nanotechnology.

Petra Moser has asserted that historical analysis suggests that intellectual property laws may harm innovation:

"Overall, the weight of the existing historical evidence suggests that patent policies, which grant strong intellectual property rights to early generations of inventors, may discourage innovation. On the contrary, policies that encourage the diffusion of ideas and modify patent laws to facilitate entry and encourage competition may be an effective mechanism to encourage innovation"

Peter Drahos notes, "Property rights confer authority over resources. When authority is granted to the few over resources on which many depend, the few gain power over the goals of the many. This has consequences for both political and economic freedoms with in a society." The World Intellectual Property Organisation (WIPO) recognises that conflicts may exist between the respect for and implementation of current intellectual property systems and other human rights. In 2001 the UN Committee on Economic, Social and Cultural Rights issued a document called "Human rights and intellectual property" that argued that intellectual property tends to be governed by economic goals when it should be viewed primarily as a social product; in order to serve human well-being, intellectual property systems must respect and conform to human rights laws. According to the Committee, when systems fail to do so they risk infringing upon the human right to food and health, and to cultural participation and scientific benefits. In 2004 the General Assembly of WIPO adopted *The Geneva Declaration on the Future of the World Intellectual Property Organisation* which argues that WIPO should "focus more on the needs of developing countries, and to view IP as one of many tools for development—not as an end in itself".

Further along these lines, The ethical problems brought up by IP rights are most pertinent when it is socially valuable goods like life-saving medicines are given IP protection. While the application of IP rights can allow companies to charge higher than the marginal cost of production in order to recoup the costs of research and development, the price may exclude from the market anyone who cannot afford the cost of the product, in this case a life-saving drug. "An IPR driven regime is therefore not a regime that is conductive to the investment of R&D of products that are socially valuable to predominately poor populations".

Some libertarian critics of intellectual property have argued that allowing property rights in ideas and information creates artificial scarcity and infringes on the right to own tangible property. Stephan Kinsella uses the following scenario to argue this point:

Imagine the time when men lived in caves. One bright guy—let's call him Galt-Magnon—decides to build a log cabin on an open field, near his crops. To be sure, this is a good idea, and others notice it. They naturally imitate Galt-Magnon, and they start building their own cabins. But the first man to invent a house, according to IP advocates, would have a right to prevent others from building houses on their own land, with their own logs, or to charge them a fee if they do build houses. It is plain that the innovator in these examples becomes a partial owner of the tangible property (e.g., land and logs) of others, due not to first occupation and use of that property (for it is already owned), but due to his coming up with an idea. Clearly, this rule flies in the face of the first-user homesteading rule, arbitrarily and groundlessly overriding the very homesteading rule that is at the foundation of all property rights.

Thomas Jefferson once said in a letter to Isaac McPherson on August 13, 1813:

"If nature has made any one thing less susceptible than all others of exclusive property, it is the action of the thinking power called an idea, which an individual may exclusively possess as long as he keeps it to himself; but the moment it is divulged, it forces itself into the possession of every one, and the receiver cannot dispossess himself of it. Its peculiar character, too, is that no one possesses the less, because every other possesses the whole of it. He who receives an idea from me, receives instruction himself without lessening mine; as he who lights his taper at mine, receives light without darkening me."

In 2005 the RSA launched the Adelphi Charter, aimed at creating an international policy statement to frame how governments should make balanced intellectual property law.

Another limitation of current U.S. Intellectual Property legislation is its focus on individual and joint works; thus, copyright protection can only be obtained in 'original' works of authorship. This definition excludes any works that are the result of community creativity, for example Native American songs and stories; current legislation does not recognise the uniqueness of indigenous cultural "property" and its ever-changing nature. Simply asking native cultures to 'write down' their cultural artifacts on tangible mediums ignores their necessary orality and enforces a Western bias of the written form as more authoritative.

Expansion in Nature and Scope of Intellectual Property Laws

Other criticism of intellectual property law concerns the expansion of intellectual property, both in duration and in scope.

In addition, as scientific knowledge has expanded and allowed new industries to arise in fields such as biotechnology and nanotechnology, originators of technology have sought IP protection for the new technologies. Patents have been granted for living organisms, (and in the United States, certain living organisms have been patentable for over a century).

The increase in terms of protection is particularly seen in relation to copyright, which has recently been the subject of serial extensions in the United States and in Europe. With no need for registration or copyright notices, this is thought to have led to an increase in orphan works (copyrighted works for which the copyright owner cannot be contacted), a problem that has been noticed and addressed by governmental bodies around the world.

Also with respect to copyright, the American film industry helped to change the social construct of intellectual property via its trade organisation, the Motion Picture Association of America. In amicus briefs in important cases, in lobbying before Congress, and in its statements to the public, the MPAA has advocated strong protection of intellectual-property rights. In framing its presentations, the association has claimed that people are entitled to the property that is produced by their labour. Additionally Congress's awareness of the position of the United States as the world's largest producer of films has made it convenient to expand the conception of intellectual property. These doctrinal reforms have further strengthened the industry, lending the MPAA even more power and authority.

The growth of the Internet, and particularly distributed search engines like Kazaa and Gnutella, have represented a challenge for copyright policy. The Recording Industry Association of America, in particular, has been on the front lines of the fight against copyright infringement, which the industry calls "piracy". The industry has had victories against some services, including a highly publicized case against the file-sharing company Napster, and some people have been prosecuted for sharing files in violation of copyright. The electronic age has seen an increase in the attempt to use software-based digital rights management tools to restrict the copying and use of digitally based works. Laws such as the Digital Millennium Copyright Act have been enacted, that use criminal law to prevent any circumvention of software used to enforce digital rights management systems. Equivalent provisions, to prevent circumvention of copyright protection have existed in EU for some time, and are being expanded in, for example, Article 6 and 7 the Copyright Directive. Other examples are Article 7 of the Software Directive of 1991 (91/250/EEC), and the Conditional Access Directive of 1998 (98/84/EEC). This can hinder legal uses, affecting public domain works, limitations and exceptions to copyright, or uses allowed by the copyright holder. Some copyleft licenses, like GNU GPL 3, are designed to counter that. Laws may permit circumvention under specific conditions like when it is necessary to achieve interoperability with the circumventor's program, or for accessibility reasons; however, distribution of circumvention tools or instructions may be illegal.

In the context of trademarks, this expansion has been driven by international efforts to harmonise the definition of "trademark", as exemplified by the Agreement on Trade-Related Aspects of Intellectual Property Rights ratified in 1994, which formalized regulations for IP rights that had been handled by common law, or not at all, in member states. Pursuant to TRIPs, any sign which is "capable of distinguishing" the products or services of one business from the products or services of another business is capable of constituting a trademark.

The Academy Industry Trouble Cooperation

Working for Mutual Benefit

Industry gets needed research, universities get funding, society gets new products and technology. It's a balancing act in which everyone has a shot at winning.

The number of research partnerships between corporations and universities has increased dramatically over the past 20 years. This trend has been driven in part by the steady decrease in federal funding for academic research. But a greater influence has been industry's need to remain competitive by outsourcing specific research projects to universities. To remain competitive in the global economy, it is imperative that corporations accelerate their innovation process.

Companies are able to bring their products to the market faster by forming partnerships with universities, which result in obvious benefits for both parties. The industry gains expertise in areas they need the most, and they have a hand in producing graduates who are better equipped to enter the business world. Universities gain needed funding, financial benefits, and more recognition from society. We cannot deny that industry has benefited immensely from these partnerships. But we also must address some of the basic issues that have arisen from such collaboration. Can we achieve a balance between industry's need to protect proprietary information and academia's need for disclosure? Can industry fund applied research without shortchanging academia's mission to teach basic research? Can university professors benefit from the businesses they help to establish without developing conflicts of interest?

Truces, Trade, and Technology

Industrial–academic research partnerships have become an important part of corporate R&D. Several basic trends have fuelled these alliances. They include the decrease in government funding of academic research mentioned above, an explosion in technology, a robust economy, and greater competition within industries. Over the past 20 years, all of these factors created an environment that fosters a codependency between industrial and academic research departments. The results of these partnerships are mainly positive for all parties involved; however, these alliances have also created new issues that may significantly affect the future of scientific research and education.

The United States' unprecedented period of economic expansion has been made possible by a unique combination of three powerful elements:

- The continuous expansion of world peace, manifested in the general reduction of military conflicts, and a period of expanding constructive relations among the most powerful nations in the world.
- The lowering of international trade barriers around the world.
- The technological revolution, chiefly anchored in the development of microelectronics and most visibly present in the proliferation of new information systems and novel technologies: the Internet, cell phones, handheld and laptop computers, over-the-counter diabetes tests, and laser surgery, to name a few.

These three trends have had a profound influence on our daily lives. The way we work, communicate, and interact has been changed in a manner that none of us would have dared to describe only two decades ago. Trade barriers and politics used to dictate with whom we did business. Today, we trade with and invest in countries such as Russia, Vietnam, China, Hungary, Armenia, and Latvia that only a few years ago were on our list of enemies or did not exist.

Totally new technologies emerged, and giant companies appeared with names that not long ago would have sounded like the names of board games or trendy new restaurants. New industries and professions that would not have been found in the most obscure crossword puzzles now are household names. Words like Celera, eBay, Lucent, Amazon.com, day trader, webmaster, and gene therapy are now common in our vocabulary. No one knows how long these three trends will continue or where and how we will end up. But for industrial and academic researchers, anything that starts or ends with "tech" makes us feel at home. This is the area in which we are all active, the area that we understand and can contribute to.

Bottom-Line Issues

Science and technology have an unquestionable significance in today's society. It may be difficult to make a quantitative connection between science, technology, and the economy, but the scientific community intuitively feels these connections do exist.

In a *U.S. News & World Report* interview, Michael Boskin of Stanford University estimated that half of all long-term economic growth in industrialized nations since World War II is due to technological progress (*1*). A recent BankBoston study shows that research at the Massachusetts Institute of Technology has had an enormous impact on the entire New England region. More than a thousand MIT-related companies in Massachusetts employ over 125,000 people and generate an excess of $50 billion in global sales. The same companies employ more than a quarter of a million people around the world (*2*).

In the United States, we live in an affluent society with high standards of living. Our infrastructure is intricate and sophisticated; people are well-educated; environmental laws and regulations are real and expanding. All of this makes operating and manufacturing very expensive. Although it would seem that this would also make us less competitive, we have actually become the most competitive nation in the world.

Our "new economy", marked by economic expansion, low inflation, and a tight behaviour market, is a direct result of the interplay between science, technology, and the economy. The huge improvements in productivity, driven by new technologies, are helping to keep inflation rates low in spite of tight behaviour markets. Technology has taught us to "do more with less". The productivity of American industry is increasing at a rate that future historians will probably call revolutionary, and the key role of science and technological innovation in this new phenomenon cannot be denied. There is no question that technology is a very powerful tool in keeping the United States competitive.

Staying Ahead of the Game

Today, more than ever, the only way for any American industrial organisation to stay competitive is to be more creative, more innovative, and faster than the competition. American industry needs to continuously introduce better and less expensive products and technologies, improve its business models, and become faster and more flexible in everything it does. Time has never been as important a competitive weapon as it is now. Time-to-market, speed of innovation—American industry is obsessed, and rightly so, with these concepts.

American industry focuses less on measuring the magnitude of its research investments and more on measuring their effectiveness. R&D productivity, aimed at being first to market with better products, has become a matter of survival. The new challenge for industrial R&D

organisations is to accelerate the product development process. We want to discover and create new products and technologies that will result in revolutionary changes, and we want to make them a little faster than anybody else does.

The mission of the industrial R&D laboratory has changed. It is no longer just an in-house facility where researchers develop new products for their firms. It has become the gatekeeper of technology, responsible and accountable for making companies technological leaders. The R&D department now comprises technology scouters as well as technology developers. Corporate managers are working hard to replace the old enemy, the "NIH" (not invented here) syndrome, with the "IA" (invented anywhere) attitude. It is no longer of any consequence whose invention it is as long it can make a significant impact and as long as our company is the first to commercialize it.

Who Benefits from Partnerships?

First and foremost, we in industry receive answers to problems that we are not equipped to answer ourselves. Occasionally, we encounter a specific invention or technology with significant commercial value, as we did with Dalhousie. Working with the academic community exposes industrial researchers to the most advanced technical thinking, new research trends, and novel experimental techniques. Dialogues with academic scientists also provide a way to test the validity of our own thinking and directions. We gain discussion partners who challenge our beliefs and conclusions.

The Patent and Trademark Law Amendments Act (also known as the Bayh–Dole Act of 1980) allowed private institutions to take ownership of the inventions generated from federally funded projects (*3*). This legislation, along with the mounting public pressure to demonstrate more directly the benefits of federally funded projects on civilian life, had a profound influence on academic research. The Bayh–Dole Act created a financial incentive for institutions that receive federal research funds to find commercial applications for their projects and made a clear-cut assignment for the ownership of the intellectual property. The act also gave industry a strong incentive to search for commercially valuable projects at universities.

In the past 20 years, the close collaboration between universities and industrial organisations helped develop products that affect our lives directly. In 1998, industrial–academic partnerships resulted in the introduction of 385 new technologies, including weather prediction software, faster modems, Internet search engines, and cancer treatments (*4*). Everyone has benefited from at least one of these important products.

Universities benefit from industrial funding. The percentage of funding that universities receive from industry has risen sharply, from 2.6% in 1970 to 7.1% in 1997 (*5*). The reduction of tension in the world led to a reduction in military spending and in turn to significantly reduced military-funded R&D, which has been partially replaced by industry-funded research. In 1998, colleges and universities were awarded more than 2600 patents, a 14% increase over 1997. Royalties from these inventions exceeded $576 million, up 29% from 1997 (*6*).

Industrial–academic collaboration also allows universities to better prepare their students to enter the industrial work force: obviously, a mutual benefit. By working on industry- funded projects, students gain greater and earlier exposure to marketing, manufacturing, business processes, and environmental concerns—factors that are of great importance to industry. These experiences facilitate the transition from academia to industry and increase productivity of these young people once they join an industrial organisation.

Regardless of the benefits of these partnerships, the university's main mission always has been, and will continue to be, supplying highly educated and trained people to work in government, public, and industrial institutions. Universities also act as centres of learning by providing a broad-based knowledge. None of the other benefits that we claim here will ever come close to being as important as these core missions.

Is There a Downside?

It is relatively easy to see how everyone profits from these partnerships. However, these alliances have the potential for some ill effects that we should not ignore. Let's examine some of them:

Does Industry Place Unfair Restrictions on Publishing the Results of Joint Research?

In a survey of more than 1000 technology managers and faculty in the United States, 39% reported that corporations restricted their academic partners from sharing results of their research (*7*). In another survey, Carnegie Mellon University found that more than 50% of corporations force a delay in publishing the results of joint research, and more than 33% of respondents reported that industry sometimes deletes information from papers before publication (*5*).

Universities and society in general have long benefited from the free exchange of the results of academic research. We have to ensure that advances in research are shared with our colleagues in public forums. Although industry has legitimate concerns about disclosing proprietary information, university scientists must be able to publish their findings. Restrictions and delays associated with joint publishing partnerships will eventually lead to slower rates of innovation. Currently, there are no universal standard guidelines or rules to govern this issue. Basically, it is being worked out on a case-by-case basis. But both industry and academia would benefit from clearer and more uniform rules and guidelines.

Does Industry Force Universities to De-emphasize Teaching the Basics of Scientific Research?

Industry places less importance than academia on making basic scientific discoveries. But when industries partner with universities, industries decide what type of research they should fund. Industries are not in the position of funding research that will not directly benefit their companies, even if the research would be scientifically significant. As a result, many universities are devoting less time to basic research and more time on applied research. Academic institutions should establish a clear policy for governing these issues. A well-drafted and published policy of this kind would have numerous benefits, including creating and communicating research priorities and attracting new faculty and graduate students.

The basic research that universities traditionally have performed has led to many technological breakthroughs. This process historically took 20 to 30 years, but the pace is accelerating. Basic research was crucial to important developments such as the Internet, advanced telecommunications, novel and better materials, and new drugs and medical treatments. Universities must continue to perform the research that leads to these discoveries.

Are Educators and University Researchers Forced into Conflict-of-Interest Situations?

Some academic researchers establish new companies as a result of their corporate or federally funded research. These scientists have a personal financial stake in the results of their research. Their dual roles as researchers and business people sometimes make it difficult to direct their research. Should they explore the areas where they feel an important scientific contribution is likely to be made? Or should they explore the areas that are likely to make a profit? Some universities forbid scientists to hold managerial positions in companies that they found, and some do not. We should have standardized and universal rules to deal with this very important issue.

Adding up the Balance

The expanding global economy and the ever-growing need for American industry to stay competitive create a pressure on industry to continue increasing the speed of innovations. Time-to-market is a new and a critically important competitive weapon of a modern firm. Industry relies more heavily now on the constructive engagement with universities to satisfy the need for improving the rate of developments of novel technologies and new product introductions. As the interests of universities and commercial enterprises intersect, researchers in academia and industry must ensure that the delicate balance of long-term and short-term benefits is maintained.

What are the Differences between Academia and Industry?

This piece is more for people who want to go into industry (Pharma/ Biotech) than who want to stay in academia. A large part of the ideas below is what I learned from a presentation by Dr. Bai Lu, Vice President of GlaxoSmithKline R&D China and a former professor at NIH.

1. *Product:* In academia, it is (big) papers. Publish or perish. The data in the paper have to be novel, solid, and significant. In industry, it is drugs. They need to be safe, effective, and marketable.
2. *Working style:* In academia, scientists can propose any hypothesis as long as they can convince the funding agencies for financial support. Most research projects are conducted in an independent manner or in small teams. Industry R&D projects do not have much freedom. They are mission oriented and aligned with the organisation strategic plan. Drug discovery requires more team work and collaborations among different departments. If the products show promising results or pass the mid/end review, investors will pour in more money.
3. *Relationship:* Academia has a traditional hierarchy structure. We report to our PIs, and our behaviour/performance will not affect other students or fellows. In contrast, the industry has a matrix structure. There exist both functional managers and project managers. The interactions among employees are dynamic and face lots of changes.
4. *Focus:* In academia, we are curious of how things work in the human bodies. Therefore, we focus on exploring the regulation mechanisms. Sometimes we have to create artificial conditions or assays to test functional outcome for a compelling story. The conclusions we draw may represent what actually happens or may not. In industry, the reliability of the drugs is the focus. The stakes are very high. The experiments are not to study mechanisms but to study the effects. Any details need to be documented carefully. False/bad data cannot be tolerated and are important for the team to decide whether to go on or to stop.

5. *Skills:* In academia, we value technical competencies, critical thinking, and analytical skills. In industry, communication and interpersonal skills are equally important. Team building and development is critical. Moreover, conflicts (schedule, resources) arise and need to be resolved.
6. *Project management:* the maturity level of project management in academia is much lower than in industry. For example, timelines in academia are quite flexible. Scope of a project can be changed at any time. On the other hand, in industry people strictly track milestones (e.g. using Gantt chart or critical path analysis) and don't do anything that is not necessary.

Chapter 6

Government-University-Industry

Partnerships

Since the 1970s the United States has seen the rise of various forms of collaboration among the sectors of government, academia, and industry. These forms include industry-specific inter-firm research consortia, government-industry technology transfer, and university-industry research centres. Yet the emergence of government-university-industry strategic partnerships is relatively recent, and often fostered by specific federal government programs. This new organisational form owes its development to recent trends in the U.S. research environment in industry, academia, and government.

Industrial research is facing pressures to decrease time-to-market for new inventions, and to conduct research aimed at specific, identifiable customer needs. As a result, traditional basic research activities in corporate laboratories have been scaled back. A survey conducted in 1997 by *R&D Magazine* found that much of this is directed basic research, closely linked to related applied research activities, rather than exploratory basic research aimed at the creation of new scientific knowledge.

To compensate, most U.S. firms now form extensive relationships with other organisations for research, including small businesses and universities. Partnerships are a way to identify and capture innovations produced by those organisations that have not been implemented by other companies.

The decline in federal research funding has had a great impact on universities, which are the major recipients of extramural federal research support. As a result, more universities have become interested in forming relationships with industry, such as conducting research for specific companies, housing collaborative research facilities, and licensing university inventions to firms.

The academic sector sees industry R&D funding as a potential replacement for federal funding, especially in view of the new interest among corporations in partnering with universities. Universities are also under pressure from another major funding source, the parents of undergraduate students, to address the perceived imbalance between research and teaching in academia. University administrators in turn are placing more pressure on professors to link research to their educational programs, and also to integrate real-world concerns into both teaching and research. These pressures may also force academia to become more applied in its research focus.

These developments mean that the United States government now shoulders more of the burden for funding fundamental, long-term research aimed at producing new knowledge. However, this responsibility is contradicted by calls from the Congress and from taxpayers for greater accountability for government, and formal measurements of program outcomes under the Government Performance and Results Act of 1993 (the GPRA).

One mechanism to link government R&D to tangible outcomes is to form closer relationships, including collaborative research efforts, with industrial and academic research organisations. Collaboration among these sectors brings many benefits, including:

- Sharing of risk and cost for long-term research.
- Access to complementary capabilities.
- Access to specialised skills.
- Access to new suppliers and markets.
- Access to state-of-the-art facilities.
- Creating new opportunities for technological learning.

U.S. agencies are becoming direct participants in R&D collaboration by forming partnerships between agency research facilities and external research organisations. This increase in collaboration calls for new mechanisms for R&D management that take into account the dynamics of working with extramural research organisations as partners rather than grantees or contractors.

Significance of GUI Partnerships for Innovation

Government-university-industry (GUI) strategic research partnerships represent an organisational form designed to integrate disparate pools of intellectual capital. In these cases, participants in the partnership bring to the table very different skills, capabilities, and organisational contexts. The alliance evolves into a shared community of innovation, where each participant retains the legacy of its origins, but joins a network of researchers that evolves its own common values, norms, and vocabulary. The knowledge from each organisation can then be integrated within the new context of a community of innovation, and applied by each participant toward its own learning goals.

GUI partnerships play a role of growing significance in national innovation systems. The total process model of innovation outlined by Professor Richard Rosenbloom of Harvard and Dr. William Spencer of SEMATECH emphasizes the importance of flows and linkages between firms and external sources of knowledge. As the global economy evolves toward knowledge-based competition, GUI partnerships are a mechanism for facilitating revolutionary innovation through knowledge fusion.

At the same time this diversity may mean that members lack a shared language of knowledge necessary for effective knowledge sharing. Viewed in the context of dynamic organisational learning, however, even such cultural gaps among GUISP participants can become an advantage. Organisations involved in successful strategic alliances engaged in learning not only at the level of technical knowledge, but also at the level of organisational structure, with participants adopting some of the organisational routines of their partners leading to greater efficiency in learning. Thus, as the gap in relative absorptive capacity narrows among participants in a GUI partnership, they face greater potential to experience radical changes in organisation and culture that can lead to more radical innovation.

GUI partnerships may also tend to foster the formation of trust more readily than purely private sector alliances. Multiple industry participants in a GUI partnership are not racing to gain strategic resources from the alliance, as occurs in some industry alliances. Two firms involved in a GUISP could receive the same knowledge from the partnership, but will use it to build very different firm-specific strategic capabilities. One indication of the special significance of GUI partnerships is that this new organisational form is emerging in different nations and different economies. This suggests that there are strong driving forces motivating these partnerships that are common across different national cultures, political structures, and economic systems. While GUI partnerships in different countries have certain unique characteristics shaped by their national environment, they tend to share processes and structures of membership, governance, and interaction that point to the existence of universal critical success factors which apply to all such partnerships.

Cases of Gui Strategic Research Partnerships

NSF Engineering Research Centres Program

An illustrative case of a GUI research collaboration is the Engineering Research Centres (ERC) Program administered by the U.S. National Science Foundation. The ERC program was developed based on a 1983 study by the National Academy of Engineering, initiated at the request of the NSF Director at that time, which recommended the establishment of a new cooperative program with the following two goals:

- To improve engineering research so that U.S. engineers will be better prepared to contribute to engineering practice; and
- To assist U.S. industry in becoming more competitive in world markets.

Establishment of the ERC program was motivated by the perception that significant engineering advances were occurring through the integration of new developments across traditional disciplinary boundaries, and that engineering education in universities no longer prepared students properly for the way in which engineering research was conducted in industry. This required that the centres established by the programs share the following objectives:

- Provide continual interaction of academic researchers, students, and faculty with their peers, namely, the engineers and scientists in industry, to ensure that the research programs in the centres remain relevant to the needs of the engineering practitioner and that they facilitate and promote the flow of knowledge between the academic and industrial sectors;
- Emphasize the synthesis of engineering knowledge; that is, the research programs should seek to integrate different disciplines in order to bring together the requisite knowledge, methodologies, and tools to solve problems important to engineering practitioners; and
- Contribute to the increased effectiveness of all levels of engineering education.

The ERC Program is managed out of NSF's Engineering Education and Centres (EEC) Division of the Directorate for Engineering. The ERC Program issues solicitations for the establishment of ERCs, each with a specific technological focus, such as Data Storage Systems or

Telecommunications Research. Universities submit proposals to host an ERC; these proposals are peer-reviewed by technical researchers and executives from academia and industry.

There were twenty-six ERCs in this program in 1999. Each ERC is funded by the NSF for eleven years, over which time each centre is expected to generate funding from sources outside the NSF, so that the centre is self-sufficient by the end of the grant period. To illustrate, in fiscal year 1994, the twenty-one centres then in the ERC program received \$51.7 million from the ERC Program Office; \$53.7 million from industry in cash, in-kind donations, and associated grants and contracts; and \$73.5 million from university, nonprofit, and other U.S. government sources. Each ERC forms several consortia involving university faculty, staff, and students, and multiple industrial firms (and on occasion government research facilities) to pursue specific research projects under the ERC's focus area. By this structure, projects tend to focus on more fundamental research of broad interest to industry, rather than on development of specific product technologies for individual firms.

The academic and industrial researchers exchange knowledge regarding the needs of industry in the research area, relevant developments across engineering disciplines, and the processes of academic and industrial research. The outputs of the ERCs measured by the ERC Program include the numbers of partnerships formed, patents filed and awarded, licenses granted to industry, and undergraduate and graduate degrees awarded to students involved in ERC projects.

Marco and the Focus Centre Research Program

The Microelectronics Advanced Research Corporation (MARCO) is a not-for-profit research management organisation chartered with the establishment and management of a new Focus Centre Research Program (FCRP) to fund pre-competitive, cooperative, long-range, applied microelectronics research. This initiative was launched in cooperation with the Defence Advanced Research Projects Agency (DARPA) of the U.S. Department of Defence, the Semiconductor Industry Association, and SEMI/SEMATECH, an organisation of semiconductor equipment manufacturers.

The FCRP concentrates on technical challenges very different from those addressed by firms and other organisations in the semiconductor industry. The parameters these challenges must meet include:

- Emphasis on the elimination of barriers via more revolutionary approaches, paradigm shifts, and the creation of multiple options.

- Long-range (beyond eight years to commercialization) research.
- Broader, less granular objectives.
- Fewer industrial business practices applied.
- Heavy emphasis on research efforts with faculty, post-docs, visiting scientists, and students.

The Focus Centres funded by the program will be virtual (or distributed) centres that span multiple universities. This will tap the best expertise across many institutions in order to build the greatest overall capability in a particular technology area. Rather than depending on only one institution to manage research in a given technology area, the FCRP will create communities of innovation linking researchers at multiple universities. The research will be long-range but still linked directly to industry imperatives by setting priorities through the National Technology Roadmap for Semiconductors, an industry-wide strategic-planning process. Industry and government support can lead to direct interaction between the university researchers and the end-users of the knowledge generated under the FCRP, contributing to a common view of technical challenges and wider dissemination of new knowledge.

MEDEA

The Microelectronics Development for European Applications (MEDEA) initiative, based in Paris, was launched on July 1, 1996 as a collaborative project under the EUREKA program. The initiative integrates microelectronics into application systems to foster the market-oriented and industry-driven needs of the electronics systems industry. Funding for MEDEA projects is split between the European Union Commission, the member states, and firms, with participating firms providing at least 50 percent of the program's budget. These member nations are Germany, France, The Netherlands, Italy, Belgium, and Austria. Nearly two-thirds of MEDEA funding will support development of applications. The MEDEA structure ensures that governmental decision making on research priorities supports the needs of industry, cementing the link between the two through its cost-sharing requirements. Also, the moderate subsidy from the European Commission leverages that investment across national borders, encouraging further collaborative research. By involving multiple firms, universities, and research institutions in MEDEA, the program can facilitate the wide diffusion of new innovations.

The Fraunhofer Gesellschaft

The leading organisation focused on applied research in Germany is the Fraunhofer Gesellschaft (FhG) and its 47 worldwide institutes.

Founded in 1949, FhG conducts applied research for industry on a contract basis, using the facilities and personnel of regional polytechnics or universities. By forging a stronger bond between academia and business, FhG aims to speed the commercial application of new technologies. The institutes receive all their financial support from industry and the German government, both paying equal shares. All contracts must be worth at least DM100,000 to receive government support. Furthermore, the exact level of funding is dependent upon the technical and economic risks of the proposal. Finally, the projects must be perceived as potentially profitable.

The FhG, as a contract research body partnering with sources of research capabilities, serves as a neutral organisation for coordinating flows of knowledge among and between its clients and research affiliates. The Institutes of the FhG themselves comprise the transorganisational knowledge management infrastructure for each technical field by managing the interactions between diverse research partners. The FhG also has the influence to spark learning in a GUI setting through this interaction.

Lessons Learned about Gui Partnership Management

A cross-sectional analysis of empirical findings from representative case studies fields a preliminary list of key considerations and respective strategic management skills that firms must develop to participate in useful GUI alliances.

Leadership and Authority

A GUI alliance also requires the identification of a lead player who has the authority and legitimacy to make fundamental decisions about the direction of the alliance and its operations. Although the lead player must enjoy the support and confidence of the other partners in the alliance, that entity must also be able to act without requiring the unanimous consent of the entire alliance for every operational decision.

GUI alliances operating as pure democracies will tend to degenerate into factions, due to the polarizing differences in organisational objectives among the partners. Often, the lead player emerges due to personalities and individual roles, not at the organisational level. For example, one GUI alliance organised under a Defence Department program ended up with a leader whose technical expertise garnered the respect of other researchers in the alliance, but whose organisational position also provided him with the authority and influence to work the management structures of the different partners.

Allocation of Benefits

A key issue for GUI alliance management is the creation of processes for the fair and appropriate allocation of the benefits from the alliances to the various partners. The most critical aspect of this is in the division of intellectual property rights from research.

A major stumbling block to numerous GUI alliances is the fundamental contradiction between the importance of well-defined and protected rights for industry partners, and the desire for the open dissemination of information by researchers. Today, the success of university technology transfer also means that some academic partners may want to own some of the IPRs that they can then market to outside organisations. For example, agreements that require universities to assign all patent rights from an alliance to the industry members will cause universities to at least hesitate, and often to refuse participation in an alliance. Creating processes for distributing these benefits to satisfy all partners is more art than science, given the competing priorities of the partners.

Stakeholder Management

Related to the above point, firms that take a lead role in GUI alliances must be skilled at stakeholder management, especially in answering the concerns of stakeholders who are not direct members of the alliance. For example, one GUI alliance sponsored by the Defence Department required the lead industry partner to take into consideration how to communicate the benefits of the alliance to Congress. This helped to assure the alliance of continued funding with minimal interference from the oversight committees involved in national security.

Life-Cycle Management

Since GUI alliances are dynamic entities, industry participants must be sensitive to how the alliance and each of its members evolves over time, and how that evolution may change the motivations for the alliance. For example, alliances must have clear processes for members to enter and exit as needed, as the alliance expands or moves into new areas and away from old ones. Also, firms must recognise that GUI alliances in general are highly situation-specific.

Changes in the underlying conditions of the alliance may render the alliance obsolete or moot. Therefore, alliances must also be managed as a dynamic, evolutionary process, with the clear recognition up-front that the alliance may outlive its usefulness and therefore must have processes in place for the graceful termination of the alliance at such a time.

Using a framework developed by Carayannis and Alexander (1998), GUI partnerships can be categorized along four variables:

- R&D Agreement (R&DA), structured as a grant, cooperative agreement, or contract;
- R&D Focus (R&DF), looking at the time-frame and nature of research outputs;
- R&D Performer (R&DP), where research is primarily conducted (among university, industry, government, or other organisations);
- R&D Location (R&DL), at the program and project levels, in terms of geographic location and organisational location (centralized or decentralized).

The resulting categorization is shown in Table 2. This analysis shows that among these three examples, GUI partnerships are intended to leverage the capabilities and resources of different research performers to address research agendas of varying time horizons and using a range of governance mechanisms. The key design issue in structuring GUI partnerships is matching the governance mechanisms, and in particular the interface mechanisms for facilitating knowledge transfer, with the capabilities and research focus of the partnership.

Some pertinent factors to consider in the structure of GUI partnerships are the differing time horizons and cultures of partners from government, university, and industry. These examples of GUI collaborations raise two significant points about this new mode of research support and conduct.

First, global pressures on national and corporate innovation provide a common motivation for the formation of the collaborative efforts, indicating that the

	ERCs	*MARCO*	*MEDEA*	*FhG*
R&DA	Cooperative Agreement	Cooperative Agreement	Cooperative Agreement	Contract
R&DF	Long-range, applied	Long-range, basic	Medium-range, applied	Short-to-medium range, applied
R&DP	Primarily university	Primarily university	Primarily industry	For-profit independent institutes
D&DL: program project	US-centered Centralized	US-centered Distributed	EU-centered Distributed	Global Centralized

Globalization of R&D has a comparable impact across nations. Implementing transorganisational knowledge management through GUI partnerships will reengineer some aspects of the national science and engineering enterprise, as barriers to knowledge sharing across economic sectors are broken down through repeated instances of collaboration. Second, the design of GUI partnerships and their intelligent transorganisational knowledge interfaces is influenced by the past history and current structure of the science and engineering enterprise in each company. Therefore, cross-national comparisons are some-what difficult, as knowledge-management practices in one culture may not apply in another setting. This suggests that further research is necessary to understand the extent to which GUI partnerships are a tool for international as well as national transorganisational innovation.

The lessons learned from GUI partnerships show that there are distinct skill sets that firms must develop if they are to derive the full benefits of the alliances from participation. GUI strategic R&D alliances constitute an ongoing process of learning, introspection, and discovery. Case studies of GUI partnerships can show the importance of learning proper alliance management skills to firm success, particularly given the specific pressures and dynamics introduced by knowledge-based competition. It can also show how these alliances are useful tools in initiating and accelerating learning at all levels within and across organisations, enabling firms to maneuver more nimbly in the complete game of business. For these partnerships to contribute effectively to firm-level and national competitiveness and innovation, the participants must develop new competencies in the mechanisms and processes for managing GUI partnerships, which are different from other forms of inter-organisational alliances.

Research in India

India and Innovation

For over four decades since independence, Indian companies had very little appetite for innovation. The well-known epitome of this lack of innovation was the Hindustan Motor's Ambassador car. Operating in a largely protected market, Indian companies invested very little in R&D, technology development, new product introduction etc. Technology licensing from abroad was the preferred route to acquire technology. Foreign firms who wished to enter the Indian market had to opt for joint venture or technology licensing. In addition, capacity licensing, which required that a producer should hold a licence to manufacture, further limited the competition in the Indian market and hence the motivation to innovate.

Pursuant to the Government of India's policy of liberalization in the early 1990s, the protected markets became open to competition. New technologies, products, services, processes and business models started flowing into the Indian market. Licensing new technology became difficult under the liberalized regime because the owners of technology no longer needed an Indian partner to access the Indian market; they could do it on their own. As noted above, the licence raj had prevented the creation of new capacity in production, so that whoever had the licence to produce monopolized the markets. Once licence raj was dismantled, creation of new capacity within the country became possible, leading to further competition in the domestic market.

Faced with competition, Indian companies have been forced to innovate in the liberalized era. It is indeed a matter of pride that, over the years, India has attained considerable success in building an environment conducive to innovation. Indian companies have competed successfully, not only in the domestic market, but also in the global market in several fields. The size and number of Indian investments and acquisitions abroad have steadily grown during recent years. Examples include Tata's acquisition of Tetley Tea (2001), Corus (2007), Jaguar (2007); Hindalco's acquisition of Novelis, Canada and so on. There are many more examples.

A recent study found that many companies and technology leaders considered India as the second most attractive country (after USA) on "the best place to innovate". The potential and inevitability of India becoming a global innovator has become a topic of active discussion in recent years. Several reports indicate that India is emerging as an important innovator, though still performing below its potential.

What is Innovation?

Stanford Professor, Robert A Burgelman describes innovation as any new product, service, production system or delivery system. One could also add new business models to this list. Innovation is different from an invention or a discovery, where the focus is limited to inventing the new or discovering the unknown. Innovation puts inventions and discoveries to practical use, economically.

An inventor is successful once the invention works, but the innovator is successful only if such working has economic value. According to the Economist, "An invention that costs US$1,000 to make can easily cost US$10 million to turn into an innovation".

Thus the key attribute of an innovation is its ability to create economic value. In other words, an innovation has to prove its worth in the marketplace. The owner of the innovation derives a competitive advantage and hence innovation is an important component of competitive strategy. This has long been realised by organisations competing in the free market. It is hence little wonder that Indian companies too have realised the need for innovation in the liberalized era.

Since Information Technology industry is of specific interest to India, it will be worthwhile to consider the growth of innovation in this sector. Between 1985 and 1991, Indian IT companies were largely performing body shopping (i.e. placing software programmers abroad) and had little understanding of even what these programmers were doing in the companies where they were placed. During the 1990s, parts of the work were brought to India using satellite communication, but there was still little scope for innovation.

The Y2K software problem (the problem feared to be precipitated in the year 2000, because of the use of two digits instead of four, in the year field in many computer applications), offered a major opportunity for the Indian IT industry to demonstrate its capability and to gain international trust as dependable source of IT solutions. The growth of ecommerce and dot com during the second half of 90s also saw many technologists of Indian origin emerge as successful entrepreneurs, venture capitalists and angels in the Silicon Valley and elsewhere.

Post Y2K, Indian IT companies started gaining increased acceptance as being capable of performing original work, especially product development. The growth of Indian market for Information technology also led to innovative products and services being produced by Indian IT companies.

All the leading Information Technology companies in India are now paying increasingly closer attention to innovation. India's biggest IT company, Tata Consultancy Services defines innovation as, "an idea that makes a material difference to an organisation's current capabilities or creates a future capability". TCS follows the broad 3-way segmentation suggested by Harvard Business School professor, Prof. Clayton Christensen:

1. Derivative or sustaining innovation, which continuously provides improvements on current services and solutions
2. Transformational improvement or platform innovation, which facilitates a swift move to visible adjacencies in terms of emerging technologies and markets
3. Disruptive or breakthrough innovation, which enables customers to access potentially game-changing markets and business models.

To drive its IT innovation engine and to cast a wider net, TCS uses a "Co-Innovation Network (*COIN*)", which is a collaborative alliance of entities across the organisation's extended ecosystem. The TCS *COIN* comprises academic institutions, research institutions, student communities, start-ups, venture capitalists, industry bodies, entrepreneurs, alliance partners, consultants and customers.

Wipro, Infosys and other Indian IT companies too talk about their emphasis on innovation to bring more value to the customer.

Innovative Economies

Till very recently, only corporate organisations had realised the value of innovation; countries had not. The forces of globalization (phenomenon by which markets become global) have forced countries to compete for resources, especially capital and manpower. In this pursuit, economies are now becoming innovative. Capital flows into economies where they get the best returns. Manpower also follows the same path, though it has certain constraints. Governments now realise that an innovation-friendly environment is a pre-requisite for the countries' economies to grow.

Reports on India Innovation

In 2007, the Economist Intelligence Unit (EIU) undertook two parallel research studies to find out "how important innovation was", "which countries innovated better than others" and "why". The first was a worldwide survey of 485 senior executives to gain a better understanding of the drivers of innovation and their relative importance. The second was a ranking of 82 of the world's economies by innovation performance during 2002-06, with a forecast for the subsequent 5 year period. The report is part of a long-range project called "Foresight 2020", undertaken on three themes – personalization, collaboration and innovation.

The study reports that innovation has a beneficial impact on both national economic growth and corporate performance. It identifies, as some of the key factors driving innovation, the emergence of high-tech clusters (e.g.: technology parks), growth of technically skilled work force and high-quality IT and communications infrastructure.

The Other Major Findings are as Follows

- Japan, Switzerland, the US and Sweden are the world's top four innovators among the 82 economies.
- China is getting substantial capital investments for driving innovation, but is not as efficient as India (and several other countries) in converting it.

- US is considered by survey respondents to have the best conditions for innovation; India is in second place
- Most valued places for innovation are countries with the following national characteristics:
  - o Robust protection of intellectual property
  - o Political stability
  - o Efficient regulatory environment
  - o Sound institutional framework
  - o Quality IT and communications infrastructure
  - o Technical skills of the workforce,
  - o Availability of scientists and engineers,
  - o Availability of university graduates.

A similar study was conducted by the World Bank in 2007. According to this study titled, "Unleashing India's Innovation: Towards a Sustainable and Inclusive Growth", India needs to tap its innovation potential, relying on innovation-led, rapid, and inclusive growth to achieve economic and social transformation.

The report recommends a three-pronged strategy comprising (a) increased competition supported by stronger skills, information infrastructure and financing (b) improved knowledge creation, diffusion, and commercialization, and (c) increased focus on inclusive innovation, to unleash India's innovation potential.

The report further emphasizes that the three-pronged innovation strategy need to be implemented in a realistic and time-bound manner, possibly by a task force of policy makers working with business and social leaders. To *capture the nation's imagination*, it may be desirable to focus on *grand challenges* such as access to clean water throughout the country, mitigating road congestion in cities and so on. A public-private oversight mechanism may be required to evaluate and address the fragmentation of India's current innovation system with regular monitoring and periodic international benchmarking, as India's innovation potential gets unleashed. If this [unleashing] succeeds, that too in an inclusive manner, then the model will be of particular interest to other developing countries and emerging market economies.

Yet another recent report on India's innovation capabilities, with a focus on the IT sector, is the NASSCOM-BCG Innovation Report 2007, which studied the innovation management in the Indian IT-ITES industry.

The Report Addresses Three Aspects of the Innovation Agenda

1. Imperative for innovation: The challenges in front of the Indian IT-ITES firms and the need for the firms to look at innovation as a 'must-have'.
2. Firm level agenda and approach for firms to spur innovation; A diagnostic tool-kit through which a firm can evaluate its current innovation maturity and the processes and mechanisms for a firm to develop a practical innovation strategy.
3. Recommendations to expand the innovation ecosystem in India: Benchmarking the Indian innovation ecosystem with global innovation ecosystems and actionable recommendations to develop India's innovation ecosystem.

The report also provides numerous case studies of both innovative firms and successful ecosystems.

Conclusion

In conclusion, it is heartening to note, the stage is set for India to become a leading global innovator. Indian companies have realised this and so has the national government. The major success factors for innovation are also in India's favour. Even the challenges posed by recent US recession and dollar depreciation should be seen as opportunities because necessity and resource crunch are effective drivers of innovation. Several technology companies are already investing in R&D in India. The Indian IT sector, which started with low value-adding activities like manpower supply has now graduated into developing technologies, products and services. It is already participating in the highly competitive centre-stage markets where innovation drives competitive strategy.

While technology is a major driver of innovation, we should understand that innovation is not about technology alone. It is also about entrepreneurship and commercial application of technology to deliver more value to the customers, at reduced costs. In the Indian context, innovation will be about addressing the needs of its large population whose purchasing power is low. Prof. CK Prahlad's theory of "fortune at the bottom of the pyramid" is of specific interest in this pursuit. India has already made breakthrough innovations in services delivery. The telecommunication sector is a good example of such value creation at the bottom of the pyramid (BoP). Similar examples can be found in the health care sector, for instance, the Jaipur foot, Arvind eye care and so on.

Information technology can be a major driver for innovation in different sectors. A good example is the concept of "Smart Green Grids", which envisages IT applications in the power sector. Government of India has asked Mr. Nandan Nilekani of TCS to submit a report on how IT can bring about innovative changes in India's power sector. Let us look forward to more such instances in the near future.

Industrial R&D in India: Contemporary Scenario

Technology/economic success of a country is deeply intertwined with its 'capabilities' (competencies) for carrying out innovation of technologies that compete at the state-of-art level in the world market. Capability development is a long term process that requires a country to pass through different phases of learning, creating the required physical infrastructure, human capital, institutions that support these activities, and creating inter-linkages among them. National capabilities are not to be understood simply in terms of the sum of firm level capabilities developed in isolation.

Porter (1990) has shown how national advantage is increasingly concentrated in particular industries and even industry segments, reflecting specific and differing sources of competitive advantage. Further detailed introspection shows that competitive advantage emerges from investment in R&D and its successful translation. A firm's R&D satisfies two functions; it not only generates new knowledge but also contributes to the firm's absorptive capacity (Cohen and Levinthal, 1990).

An underlying commonality of industrialized economies is investment, firms therein undertake in R&D. A sharp distinction can be observed between developed and developing economies in terms of the intensity of investment in R&D and also in the major sources from which the investments are emerging. Almost 70-80% of investments in R&D in developed economies are accounted for by its industries whereas in developing countries the government accounts for this proportion of investment. A firm invests between 5 to 10% of its sales in R&D in industrialized economies (in some knowledge intensive industries the percentages are much higher) whereas only a few firms invest in R&D in developing economies. Among the firms investing in R&D, only in some sectors (such as ICT, pharmaceuticals) R&D as percentage of sales is observed to be 1 to 2% (only for a few isolated firms, one can observe higher degree of investment).

Protectionist barriers (fiscal and non-fiscal), was one of the reasons for Indian firms not having the required push to invest in R&D.

However, this was not the only factor. Indian firms operated on a small capital and were miniscule entities in comparison to global firms (MNCs). There were many regulatory barriers, rules and regulations, government controls that also acted as an impediment for Indian firms to expand. They directly or indirectly affected firms focusing attention in R&D.

However, there has been a significant shift in the last few years. Liberalization of the economy that began in the 1990s has become more institutionalized, greater integration with world economy has taken place, and many firms have established global footprints. Firms particularly in the pharmaceutical sector have been compelled to invest in R&D due to India's adherence to TRIPs agreement, etc.

The Present Study

The present study investigates the R&D investment scenario in India with specific focus on industrial R&D. In the first part we examine international R&D investment trends i.e. in major industrialized and emerging economies. The international investment provides a benchmark for Indian R&D investment. In the second part of the study, we examine R&D investment by public limited firms in India. Examination was done for 2006-07. Average data was taken to mitigate the effect of any idiosyncratic fluctuations. Broad trends for earlier years were analyzed to get a proper perspective of contemporary investment trends.

Novelty and Justification of the Present Study

R&D Statistics periodically brought out by the DST (Department of Science and Technology) is the prime source for assessing the intensity and extent of R&D undertaken in the country. DST uses different data sources for this purpose. Primary survey is used for collecting R&D statistics in industrial sector. Information is solicited from R&D units recognised by DSIR (Department of Scientific and Industrial Research). These R&D units include public and private limited companies. This compilation by DST is important as it provides indication of the R&D activity of the country. However, there are limitations in using these statistics for gauging the current scenario. One of the main drawbacks is that the data is dated. The latest available report by DST is "R&D Statistics 2004-05'; this captures industrial R&D expenditure data up to 2002-03. Also restricting the survey to data collection for R&D units recognised by DSIR leads to missing gaps. A recent study (Bhattacharya, Sharma and Lal; 2007) sponsored by NSTMIS (DST) and conducted by NISTADS has shown that there are 1,208 public ltd. firms involved in R&D in India but were not recognised R&D units. The primary reason behind their non-inclusion in DST statistics was that these firms had R&D units/in-house activity not recognised by DSIR. Non-inclusion of such firms has strong bearing in estimating the R&D expenditure and it underscores the inventive/ innovative activity of the country. For example in 2002-03, inclusion of the R&D expenditure of these 1,208 firms pushes the national R&D expenditure during this period up by 3.7% and industrial R&D expenditure up by 16.3%. The 1,208 firms have also undertaken a large number of technological as well as non-technological innovations that reasserts India building up technological capacity/capability.

The present study on assessment of industrial R&D in India is based on capturing data from various public sources including company reports and red herring listing. This to an extent overcomes the constraints of using DST R&D Statistics to reflect the contemporary industrial R&D scenario in the country. However, capturing data from public sources was confined to public limited companies, because they divulge their detailed data (i.e. as per legal requirements only public ltd. Firms have to submit details of their various activities including R&D to the Ministry of Company and Law Affairs). The limitation of this study is mainly on two aspects. Firstly, private firms do not have legal binding to submit detailed data of their various activities and thus sketchy account of their R&D expenditure and related statistics can be gathered from secondary sources. Thus, these firms were not captured in this study. Secondly, primary survey provides valuable insights which cannot be captured by secondary sources. However, a good estimation of contemporary scenario of industrial R&D activity can be obtained by investigating public limited companies as studies have shown that they are the major driver of industrial activity in the country.

Method

Target population and sample size: The Department of Company Affairs lists approximately six lakhs and eighty-five thousand companies comprising of public and private ltd. companies. The disclosures are not available for private limited companies. Details are available for 75-80 thousand companies that are public limited companies. Further approximately 10,000 companies are there that have time series data available for at least three years. It is possible to get from CMIE, through their Prowess database, the time series data of the above 10,000 companies. Prowess database has been extensively used to assess the industrial scenario, investigate trends, performance and construct indicators based on this data source to determine the 'health' of industrial performance.

Among the reasons of using this database for the above assessments is that these 10,000 or so companies contribute 70% of industrial revenues and are thus indicative of the industrial activity of the country. This motivates us to use this data source to examine industrial R&D in India.

R&D Activity: International Scenario

R&D represents the most developed, widely available, and internationally comparable statistical indicator of industrial innovation activities. It comprises creative work "undertaken on a systematic basis in order to increase the stock of knowledge in all fields and use this knowledge base to devise new applications" (UNCTAD, 2005). R&D spending of a particular country has been used by many organisations (UNCTAD, 2007; World Bank, 2007; and World Economic Forum, 2008) to measure the competitiveness of countries. According to World Economic Forum, the most competitive country in theworld ranked on the scale of 1-7 (1=least competitive, and 7=most competitive) among 130 countries at present is the US (5.74), followed by Switzerland (5.61), Denmark (5.58), and Singapore (5.53). India (4.33) stood at 49th rank out of 130 countries. China's (4.70) rank on this index is 30th (improved from 34th rank in 2007-08), whereas India slipped to the present position from 48th rank in 2007-08. In calculation of competitive index, R&D expenditure acts as an important component.

India is the 4th largest economy of the world in PPP (purchase power parity) terms after US, China and Japan. However, it fares poorly in the world map of R&D spending.

Table: *Global R&D funding, 2006*

Countries	*GDP, PPP (US $ billion)*	*R&D, PPP (US $ billion)*	*R&D as % of GDP*	*R&D as % of world*
Americans	15,155	374.9	2.47	35.70
United States	12,416	343	2.76	32.70
Asia	19,203	387.2	2.02	36.90
China	8,815	141.7	1.61	13.50
Japan	3,995	136.7	3.4	13.00
India	3,779	38.8	1.03	3.70
Europe	14,072	264.3	1.88	25.20
Rest of world	2,073	23	1.11	2.20
Total	50,503	1049.4	2.08	100.00

Source: *Global R&D Report 2007*

Table: Share of Total Global R&D Spending, 2006-2008

Countries	2006	2007	2008 (estimated)
Americans	35.70	34.5	33.1
United States	32.70	31.4	30.1
Asia	36.90	38.8	40.8
China	13.50	15.6	17.9
Japan	13.00	12.8	12.4
India	3.70	3.7	3.7
Europe	25.20	24.6	23.9
Rest of world	2.20	2.2	2.1

Source: *Global R&D Report 2007*

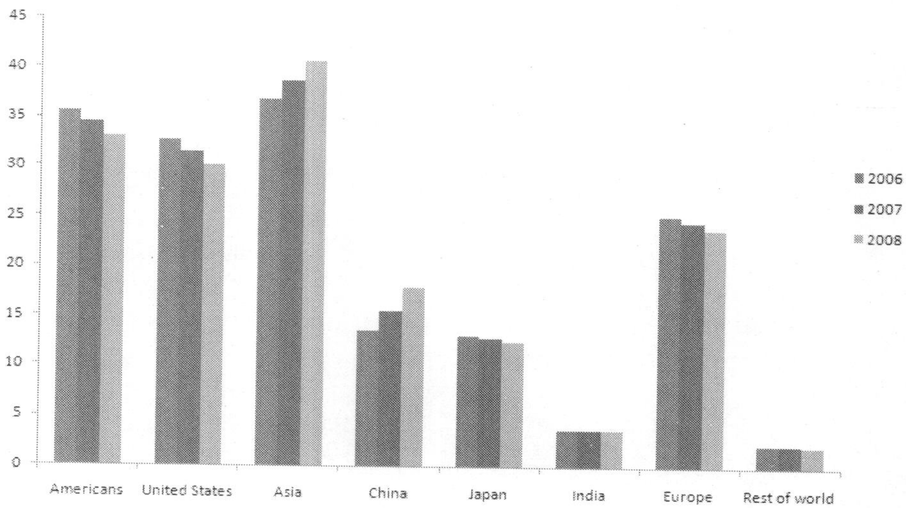

Figure: *Share of Global R&D spending*

Source: *Global R&D reports 2007*

The low investment in R&D is an indication that India is still involved in activities that are not creating higher value at different levels. This assertion can be made as expenditure in research is an indication of commitment of a firm/research organisation to search for novel ways of producing/creating new products. It can also be observed from Figure that India's spending has remained constant from 2006 to 2008. China shows upward trends. The indicator Gross Domestic Expenditure on R&D (GERD) is used frequently to measure commitment of a country in R&D. This indicator is measured in terms of R&D spending as percentage of GDP for a country.

Table: *GERD in Select Countries*

Countries	***GDP, PPP US $ trillion***	***GERD PPP US $ billion***	***R&D % 0f GDP***	***GERD PPP US $ billion***	***GERD PPP US $ billion (projected)***
United States	12.42	343.00	2.76	353.00	365.00
China	8.82	141.71	1.61	174.96	216.82
Japan	4.00	136.69	3.4	143.50	150.38
Germany	2.43	63.54	2.5	64.61	65.69
France	1.85	42.14	2.2	43.98	45.99
India	3.78	38.85	1	41.81	45.00
UK	2.00	37.54	1.9	40.08	42.82
South Korea	1.06	34.73	2.6	37.73	41.00
Canada	1.08	23.06	2	24.53	26.00
Taiwan	0.68	17.91	2.2	19.85	22.00
Sweden	0.29	11.83	3.9	12402.00	13.00
Israel	0.18	9.25	4.5	10.12	11.00
Switzerland	0.27	8.26	2.6	8.62	9.00
Finland	0.17	6.00	3.5	6.37	6.70
Denmark	0.18	4.71	2.6	4.91	5.11

Source: *Global R&D Report 2007*

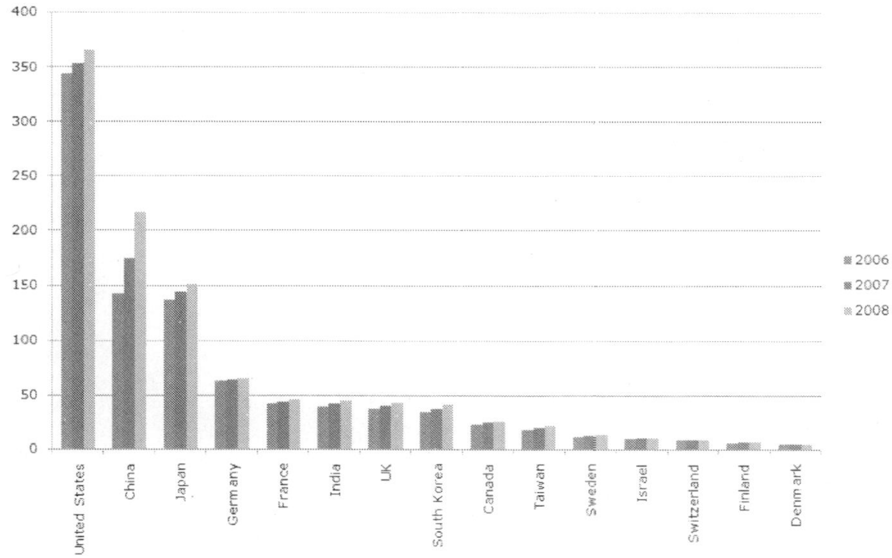

Figure: *GERD for selected countries 2006-2008*

Source: *Global R&D reports 2007*

USA is clearly the global leader. But, it is surprising to see the strong positive transition of China. In 2007 it was the 2nd ranked country. There is more positive outlook for 2008. India also is in the top league of countries.

The above assessment of GERD is in PPP terms. The actual expenditure by each country in R&D as a share of GDP is shown in Figure.

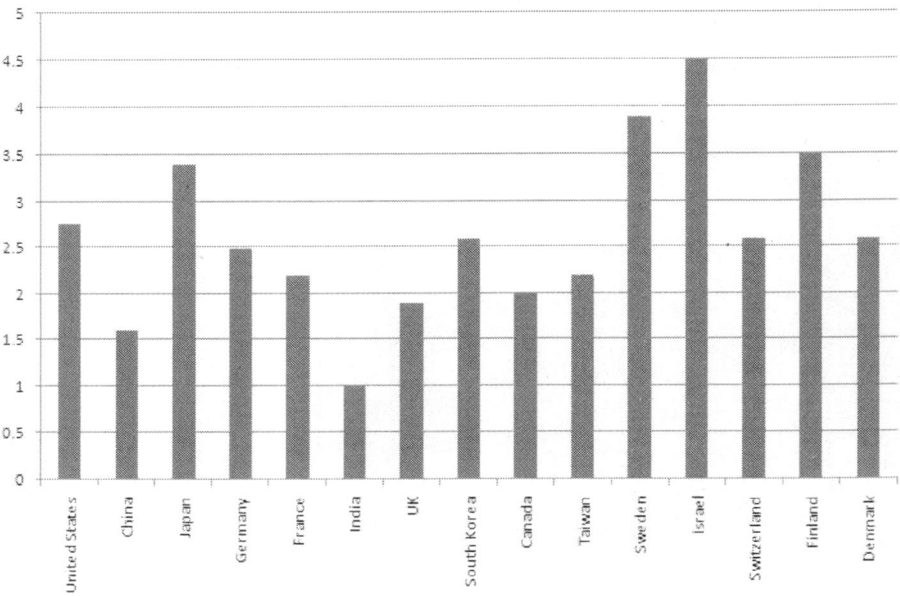

Figure: *R&D % GDP for selected countries (2006-2008)*

Source: *Global R&D reports 2007*

Figure shows that in comparison to other countries India's R&D expenditure is below 1%. Developed countries generally cross 2% threshold. India, Brazil, Argentina, Russian Fedration still have percentages between 0.5 to 1%. Figure exhibits sources of R&D funding in different cuntries; this figure plausibly provides an answer to this.

Government is the major source of funding in India, Brazil, and Hungary. Business R&D is the major driver for R&D investment. This is borne out from the fact that countries like India where the major source of R&D investment is from the government have GERD between 0.5 to 1%, whereas it touches much higher levels for countries that do not rely on government as the primary funding source.

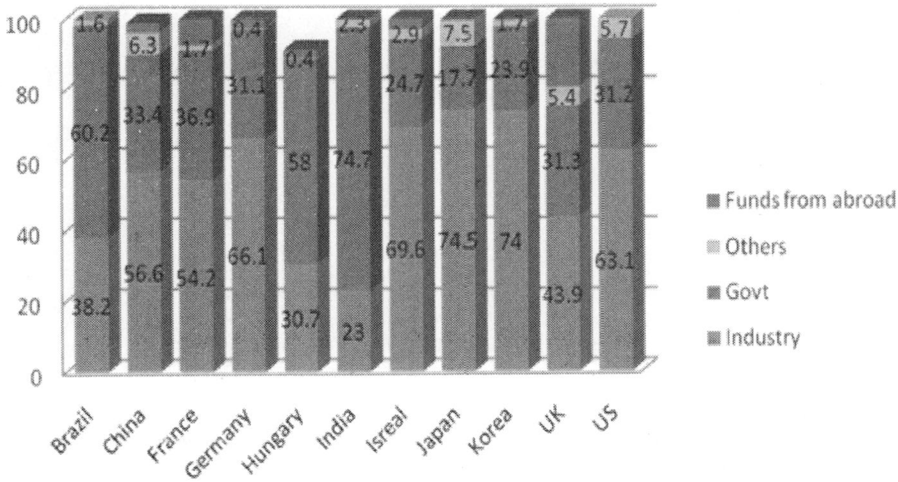

Figure: *Source of funds (%) for select countries*

Source: *Global R&D reports 2007*

R&D investment is an important component in the innovation chain. This is truer in an industrial setting where R&D investments are done with innovation as the final goal.

However, translation of R&D investment to the creation of novel processes/products or improvements in existing products is a highly uncertain, complex process. Among the indicators that shows successful process of translation is patenting activity. Patents indicate in general measure the inventive activity.

Patenting particularly from USPTO has been used as yardstick to measure the competitive capability of a country, and is widely used for inter-country comparison on R&D productivity. Patents granted in the US for foreign countries are especially important because it is the single most important export market.

According to patents granted during 2005, India's position is weak in comparison with other emerging economies of Asian origin e.g. Taiwan, Korea, and China.

One major difference noticeable in Figure-5 is that most of the patents granted to inventions are for respective local firms (e.g. country institutions) in case of Israel, Korea, and Taiwan. In case of China and India, it is MNC firms who have been granted majority of the patents. Maybe it is a pointer to the fact that MNCs in these two countries are able to use the innovative capability of the local scientists better than the local S&T institutions.

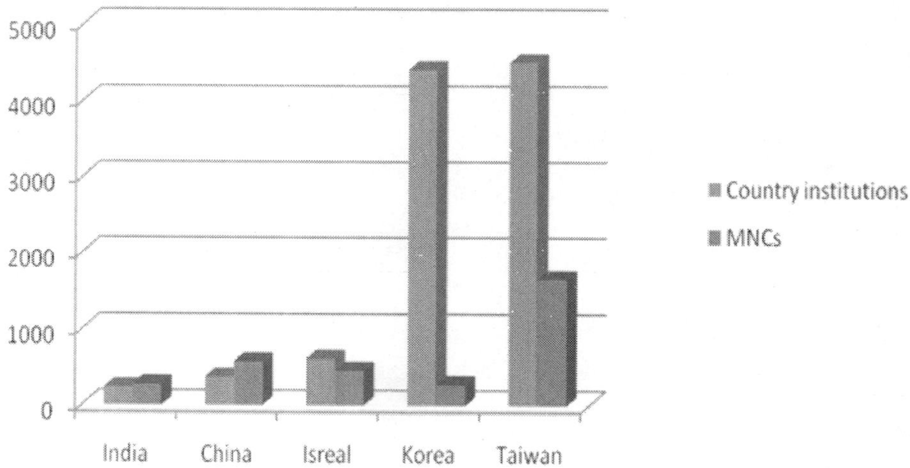

Figure: *US patents granted to inventions of various countries*

Source: R&D India, Newsletter October 2006, DSIR, New Delhi

High technology export is another useful measure to gauge the capability and competitiveness of a country.

The results of R&D spending often reflect in a country's high tech exports especially its proportion to the overall total manufacturing exports. As per the data shown in the table, in 2005 India stood at 39th rank in the world as far as the value of high tech exports is concerned. The US is on top of the world followed by China at number two and Germany at number three.

But when high tech exports are calculated as proportion of the total manufacturing export, India has even lower rank at number 54. China's rank (11th) was much higher than India's. During the same period, India managed to register only 4.88% high tech exports of its total manufacturing exports, whereas the same figures for China, US, and Germany are 29.81%, 32.29%, and 17.22% respectively.

India's major source of R&D funding comes from government. The stark contrast with developed and some emerging economies is the involvement of industry in R&D. Table 4 exhibits business R&D expenditure for selected countries and shows this stark contrast.

Table: *Select Global Scientific and Technological Indicators, 2005*

	India	*China*	*Brazil*	*USA*	*Japan*	*Germany*
High tech exports	2840 (39)	161603 (2)	5929 (33)	216016 (1)	124045 (4)	131838 (3)
High tech. Exports as % of manufacturing exports	4.88 (54)	29.81 (11)	11.59 (37)	32.29 (8)	23.68 (15)	17.22 (24)
Business R&D expenditure (US $ million)	851 (34)	15876 (6)	2234 (25)	219226 (1)	101458 (2)	048199 (3)
R&D expenditure per capita (US $)	3.6 (58)	18.3 (50)	30.8 (44)	1064.3 (6)	1060.3 (7)	828.4 (12)
Business R&D per capita (US $)	1.94 (47)	8.22 (27)	3.70 (40)	18.68 (9)	23.97 (4)	17.51 (11)

Note: Figures in brackets indicate the comparative global rank.

Sources: *1. World Development Indicators 2. UNESCO and OECD main S&T indicators 2005*

Industrial R&D-Indian Scenario

Sakakibara & Cho (2002) identified three types of organisations engaged in R&D activities: Private, Government, and Cooperative. Under private R&D they include listed (public funded) as well as non-listed firms. It also includes foreign firms undertaking R&D/foreign R&D centres and again may be listed or non-listed entities.

Government R&D on the other hand, is a contribution to research conducted in universities and national research institutions, while cooperative R&D primarily involves technology associations that promote R&D. We can see a similar distinction in India. India has a huge R&D infrastructure with 400 national laboratories, 1300 recognised in-house industrial units, besides several government departments and private institutions and foundations engaged in scientific research.

R&D is also undertaken in the 358 universities in the country. There are approximately 500 Foreign R&D centres in India. In spite of this impressive R&D infrastructure in the country, the amount of funds directed for R&D is below 1% of GDP. However, positive trends are seen. The National R&D expenditure in 2005-06 was Rs. 28,776.65 crores and has been projected to attain a level of Rs 32,941.64 crores in 2006-07 and Rs 37,777.90 crores in 2007-08 (2008, R&D Statistics at a Glance). The share of R&D expenditure as a percentage of GNP has also increased from 0.58% during 1990-91 to 0.80% during 2002-03 to 0.89% in 2005-06. Industrial R&D expenditure comprising both public and private sector was approx. 8,748.20 crores.

The investment in R&D has more then doubled for private sector industries in 2004-05 from that in 2002-03. For 2005-06 private sector investment was Rs. 7,444.21 crores and is expected to reach the level of Rs. 11,192.86 crores in 2007-08 (ibid).

The industrial sector spent 0.55% of their sales turnover on R&D activities in 2005-06. Besides regular R&D budget allocated to various organisations, extramural funding is also provided by scientific departments/agencies to R&D organisations to build general R&D capabilities and provides special encouragement to scientists to pursue research career.

The extramural R&D funding commitment by Central government S&T departments/agencies was Rs 448.69 crores in 2002-03; as per the latest available statistics (2005, Directory of Extramural Research & Development).

There were 2,718 projects approved for funding during 2002-03. The maximum funding was in Engineering and Technology (38.15%). DST was the major funding agency, accounting for 39% (Rs. 176.56 crores) of the total extramural funding in 2002-03.

As outlined in the beginning, R&D has never been a major concern for Indian industry. Aided by government policies that protected them from outside competition, most companies saw little need to spend money on research.

There was not much demand of the public R&D either. Innovation was not a priority and there was a general disinterestedness of the industry to develop products. Re-engineering was the key concern and with not much commercial safeguards for innovative products, incentives for innovation were not there in the industry.

Liberalization and subsequent opening up of the Indian economy from 1991 onwards are beginning to make significant impacts. Lowering of customs duties has played a key role in this process of facilitating and encouraging investment in R&D. Starting in 1994, for example, the tax on equipment associated with R&D activities was reduced from 50% to 25%. Another significant development has been the amendment of the patent act. The new act Patent Amendment Act (2005) allows for filing of process and product patents in all technological categories/

sectors. Foreign investment and entry of multinational companies with large R&D centres, corporate research centres and joint efforts with Indian partners are effecting the change.

We determined the public limited firms that had reported disclosures for at-least three years and those among them who had made expenditure under R&D (using Prowess database).

There were 10,064 public limited firms (in the current Prowess database 2008 version) satisfying the criteria of at-least disclosing their audited statements for three years to the Registrar of Company Affairs.

Table highlights the firms undertaking R&D investment within this set in different periods of time. Sales and R&D intensity is also given in this Table. R&D intensity is defined as R&D divided by sales. Normalization of R&D by firm sales controls for the effect of firm size, which affects the return per unit of R&D effort.

Table: *R&D firms, 1990-2007*

Year	*Number of firms*	*R&D expenditure (Rs. crores)*	*Sales (Rs. crores)*	*R&D* intensity*
1990	44	74.57	152168.9	0.049
1991	83	135.42	179743.4	0.075
1992	258	324.72	224824.4	0.144
1993	505	582.79	275970.7	0.211
1994	613	714.44	317761.9	0.225
1995	853	1116.12	388437.9	0.287
1996	917	1590.24	484140.3	0.328
1997	1001	2080.03	535698.9	0.388
1998	961	1785.69	568695.5	0.314
1999	969	2851.23	635457.5	0.449
2000	933	2219.33	748025.3	0.297
2001	930	2446.86	877662.4	0.279
2002	1068	3003.47	877667.13	0.342
2003	1099	3868.09	968885.39	0.399
2004	1070	5098.99	1139574.9	0.447
2005	980	6074.17	1358880	0.447
2006	966	7635.28	1608181	0.475
2007	918	8596.26	1837312.7	0.468

*R&D expenditure/sales

Source: *Constructed from Prowess database*

Table 5 shows significant positive growth in number of R&D firms from 1990 to 1995 (we define a firm as an R&D firm if it has undertaken R&D investment). The growth trend is slower after that with minor negative fluctuations in some years also. However, absolute value of R&D investment has significantly increased over the years. There has been almost a 770% increase in R&D investment in 2007 from that in 1995; although the increase in number of firms undertaking R&D investment has been marginal. The number of R&D firms in 2000 was more than that in 2007, however R&D investment in 2007 was 387% more then that in 2000. The R&D intensity has not shown this high growth rate as sales have also significantly increased over the years. The proposition that R&D investment contributes to sales is supported by this empirical data.

Table: shows the breakup of R&D investment for the aggregated period 1990-2006 in terms of ownership group: Indian and Foreign entity. Other indicators are also given in this table.

***Table:** Firms Exhibiting R&D Investment (1990-2006)*

Firms	*No: of Firms*	*Sales*	*R&D*	*R&D Intensity*	*Import*	*Export*
Indian Entities	1472	43,02,348.1	22,514.6	0.52	7,75,668.6	6,65,085.2
Foreign Entities	195	10,82,688.4	4,892.4	0.45	1,58,776.9	1,13,102.0

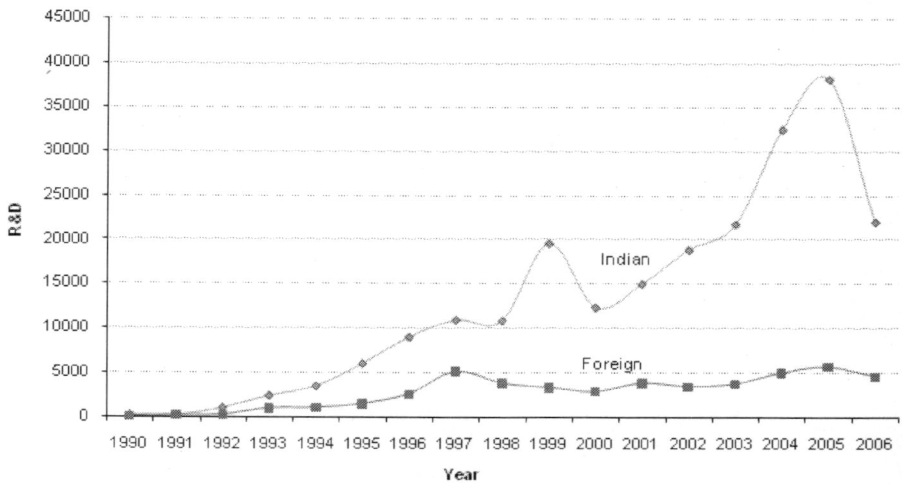

***Figure:** R&D Expenditure by Indian and Foreign Entities (1990-2006)*

Note: R&D in Rupees Million

Source: *Prowess database (CMIE)*

The broad expenditure statistics of public limited companies as shown by Table and Figure is much below the expenditures made by industrial sector in developed economies (refer section on International R&D Trends).

Even industrial sectors in emerging economies are making high levels of investment in R&D. China's high investment by industry is a case in point. New Science and Technology Policy 2003, envisages enhancing investment on R&D by 2% of GDP with increased participation from industry.

Thus on one hand we do find top multinationals locating their R&D centres in India. TIFAC report on 'FDI in the R&D sector in India' has given detailed statistics of 100 FDI companies with R&D centres in India.

These FDI companies are in different sectors % pharmaceuticals (drug discovery services, new dosage formulations, etc), ICT (embedded software, chip design, etc), processed foods etc. The report shows the 'successes' of these R&D centres in terms of generating proprietary technology.

On the other hand in spite of a few firms reaching international levels in terms of sales, clientele, delivery, acquisitions and their focus on becoming knowledge driven entities, the SME's are still struggling to adjust to the changing scenario.

Many of them do not have the required capital to undertake the transition. But the main hindrance is the reluctance to make long term investment in R&D, improving quality standards, and move away from re-engineering.

Thus, we still find that R&D in India is mainly funded by government sector. Without industrial sector investing in R&D it is not possible for the country to achieve R&D investment of 2% of GDP.

Characteristics of Firms Undertaking R&D in 2006-2007

There were 1,055 firms from a population of ~10,000 firms (refer 'Method' section for details) that had made investments in R&D for the period 2006-07.

This was the sample for the present analysis. Below table shows the distribution of the selected 1,055 firms in terms of incorporation year.

Table:* *1055 R&D Firms distinguished in terms of Incorporation Year

Incorporation year	Number of firms	Major economic activity
Before 1900	20	• Chemical products (4) • Food products and beverages (2) • Textiles (2) • Non-metallic mineral products (2) • Electricity supply (2)
1901-50	163	• Chemical products (30) • Food products and beverages (19) • Machinery and equipments (17) • Non-metallic mineral products (15) • Diversified (10) • Automobile spare parts and ancillaries (9) • Electrical machinery and equipments
1951-60	102	• Chemical products (24) • Machinery and equipments (14) • Automobile spare parts and ancillaries (8) • Food products and beverages (7)
1961-70	128	• Chemical products (32) • Machinery and equipments (19) • Automobile spare parts and ancillaries (14) • Basic metals (11)
1971-80	152	• Chemical products (50) • Textiles (11) • Basic metals (10) • Automobile spare parts and ancillaries (9)
1981-90	278	• Chemical products (92) • Automobile spare parts and ancillaries (26) • Rubber and plastic products (20) • Electronic equipments (18) • Machinery and equipments (16) • Computer software (13)
1991-95	125	• Chemical products (38) • Computer software (13) • Food products and beverages (10) • Textiles (10) • Machinery and equipments (16)
1996-2000	66	• Chemical products (15) • Computer software (07) • Automobile spare parts and ancillaries (07) • Food products and beverages (05) • Wholesale trade (05) • Non-metallic mineral products (06)
2001-05	18	• Chemical products (06) • Automobile spare parts and ancillaries (4) • Non-metallic mineral products (02)
2006-07	3	• Petroleum products (01) • Chemical products (01) • Computer software (01)

Note: Figures in brackets refer to number of firms.

It is interesting to note that many of the firms were incorporated more then fifty years ago. It is also an interesting finding that the number of firms incorporated after 1995 was less then the earlier periods.

It is however not possible to ascertain when individual firms undertook investment in R&D. Chemical sector dominates the sample i.e. majority of the firms belong to the chemical sector.

Automotive, Food & Beverages, Textiles and Software are the other visible sectors. Software firms are visible from 1991 onwards reflecting their presence in Indian industrial activity.

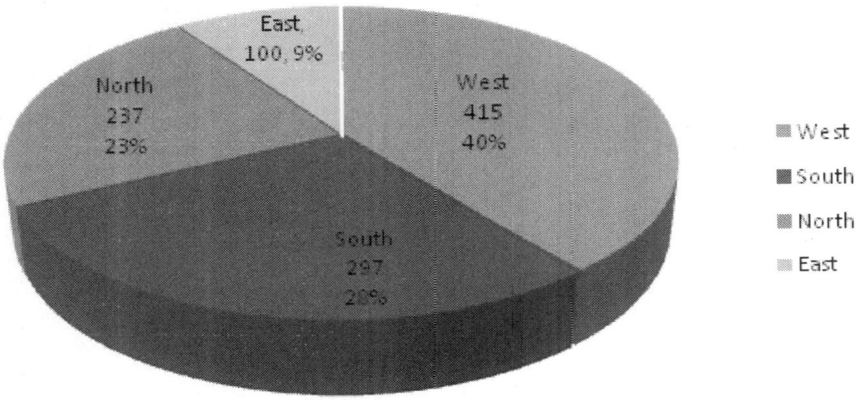

Figure: *Region wise distribution of R&D firms, 2006-07*

Table: *Distribution of R&D Investment in terms of Ownership Group*

Ownership group	***No. of firms***	***R&D expenditure (Rs. Crores)***	***R&D expenditure (Rs. Crores)***	***Average R&D expenditure (Rs. Crores)***
		2006	2007	2006-07
Business Group	529	4362.96	5694.29	5028.63
Private Indian	361	1561.44	1005.94	1283.69
Private foreign	88	502.45	458.25	480.35
Central government-commercial enterprise	57	1187.48	1349.11	1268.30
State government-commercial government enterprise	19	18.23	16.96	17.60
Cooperative sector	01	0.28	0.27	0.28
Total	1,055	7,632.84	8,524.82	8,078.83

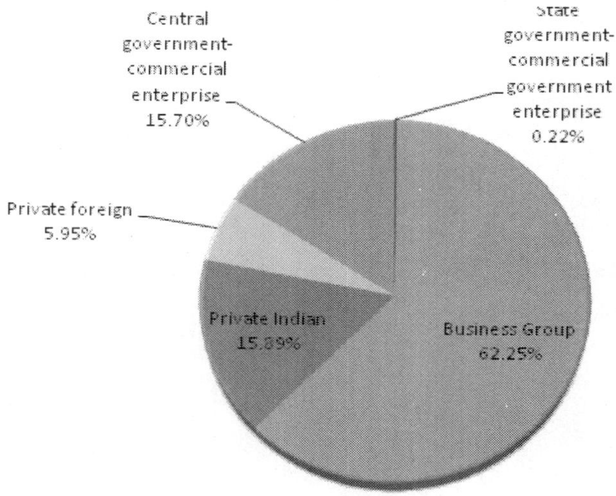

Figure: *Average R&D expenditure (Rs. Crores) of 1,055 R&D firms according to ownership group, 2006-07*

92% of the firms have private ownership (comprising of Business group, Private Indian, Private Foreign) signifying their dominating the industrial activity. Only 8% of the firms were from government and cooperative sector.

Table: *R&D intensity of firms with respect to R&D expenditure (2006-07)*

R&D expenditure *(Crores)*	***No. of firms***	***R&D Intensity***
>100	20	49.35
>50 & < 100	12	4.32
>1 & <50	306	2.32
<1	434	0.64

Table: *R&D Intensity and Sales (2006-07)*

Average sales *(Crores)*	***No. of firms***	***R&D intensity***
>10,000	21	0.41
>5,000 & < 10,000	15	0.35
>1,000 & <5,000	97	1.23
>500 & <1,000	111	1.05
>100 & <500	275	0.90
<100	253	6.00

Table above shows that R&D intensity is much higher for small enterprises. There is not much difference in R&D intensity for medium and big enterprises. However, dominant firms in the economy (sales > 5,000 crores) have lower R&D intensity. In other words resource allocation in R&D do not communsurate with the sales of large enterprises. The broad indication is that small firms are trying to become more innovative then the larger firms. Table highlights a different set emerges when we take sales in consideration.

Table below shows the number of firms in each sector and R&D intensity therein. The firm in each sector with FPS (Foreign Promoter Share) is also shown.

Table: *R&D intensities of different sectors of Indian R&D firms (2006-07)*

Sectors	*No. of firms*	*R&D intensity*		*Average R&D Intensities*	*Number of FPS firms*	*% of FPS firms*
		2006	*2007*			
Pharmaceuticals	115	7.08	6.74	6.91	26	22.61
Chemicals	303	2.56	2.42	2.49	71	23.43
Food products	68	3.43	0.37	1.9	9	13.24
Motor vehicle	85	1.71	1.81	1.76	25	29.41
Electronics	37	1.71	1.25	1.48	8	21.62
Machinery	92	0.93	1.72	1.33	25	27.17
Software	37	1.15	1.15	1.15	9	24.32
Rubber & plastic	47	0.59	0.59	0.59	12	25.53
Basic chemicals	97	0.61	0.31	0.46	17	17.53
Electrical machinery	44	0.41	0.33	0.37	10	22.78
Other food products	46	0.37	0.33	0.35	7	15.22
Textiles	49	0.19	0.31	0.25	10	20.41
Basic metals	45	0.15	0.18	0.17	8	17.79
Non-metallic	53	0.16	0.11	0.14	11	20.76

It can be observed that R&D intensity is very high in some sectors, much above the average R&D intensity of 0.4 of the 1,055 firms in the sample. Sector wise R&D intensity broadly mirrors global trends; however the baseline and celing levels are much higher in developed economies.

The table also shows sector wise FPS distribution. Motor vehicles and Machinery are two sectors that attract maximum FPS share. In other words, foreign participation is more in these two sectors then the others. However, it should be noted that these are aggregated statistics and may strongly be influenced by outliers.

***Table:** Distribution of firms w.r.t Foreign Promoter Share, 2006-07*

Number of firms	***FPS (%)***	***R&D intensities***
118	<=25	0.91
30	>25 and <=50	0.75
57	>50 and <=75	0.49
26	>75	1.68

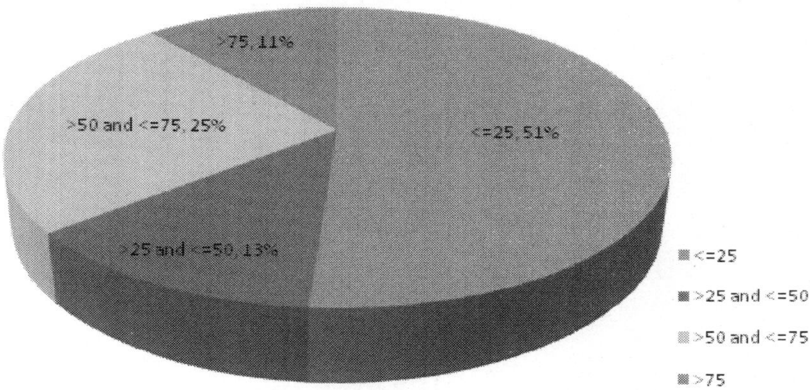

***Figure:** Distribution of firms w.r.t Foreign Promoter Share, 2006-07*

In terms of holding, we observe 83 firms have FPS above 50%. These firms primarily should be placed under foreign firms as effective controls of these firms are outside the country. R&D intensity highlights an important policy relevant aspect. It shows that R&D intensity of firms with high FPS share (>75%) have the maximum R&D intensity in comparison to other categories. The average R&D intensity of firms with no FPS share is 0.63. Thus two points emerge: (a) Firms with FPS have higher R&D intensity then those attracting no FPS. This implies FPS is an inducement for a firm to put more allocation for R&D as a percentage of sales. (b) Very high FPS share is a strong inducement. The findings of Chang (1985) that "Foreign R&D investment has played a key role in increasing the overall R&D picture in many advanced as well as developing countries" holds true for this snapshot analysis.

The above analysis has so far shown the average R&D investment pattern and related statistics derived from them. To observe the major drivers of the above trends, we investigate the top fifty firms in terms of R&D Investment and Sales.

It can be observed that pharmaceutical firms are dominating the above group. Thus the high R&D intensity of this sector (as observed earlier) is a contribution from not a few isolated firm but it is more pervasive. Refinary firms are dominating sales in comparison to other firms in the above set. Software firms and automobiles are also prominently visible among the top fifty firms.

Summary and Discussion

The paper dwells on two perspective of India's R&D investment. First India's R&D investment pattern is compared with global trends. In the second part, the industrial R&D investment pattern is analysed from a sample taken from the poulation of public limited firms.

International Scenario: India is presently the 4th largest economy of the world (in PPP term) and a favoured destination of global R&D firms. Many Indian firms have created global footprints. In two sectors that have potential of driving the world economy i.e. ICT and biotechnology, India is among a few emerging economies to make its presence felt. However, inspite of these impressive statistics, Indian industrial R&D investment is still at a nascent stage. India compares poorly with industrial economies in terms of R&D spending. Unlike India, the major driver of R&D investment in developed economies comes from the industry. This is true even in case of China, where industry accounts for 57% of R&D investment. India's R&D investment from industry was 23% in 2007, which was even less than industrial investment in Brazil (38.2%).

Lessons learnt from international assessment of R&D investment are: a) India needs to increase resource allocation in R&D as % of GDP considerably, to 2% from the present level of 1%. This is minimum benchmark of developed economies; (b) to attain this level the industry should become a major player as is the international trend. R&D investment from industry should at least match the contribution made by government.

R&D investment drives the innovation process. An indirect indication of its effectiveness can be gauged from the firms' patenting activity and its creation of value added products. High technology exports and patenting activities are considerably lower for India. This may be a reflection of India's low investment in R&D.

Industrial R&D-Indian Scenario: This was based on a population of 10,000 public limited firms. These firms account for 70% of industrial revenue in the country. The number of firms involved in R&D activity has increased 20 times in 1995 from the level in 1990 (i.e. from 44 firms to 853 firms). In the later periods, there was not a major change in the number of firms involved in R&D activity. There has been almost

770% increase in R&D investment from that in 1995. Thus firms involved in R&D have significantly increased their R&D investment. R&D intensity has increased from 0.05 in 1990 to 0.47 in 2007.

1,055 firms had made investment in R&D in 2006 or 2007 or in both the years. This was the sample chosen for further indepth study. Statistics was based on the average for two years: 2006 and 2007

Key Findings

Chemical sector emerges as the dominent sector in which firms had made R&D investment. Automobile, Food & Beverages and Instrumentation are the other sectors where firms had made R&D investment. In the later period there is emergence of software firms. Western region is the major centre of industrial activity. Small firms (sales < 100 crore) are the key drivers of R&D activity. Firms in this category devote almost 6% of their sales to R&D (this is on an aggregate) as compared to range of 0.45 to 1% for firms from other categories (sales above 100 crores). R&D intensity is high for pharmaceutical industry (6.7%) and Chemicals (2.42%). Textile (0.19%), Basic metals (0.15%) and Non-metallic (0.16%) are hardly contributing to R&D. Software sector has moderate investment intensity (1.15%). Foreign promoter share (FPS) acts as an inducement for R&D investment. Firms that have FPS > 7.5% have R&D intensity of 1.68% in comparison to firms with no FPS (0.63%).

We should be cautious in making any generalized interpretation from the above findings. Firstly, these statistics emerge from a snapshot analysis of average activity in two year period 2006-2007. Secondly, the firms are restricted to public limited entities. But at the same time the findings of this study are important in the indicative sense.

Bibliography

Archer, David; Cameron, Alex: *Collaborative leadership – How to Succeed in and Interconnected World*, Butterworth Heinemann, NJ, 2008.

Bently, Lionel: *Trade Marks and Brands: An Interdisciplinary Critique,* Cambridge University Press, Cambridge, 2008.

Bhattacharya, S; Sharma, S.C; Lal, K: *Study of R&D and Innovation Activity of Firms in India,*.National Institute of Science, Technology Studies for Department of Science and Technology, Government of India, 2007.

Brown, Terrence and Ulijn, Johannes: *Innovation, Entrepreneurship and Culture: The Interaction between Technology, Progress and Economic Growth*, Edward Elgar, Cheltenham, 2004.

Burk, Dan L. and Mark A. Lemley: *The Patent Crisis and How the Courts Can Solve It*, University of Chicago Press, Chicago, 2009.

Cappellin R. and Wink R.: *International Knowledge and Innovation Networks Knowledge Creation and Innovation in Medium-technology Clusters*, Edward Elgar Publishing Limited, UK, 2009.

Chrislip, David: *The Collaborative Leadership Fieldbook - A guide for citizens and civic leaders*, Josey Bass, NY, 2002.

Cohen, W.M. and Levin, R.C.: *Handbook of Industrial Organisation*, Elsevier, Amsterdam, 1989.

Dowd, Raymond J.: *Copyright Litigation Handbook,* Thomson West, 2006.

Greenhalgh, C. & Rogers M.: *Innovation, Intellectual Property, and Economic Growth,* Princeton University Press, New Jersey, 2010.

Kanter, Rosabeth Moss: *Rosabeth Moss Kanter on the Frontiers of Management*, Harvard Business School Press, NJ, 2003.

Lai, Edwin: *"The Economics of Intellectual Property Protection in the Global Economy"*, Princeton University, UK, 2001.

Lessig, Lawrence: *"Free Culture: How Big Media Uses Technology and the Law to Lock Down Culture and Control Creativity"*, Penguin Press, New York, 2004.

Lindsey, Marc: *Copyright Law on Campus,* Washington State University Press, 2003.

Middleton, Julia: *Beyond Authority – Leadership in a changing world,* Palgrave Macmillan, 2007.

Nimmer, Melville; David Nimmer: *Nimmer on Copyright,* Matthew Bender, NJ, 1997.

Packard, Ashley: *Digital Media Law,* John Wiley and Sons, NY, 2010.

Patterson, Lyman Ray: *Copyright in Historical Perspective,* Vanderbilt University Press, UK, 1968.

Perelman, Michael: *Steal This Idea: Intellectual Property and The Corporate Confiscation of Creativity,* Palgrave Macmillan, Chicago, 2004.

Porter, M.: *The Competitive Advantage of Nations,* The Macmillian Press Ltd., London, 1990.

Rand, Ayn: *"Patents and Copyrights" in Ayn Rand, ed. 'Capitalism: The Unknown Ideal,'* New American Library, New York, 1966.

Reffo, Gerry; Wark, Valerie: *Leadership PQ: How Political Intelligence Sets Successful Leaders Apart,* Kogan Page, UK, 2014.

Rife, by Martine Courant: *Convention, Copyright, and Digital Writing,* Southern Illinois University Press; 2013.

Rubin, Hank: *Collaborative Leadership: Developing Effective Partnerships for Communities and Schools,* Corwin Press, US, 2009.

Spooner, Lysander: *"The Law of Intellectual Property; or An Essay on the Right of Authors and Inventors to a Perpetual Property in their Ideas",* Bela Marsh, Boston, 1855.

Steinberg, S.H. & Trevitt, John: *Five Hundred Years of Printing,* The British Library and Oak Knoll Press, London and New Castle, 1996.

Story, Alan; Darch, Colin & Halbert, Deborah: *The Copy / South Dossier: Issues in the Economics, Politics and Ideology of Copyright in the Global South,* Copy/South Research Group, 2006.

Tapscott, Don; Williams, Anthony D.: *Wikinomics: How Mass Collaboration Changes Everything.* Atlantic Books, NY, 2006.

Vaidhyanathan, Siva: *The Anarchist in the Library: How the Clash Between Freedom and Control Is Hacking the Real World and Crashing the System,* Basic Books, New York, 2004.

Verloop J.: *Insight in Innovation: Managing Innovation by Understanding the Laws of Innovation,* Elsevier B.V. , Netherlands, 2004.

Wagner, Stephen: *Managing Innovation: The New Competitive Edge for Logistics Service-providers,* Haupt, Vienna, 2008.

Wesley, M. Cohen and Daniel A. Levinthal: *Absorptive Capacity: A New Perspective on Learning and Innovation,* Administrative Science Quarterly, 1990.

Index

❑❑❑